KENNETH BORDEAUX

BACK TO THE *Spirit* OF GREED

W.M.A.G.A

"What Made Americans Greedy Again"

WORKBOOK PRESS LLC
187 E Warm Springs Rd,
Suite B285, Las Vegas, NV 89119, USA

Website: https://workbookpress.com/
Hotline: 1-888-818-4856
Email: admin@workbookpress.com

Ordering Information:
Quantity sales. Special discounts are available on quantity purchases by corporations, associations, and others. For details, contact the publisher at the address above.

Library of Congress Control Number:
ISBN-13:   978-1-958176-85-6 (Paperback Version)
               978-1-958176-86-3 (Digital Version)

REV. DATE: 08/10/2022

Dedicated to the People Who Lost Their Loved Ones in the Racially Motivated Mass Shooting at the Grocery Store in the City Where I Was Born -

Buffalo, New York

Six days after I submitted the manuscript for this book to the publisher, I was getting ready to enjoy a beautiful Saturday afternoon hitting golf balls at a driving range in Colorado. As I pulled up to the range my cell phone began ringing and it was my dear Uncle in Rochester, New York who said, "Son, I just got off the phone with your two of your cousins in Buffalo…you need to call around to make sure that all your family is o.k., there has been a racially motivated mass shooting at the TOP's grocery store on Jefferson, Ave and ten people have been killed." After a few more words of speaking to him my sister was conferenced in on the phone. I began calling another cousin from Buffalo who lives in Atlanta to recruit her to help making calls to family. I knew this alleged grocery store very well. It was the place that I knew where a conglomerate of my family members shopped and lived nearby. I cannot begin to tell you all just how close our family came to having at-least five different family members that was either diverted or was running late to get to that store on that Saturday afternoon. Later that evening I realized everything that I had already written about and sent to the publisher had manifested again six days later in the very city that my mother and father gave me birth. Therefore, I decided to reach back out to my publisher to dedicate this book to the family, friends, and community of people in Buffalo, New York who are grieving the loss of someone from this horrible act of "Racism, White Supremacy and Replacement Theory" fear that turned into mass murder in the place I was born. Because of this despicable act, what I have said in these pages are even more determined as a believing author and activist to expose this spirit and call it what it is "RACIST." This country has a diabolical spirit of racism and white nationalism that goes back Four-Hundred years that needs to be eradicated. It is going to take everyone's effort to get rid of it, including our religious leaders who have been way too silent and cowardly on this issue for far too long. It is time for all the Clergy across America to stand up in their synagogues and churches to teach their people that racism is demonic, and it has no place in America! I ask you all to please pray for the healing of the people of Buffalo, New York and every city across this nation who have suffered from the results of a Mass Shooting in their community. It is in their honor that I dedicate this book.

Back To the Spirit of Greed

"What Made Americans Greedy Again"

W.M.A.G.A

TABLE OF CONTENTS

Back To the Spirit of Greed

"What Made Americans Greedy Again"

W.M.A.G.A

Acknowledgements

I would like to start out by saying that drafting this book was a little different from the other four books that I have written in the past. There were a few people whether they realized it or not that participated in my efforts once they knew what I was writing about. I would like to acknowledge each of them for what they have done to encourage me that I believe only enhanced what I was writing. They forwarded news articles and YouTube videos that I was able to review. Some of those news articles and videos I chose to include in the book since it went right along with what I was saying in the subsequent chapters. Not all of it was articles or videos but it was continuous conversations I had with them that gave me more perspective in what I was able to use to make better sense. It pays as an author to bounce your thoughts off other people that you can trust because it helps you get clarity on what you are really trying to say to your readers. Everyone hears differently and that is something that as a writer I want to be very mindful of as I release books to the public. I want to first thank my uncle, Bishop Dennis C. Bordeaux of Rochester, New York for lending his ear and support to me while drafting this book. He was born in the late 1940s and knows a lot about the history of the race issues about which I am writing. My uncle was able to not only weigh in on a greater perspective of what he went through but what people like my grandfather (his dad) who was a business owner in Lackawanna, New York had to navigate through with racism. Thank you, uncle, for the articles, conversations, and videos that you sent me to help with my understanding. I have used some of them in the following chapters where they were appropriate that would help bring clarity and make sense to the readers. I have to say that it does make me feel confident that I can write on such a controversial subject as this while being supported by our most senior family member. It only brings validation for I know that you would be the first one to correct me if I was wrong in what I was writing. Secondly, I would like to thank one of my good eldest friend James Clark of Denver, Colorado. Like my uncle, you too were born in the late 1940s and was able to speak to me from an older generation perspective on the race and church culpability issues in America. We have been great friends since the mid-1990s, and you have been with me every step of the way in terms of what I have felt God has called me to do. You have seen every high, every low and watched me stay focus to bounce back to continue to be productive in this life. Thank you too for your support and input to this project by sending me articles and videos to review. As I did with my uncle's, I also included some of what you sent me and placed them in chapters that will make sense to the readers. I would say that having your input has made me feel more relevant as to what I have been doing in drafting this book. As a dear friend, I do know that you too would correct me if I was addressing the race, political and church leadership issues wrongly in America. It pays to have great friends older and have lived longer in this world than myself when wrestling to write about such sensitive information. Thank you for your friendship for so many years and at the end of the day, I hope this project will make you proud. Thirdly, I want to thank my good friend Pastor Michael Fabe from South Africa. I will say that you do not realize how talking to you helped me bring balance to what I said in these chapters knowing that you grew up under Apartheid in your country. The goal of this project was to address the issues and not lose the readers with unnecessary emotion. Where I needed to use it, I made sure it was there. But if we are honest, talking about racism, politics and the church is a very emotional subject for most. I just wanted to say thank you for sharing with me your perspective as a person who was born outside of this country and have lived it in South Africa dealing with apartheid. I want you to know that it will be obvious in this book where I used one of your quotes to me, but it was a good one that I felt spoke directly to what I have been trying to say about us as people if we do not work to change ourselves. Thank you too for your friendship, laughs and jokes during this entire process in drafting this book. I promise you if I ever meet *Denzel Washington* personally, your favorite actor, you will be the first person I call. I quoted him as well in a proper place in this book. Fourthly, I would like to thank my cousin Sondra Brooks. Cousin, the conversations, and input that you sent me was timely. It really made me sure that I was on the right path, and it helped me to know how to close this book in a way that was fitting. I thank you for assisting me with the book launch, social media interviews and speaking engagements. I am so blessed to know that this kind of talent and service is within the family. You Rock! Fifthly, I want to thank my oldest brother Jeffrey Bordeaux, Sr. I know that we have had these discussions before in the past, but I really got more clarity in how you have experienced racism and your historical knowledge of it in America. I always knew that you were very deep in your thoughts and understanding. I want to thank you as you little brother for lending it to me and giving me some of your time. The research and information that you were able to share has been impeccable. The knowledge you had about our grandfather that our grandmother passed on to you was invaluable. Unfortunately, he died at such an early age, and therefore you were the only grandchild that he got to lay eyes on before the rest of us came along. I am glad she told you whatever she remembered about him and his life. Sixthly, I want to thank my wife Maria for her unselfish support in observing me work on this project during the day, nights, and weekends. I know there were times that you would have rather had me sitting next to you watching a *British Movie*, but you knew what I was working on as an author was important work. I now have time to make all that up. This was the first book you seen me put together from start to finish. I want you to know that even talking to you about some of these things that we face as Black men and women in this nation helped me a lot. It was great to hear life from your perspective as a Black woman who was raised up in a white family and had the benefit of experiencing both worlds. I want you to know that your perspective also brought to me great discernment into what I said and how I said it to accomplish my goal which was to gain the genuine attention of the reader. Lastly, I want to acknowledge someone different that I never done before in any of my other books. I want to acknowledge a young lady that I dreamed about that I know Lord showed me in the preliminary stages of drafting this book. I did not know her or ever seen her before I dreamed about her life. For simplicity's sake for the reader, I will call her *"The Runner."* I know there are some people that think that dreams

3

do not have any real significance. But it was the dream about her that I had in the pre-text of drafting this book that I could not shake. I do not know if you were a real person that once lived or not. I realize that you could have been one of my ancestors: great-great-great-great grandmother, auntie, or cousins. Nevertheless, I do know it was this dream that seemed real about you that motivated me to keep authoring this book and address the history of violence, racism, slavery, and bigotry in this nation towards Black people. Unfortunately, within the past several years there has been so many that have tried to ignore or erase this ugly past when Black men or women speak up against it as if we have not let things go. They do not realize when our society embrace, ignore, or support those who are racist that the memories of our nation's ugly past is only around the corner from our minds. What I do know is that I saw you running as fast as you can on a beach front that I am familiar with in South Carolina. I have been their several times on vacation and saw you running from a slave ship full of British Colonial sailors chasing you close to shore. I could not get the vision of my mind with you pulling up your dingy white dress with your left hand, your head wrapped, while these shrewd men who were laughing, mocking, and jeering at you for sport. I could clearly see you running for your life at a high speed that would have outrun most men. It was like they were toying with you and thought everything was funny. Like most racist men they did not take you seriously when they should have done so. I could see in the dream that you were a short woman, beautiful Black skin, sweat pouring down your face, arms and legs. I could feel your anxiety in my sleep for I wanted to help you get away, but I could not. I never forgot that feeling of helplessness from time to time as it motivated me to keep drafting this book until completion. I could see that you could not have been much more than 17 years of age at the time as you tried to escape those wicked men trying to capture you. Even during your struggle to get away, I could see your real gift and talents that those who were chasing you could not see. In modern times you would have easily been on a U.S. Olympics Women's Track Team and would have made this nation proud. But as you ran, I could see coming from a small distance behind you another British Colonial male riding a pale-white horse. Now I knew why the men on the ship that was close to shore were laughing, mocking, and jeering. They knew that you could have easily outrun their ship and gotten away, but they also knew you could not outrun the man on the horse coming up behind you. I could see the fear and determination in your eyes to get away. I also could see that you knew that if you got caught that you would be taken back to your slave camp or given to the men on the ship to pass you around like a piece of meat or something worse. As the rider caught up to you as you ran north on the sandy beach front, I woke up and I never forgot this dream or your face. In truth it was really because of you that I was determined to finish this book. Although it was a dream, I know that things like this did happen to our beautiful Black African women in this country for hundreds of years. I no longer have that horrible feeling of wanting to help but could not for I know that this book is the help that you wanted many to come to know. For they will come to understand the atrocities that was done to Black women like you, but they have not gone unnoticed by God. For every one of those men who chased, abused you and others like you will have to stand before the seat of judgement when this life is over and given an account. As the scriptures say in 2 Corinthians 5:10 *"For we must all appear before the judgement seat of Christ, that everyone may receive the things done in his body, according to what he has done, whether it be good or bad."* I will say to you: *"Man may get by, but he never gets away!"*

Back To the Spirit of Greed

"What Made Americans Greedy Again"

W.M.A.G.A

Letter to the Readers

"Time Is Up"

Dear Readers,

    I chose this time to open my book with a simple letter to let everyone know that I did not author this book to hurt or harm anyone but only to release the facts as I know them. I want to try to allow all my readers to hear the heart of a man who is a husband, father, grandfather, and a coach to many young people. My desire is to unveil truth and find answers that will bring accountability to all of us so that all our children and children's children will live in a better world moving forward. We as American's have been through a lot in the past five years. I realized that ever since the death of George Floyd on May 25, 2020, it has been like something broke in America that is almost unexplainable. On January 1, 2019 I was spiritually heightened while sitting in Church service to start informing a lot of my African American friends and family of the significance of the year of 2019. As I watched churches around the country have their normal Watch Service Night or New Year's Eve service declaration the best is yet to come…I was feeling something different as I sat quietly. I was sitting there thinking could this be a year of significant importance for all Black people in America. I had never had that thought before that night. Could it be a time for us to watch and pray? For the first time, I realized that night that January 2019 became the mark of the 400-year anniversary since the first ship docked in Virginia with twenty-three slaves from Africa. I could not rest in my spirit that night or the first few months of the thought of that year being something special. Something was letting me know that 2019 would be a pivotal year to pay attention to for all Black people in the United States. As I informed others, many of my friends started seeing what I was saying and accepted the challenge and to start paying attention to what would be happening that year. My friends appreciated me reminding them of fact that it has been four hundred years since the first slave ship docked these shores. I also reminded them that God told Abraham that his people would serve in a land not their own as slaves for four hundred years and after wards would come out with great possessions. For the first time, the Covenant that the Lord made with Abraham in the book of Genesis 15, specifically in verses:13-16 became so real to me as its say's *"Then the Lord said to Abram, know this for certain: Your offspring will be aliens for four hundred years in a land that does not belong to them and will be enslaved and oppressed. However, I will judge the nation they serve, and afterward they will go out with many possessions. But you will go to your fathers in peace and be buried at a good old age. In turn here, for the iniquity of the Amorites has not yet reached its full measure".* I encourage you to read the entire chapter 15, in fact, you really would need to read Genesis Chapters 12 – Chapter 15 to get the full understanding what God promised to Abraham. Nevertheless, I noticed that there was no prophet or preacher in the Church saying anything in the year 2019 about the four hundred years of enslavement and oppressions for Black people being over in this nation according to God's word. I know that they knew this biblical history and had made other text in the bible relative to things in modern day times. Why were they not preaching this revelation during a time of racist upheaval and police brutality towards Black people? The year 2019 would have been the perfect time for preachers across America to warn the racist about their attitudes towards people of color if they would have done the math. It was like that for four hundred years of mistreatments from the hands of others in a land not our own was now jumping off the page of the bible to me and others. Nevertheless, I prayed in the beginning of that year before life would take on a normal pace and busyness. I remember sitting in church that year at times listening to the message and wondering if anyone in the pews knew what I was sensing in my spirit about America and what the year 2019 could mean? I wondered if my white brothers and sisters in Christ understood what that year could mean for Black people in accordance with the prophetic words God had spoken to Abram in Genesis 15? I remember feeling very encouraged and a weight of relief that was indescribable. In a sense I was feeling liberated for some reason. This was a different type of liberation that I have never felt before. I felt sure of my mission, purpose, and reason for living at such a time as this. I felt extremely fortunate as a middle-aged Black man who has been here since 1963 and have seen a lot of things in this country dealing with racial issues. I realized that I was fortunate to have the experience and knowledge that I possessed. During the past 35 years of my life, I had attained a lot biblically, spiritually, educationally, and historically concerning that matter. For the first time, I felt like something right was on the horizon for Black people in this country, but I did not know what it was and how it would come about. What I did know is that the unchecked abuse, unfair treatment, crimes, and injustice towards Black people was ending. It was over and time was up! I could not talk about it with a lot of people because I did not feel like it included them. I knew we had huge racial problems in this country that were real and systemic that needed to be solved that had not been for years. I knew we were living through a time of rabble-rousing, instigating, and inciting white supremacy in our nation by the former President whenever he saw fit. Despite his efforts to divide us and not unite us, there was a self-assuredness within me that the revelation I received. That revelation was that it had been exactly four hundred years since the first Black people had been cargo at the belly of a slave ship to America. Surely at this 400-year mark that I did not realize that I was born to see such a time. Let me say for the record that I did not think that Black people were going to get on planes or boats and head back to Africa. What I did know is that something was getting ready to break off the lives of every Black person in the U.S.A; and boy was I right! I would say to my friends in 2019, *"Keep your eyes and ears open, let's not miss what God is doing this year."* Life got busy as I was preparing wedding plans for October 2019 with my fiancé, and I had stopped thinking about what was in my spirit in the earlier months. My fiancé and I had a busy year with wedding plans and got married on October 6, 2019. We started our lives living together in our new place right after the honeymoon. Three months later in January 2020, the infamous former NBA Los Angeles Laker Player, Kobe Bryant, his daughter, and several others would die in a helicopter crash that would shock the world. A month after that COVID-19 would hit our nation. People would be sent from their jobs to work from home. Schools closed and kids were sent home to learn virtually. Restaurants and hotels would close, and only essential workers would be in buildings. The racial divide in our country would get worse that year while most people were isolated in their homes. Early that year, a young Black man by the name of Ahmaud Arbery was out for a Sunday afternoon run in Georgia and ended up running for his life. Three white men who suspected him of breaking into a house chased him down in vehicles. When they could not subdue him, he was shot at close range with a shotgun and killed. The video of that chase and struggle was all over cable news, social media and went around the world. Then a young Black woman in Kentucky, Brianna Taylor was riddled with bullets from a botched police raid that left her dead in her apartment. If that were not enough to get over after being stuck in the house for months, the Corona Virus had killed over a hundred thousand people. Then a news video goes viral with police officers killing another Black man. George Floyd was murdered on May 25, 2020, by a white police officer in Minneapolis who had his knee on his neck for about 9 minutes and 30 seconds in broad daylight. A young teenage girl who was 17 years old at the time video live the incident on her cell phone. I sat glued to the television and could not believe what I was watching. Later that evening the entire world was watching on television Black Lives Matter protests, riots, the burning of a police precinct and looting of stores against his death all over this country. It was a crazy Memorial Day weekend in America. George Floyd's aunt *'Angela Harrelson'* described it best about the American climate back then in her new book *"Lift Up Your Voices:" 'The corona virus pandemic had most Americans under stay -at-home orders in May 2020. Millions of people sat in and watched on their TV for more hours than they were used to. They were in a position to see a video of something most of them never seen before: a modern-day lynching.'* At that time, I was reminded of my thoughts at the New Year's Day church service just a year before in January 2019. I remembered how I was telling my friends and family that Black people really need to pay attention and keep their eyes open for something was on the horizon in this nation for us as a people in the early months of 2019. I was right! I realized after George Floyd's death that it was time for accountability when it comes to injustice, racism, and violence towards people of color in America. I started seeing that the *"Time was Up"* for how things had been legally overseen towards us for four hundred years. I knew that things were changing. I began to think, God had ended the mistreatment of the Israelites after four hundred years and judged Egypt in Pharoah's day. It started to look to me that is what was going on in our modern times in America towards Black people. It came clear to me that the four hundred years that I was thinking about in 2019 had to do with this nation ending the abusive and racist treatment of Black people without accountability in America. I then noticed that the scripture did say, *'I will judge the nation that they served."* In other words, I saw that our *'Time was Up'* for the violence towards Black people without accountability. I then realized that this was what I was feeling in the New Year's Eve Church service in 2019 that I could not it explain. It all made sense to me now. I saw that the historical unchecked abuse towards Black people from now on will all be judged! Those non-accountability days were over. The world was becoming aware of it and things were changing. I realized that America, just like the Amorites in the day of their wrong doings had come to her boiling point." *It was now a Time of Judgement!"* In other words, racism in America towards Black people without accountability would no longer go unchecked. God was no longer tolerating racist people persecuting and mistreating Black people in America while they wear His name, His Son's name, and symbols of the cross around their necks, hats, or T-Shirts. I remembered at this time a dream had on November 28, 2016. I heard his voice say in the dream that *"the division that came to this nation was not of my doing."* I kept what I heard to myself and just watched and prayed as events unfolded that proved what I saw and heard in the dream was true. I journaled the dream and the events that came after it so I can refer to them later. The fact is that the year 2020 was hell in America. The issues of COVID-19 and all the protests in major cities were insurmountable. People everywhere of all races stood up, protested the racial injustice, videos that they were seeing nightly showing police brutality, and white nationalism. Even little children recognized the chaos in our country between the summer protest, COVID-19 and having to stay at home with virtual learning. I have seen messages from different teachers who have reported that the kids have been stressed out since 2020. I knew at this time America's dirty laundry was being exposed to the world through social media, internet, and cable news. I know that many believers do not like to hear the word judgement, nevertheless this nation and its Church was on display for its duplicity. One may say, *"why the Church?"* I will tell you why the Church. In the same moment of the dream in November 2016 that the Lord told me that the division that came to this nation when Donald Trump became President was not of his doing. He also told me that *"And the Church was not Innocent."* That means, the Church was culpable in what was going on in our nation. I was puzzled when I heard what He said and started doing my research as to why God would say *"And the Church was not Innocent."* I later recognized that the Church is not innocent because He would later say to me that the Church has been *"culpable"* in watching the racism arise in this nation for hundreds of years and have not preached against it. So that means that God has been watching His preachers in America for four hundred years and witnessed Himself what they have not done. That is not good! I looked up the word *culpable* since it not a word that I use and it means, *"deserving blame, guilty, at fault, responsible and answerable."* The explanation of the definition said, *"sometimes you're just as culpable when you watch something as when you actually participate."* Wow, that is a shocker! Who is preaching that sermon? If you do not believe what I just said about the *"Church Is Not Innocent"*, because it has been *"culpable"*, then let's look at what the

American Journalist John Harwood said about the Republican Party and Evangelical Christians on December 27, 2021, on cable news. John, who is lifetime journalist said, *"This is yes about Trump and the grip he has over the party, but it extends far before Trump has ever come on the scene. This is significantly about a Republican Party, a group of people, principally white evangelical Christians who think the country that once reflected their aspects of their culture is now slipping away from them economically, culturally, and demographically. They think we are on our way to becoming a majority minority country and the Fear and Desperation of those white conservatives most notably Evangelical Christians is fueling the desperation within the party. They are fueling the M.A.G.A movement. Donald Trump road those fears and desperation into power. His promise was to roll back the changes and 'Make America Great Again.' And that is significantly of what we are talking about here."* Say what? The Evangelical Christians are fueling the M.A.G.A movement! That sounds culpable and not innocent to me. We can see just from that statement alone how much the Church participates in the division that came to this nation that was not God's doing. It was those who was behind, supported and was complicit with the M.A.G.A movement. In fact, one recent report shows that 78 percent of the Republican Party to this very day think that the January 6th House Committee investigating into the Capitol attack is a waste of time. Many of them function as if they had no eyeballs on that day when our democracy was under attack by the so-called the *"righteous vs unrighteous."* Therefore, the Church is far from innocent because how she has managed racism in America for hundreds of years by being silent about it. We will see that *"What Made Americans Greedy Again"* was the need for economic, political, cultural, and demographic power. It was a strategic plan to control all branches of our government (Legislative, Executive, Judicial), along with the need to control our FBI, Military, Courts, and Votes. The Church in America refuses to see with her eyes, hear with her ears and call out racism towards Black people in this nation. It was the Church's own fear and desperation of what the Evangelicals thought was slipping away from them culturally, demographically, and economically that caused them to ignore the obvious racial injustice in this nation. Why would the Church fear Black and Brown people that come into leadership in this nation? Instead of saying something about it in their pulpits, they either ignored it, kept quiet, complicit, or said dumb statements that made things worse. What the Church did not realize about Black people is if the Church can't see us leading in this nation that is like saying to us that we are good enough to have the gospel preached to us, bring us to salvation and be baptize as members of their congregations. But when it comes to leadership, we are unqualified and a threat to be feared. In other words, we are to be feared when we become President, Vice President, Senators, Congressman, Mayors, Chief of Police, Lawyers, Judges…etc. How can the Church be involved in this kind of hypocrisy ever reach us if they show fear and desperation towards us when we become national, local, and state leaders? If that is not hypocritical, I do not know what is. God does not give us a spirit to fear but the Church clearly had a spirit of fear and desperation for power from 2008 to 2020. Therefore, it caused her to behave out of character openly for all to watch. The Church does not realize that people are not stupid; we know what we see! In 2020, it became obvious to me that this was exactly what was happening in this nation. The fear and desperation to go back to conservative white power for the evangelicals is what they desired since 2008. The birth defect of slavery, racism, bigotry, and white supremacy in America had boiled over for the entire world to see. This nation did not understand that Black people time was over for being abused and God's deliverance is here to stay. The evangelicals did not understand that Black people had always been some of God's people and some of the first to believe in Christ. There was no way that God was going to continue to watch them be persecuted in this nation indefinitely. If you do not believe me that Black people were some of the first to believe in Christ, read the story about Philip baptizing the Ethiopian Eunuch who oversaw all the treasury for the Queen of Ethiopia. He baptized him in a pool of water that was in the desert in Acts 8:26-40. This is the reason Black people need to stop letting other people tell the story of Christ and read to understand it ourselves. Christ was described in the bible to have woolly hair and dark skin which is closer to what Black people look like not what we have seen and been told about Him by European scholars. The hairs of his head, it says, *were white as white wool, white as snow; and his eyes were as a flame of fire; and his feet like unto fine brass, as if they burned in a furnace; and his voice as the sound of many waters (Revelation 1:14-15).* The point of this letter is to say, America should have taken care of the racial issues in this country a long time ago instead of waiting until everyone's cell phone, radio, newspaper, computer, I Pad, and television in the world could see our true nature in real time. The protest broke out in the summer of 2020 for weeks world-wide. There was no getting away from it no matter what you tried to watch on television. Every Police department, Legislator, Mayor, Chief of Police, Governor, Congressman, Senator, City Official, Corporation, Professional Sport Organization was being called into account. There was no dinner table where it was business as usual, and people could just pass the potatoes and ignore it. The senseless murder of George Floyd by a police officer was in your face nightly for all the world to see. Why those police officers did that to George Floyd and think they could get away with it I will talk about later in the book. I will tell you what caused it to happen. It was a 400-year broken legal structure in this country that made them think that they could kill a Black man in broad daylight and not be held accountable. Unfortunately, the time for that old structure had ended in 2019 and a lot of police officers are now finding themselves being indicted with charges or facing prison time. The message has been so loud and clear that police departments cannot keep police officers on the force. They are leaving and retiring at record numbers to the point that some cities are now producing thousands of dollars bonus money for police officers to stay on the force. The horrible years of racial injustice and harsh treatment of Black people in America that came from a history of slavery and white nationalism was on trial. In the summer of 2020, I began to reach out to my family and friends who had enough. They were so tired of these vicious acts towards Black people, and I began to tell them that the time was up. God is now judging America publicly! I have never been a doom and gloom person, but this was not doom and gloom what I was sensing, it was reality! The lynching and abuse of Black people in America without accountability was over at the close of 2019 and most people just did not know it! For example, the nation of Israel did not suffer at the hands of the Egyptians not one day past four hundred years; therefore, what would make anyone thinks that Black people would suffer in America a day past four hundred years without accountability? The bible says that the Lord heard the Israelites cry and call. He responded by sending Moses and Aaron to deliver them out of the hands of the Egyptians. Let me say that this was not the first time that God had heard their cry and call. He had heard their cry and call many times during the 400-year period under the control of the Egyptians. Let me make it clear to you that the reason He delivered them because their *"Time was Up!"* The four hundred years He had spoken to Abram that they would suffer in land not their own was over! Know that God is a covenant God. When he say's four hundred years He does not mean 399 or 401, He means four hundred! Never have I heard this truth made by any preacher in their messages all the years I heard Genesis Chapter 15 in a sermon. Just like the Israelites *(Abraham's people)* four hundred years was over for slavery with the Egyptians back then, Black people time of four hundred years of racist treatment and persecution from white nationalist in America is over! When things are over, it is over! God will then start judging the situation like He did with the nine plagues and the Red Sea drowning of the Egyptians. We are now starting to see many police officers, chiefs of police resigning, and others being charged with crimes that would not happened before in the past. We are now seeing a time of judgement for those who have treated Black people with contempt and the persecutors see it, feel it, and know it. Just to name a few incidents: who would have ever thought that the police officer that killed George Floyd would be indicted and found guilty on all murder charges and put away to prison? Who would have thought that a jury panel of 11 whites and 1 black would convict 3 white men in the Georgia South for the killing of Ahmaud Arbery? That has never happened in this country. Whoever would have thought that the police officer who killed Dante Wright would be found guilty of first and second-degree manslaughter? I guess God must have heard the cry and call of all the people that protested in the streets around the world in the summer of 2020. Things are changing, something is going on. We have never seen so many police officers and racist people stand accountable in this nation for their crimes. Even if you are racist, you would still have to appreciate what I am writing in this letter and how I break it down. It can challenge you to look at your ways. What we do not understand as people about God. There is a time where He talks to us to get our attention to reason with us to turn from our wicked ways. If we do not respond to Him during that time, He is patient and long suffering but after that He is not talking anymore. He begins to judge the situation. Just like your parents did when you were kids. They keep telling you to go to bed and go to sleep, but you keep playing. After a while, your parents are not talking anymore. They just come up in the room and manage the situation. I know this may not be making some reader's feel comfortable but that is not my objective in drafting this book. This book is for every person in America to realize that from now on God is the one who is judging all these situations and we better pay attention to it. God is dealing with the racism, inequality towards Black/ Brown people in America and giving them a voice. This letter in this book is not to make anyone feel bad, but it is to warn those who do not believe that water is wet and wants to continue in their racist ways. Just remember that the one man that shot and killed Ahmaud Arbery did not go to prison alone. Two other men who were *culpable* went to prison with him for life. They both were considered by the mostly white jury that they were a *'party to a crime.'* I am going to reiterate that we need to pay close attention as to who is really judging all these situations moving forward. Likewise, Pharoah did not realize that it was God judging him and Egypt with the nine plagues. He later continued to pursue the Israelites after they were let go. He ended up drowning in the Red Sea with all his army. I am sure if Pharoah knew then that it was really God who was judging the situation, he would have let the Israelites go their way with no problem. The Church needs to get rid of its appearance of being culpable with racism and division in America for political purposes. Churches everywhere need to standup and be what the Father expects of us and call a spade a spade. If you are reading this letter and still think that we are in the days when you can *walk, sit, or stand* with racists folk and not be held accountable, then continue to do what you do. Let me remind you what one of my favorite verses in the bible, it says in Psalms 1:1 *"Blessed is the man that walk not in the counsel of the ungodly, nor stands in the way of sinners, or sit in the seat of mockers."* A word to the wise, especially Christians. We need to put a check on where we *walk, stand, and sit*! That is half of our problem. Those that have been culpable *(including Church folk)* now know that there are consequences for their ways. It is time for people, the Church, to grow up, repent from their wicked ways and learn to love everybody; *"A house divided against itself cannot stand,"* Jesus said in Mark 3:25. America and our democracy will fall if we keep thinking we can play with the *disease of racism* and *white nationalism*. Understand that loving everyone does not mean that you agree with everything they do. Give me a break, just look around your own family. We still love our family, children, and friends even if we disagree with their way of life. Loving people means that you know how to give all human being general RESPECT! It means that you are grown up and know how to give people space to learn that they need to change their ways after talking to them. Lastly, if the Evangelical Church really wants to repair her reputation it needs to acknowledge that it has been culpable with this whole mess toward race in America. Ever since the Capitol Building Insurrection the Evangelical preachers are now trying to make attempts to change their image. Instead, they need to put those efforts into changing their hearts. That is what is going to help heal this nation. Join me in reading my book." *Back to The Spirit of Greed...What Made Americans Greedy Again (W.M.A.G.A)."*

Stay Kingdom,

KB

Back To the Spirit of Greed

"What Made Americans Greedy Again"

W.M.A.G.A

Introduction

"The Great Divide"

In the first six months of the year 2017 I went back and forth to New York City several times supporting one of my best childhood friends John Douglas Thompson, Jr., who is well-known in the city as a Broadway Show Actor. In 2017, he was the leading actor in an old August Wilson play called Jitney. The play was revitalized and directed by Reuban Santiago-Hudson at the Manhattan Theatre Club Samuel J. Friedman Theatre. It was a great play and a hot box office ticket that year. Because of its success I would again fly back to NYC in June 2017 to see him, the producer, the cast honored at the Tony Award Show for they had picked up several nominations. My friend John was nominated for best featured actor in a play, and I was super proud of him. His sister and I attended the award show and festivities with him, and I even got a chance to walk on part of the Red Carpet, can you believe it? While at the show, after one of the commercial breaks the former Vice President Joe and Jill Biden who had just left the Oval Office in 2017 was introduced to the crowd in Radio Studio Hall. I watched in amazement at the resounding standing ovation that the entire theatre gave them for several long minutes. I did not know the Biden's but had only seen them on television like most people during the Obama Administration. It became clear to me that day that these two individuals where well known, loved, and respected by the people in New York. It was one of those few moments in my life that I knew that I was fortunate to be there and witness what I was seeing. While this was happening the new Presidential Administration of Donald Trump had only been in office five months. As I was sitting in this crowd, I saw all these people cheer and applaud on their feet in an unusual manner. It was loud and long. Later that evening while I was at the Tony Awards After Party in a beautiful hotel with my childhood friend John. He went to get something to drink, and I ended up to my surprise standing right next to Joe and Jill Biden in another massive crowd at the hotel. I noticed their secret service agent and had previous experience collaborating with them in the Air Force. I knew their protocol, respected his position, and immediately turned to their secret service agent and asked him if I could take a selfie-picture with the Bidens. He gracefully smiled and said 'Yes'. I took a picture with Jill and Joe separately. I shook the former vice president's and vice first lady's hand. I thanked them for their service to the country during the Obama Administration and allowed other people to speak to them. It was so surreal. I walked away thinking to myself *"Could I have just shaken the hands of the next President and First Lady of the United States?"* Only time would tell. Well, my intuition was right. Four years later, the Biden's would overtake the White House as President and First Lady. At the time I took a picture with them I knew that they had no plans for running again for public office for they had just lost their son Beau in 2015. I say this because I had a strong feeling that I would be writing more politically on the subject of *"The Spirit of Greed* "at the end of 2016 during the Obama Administration right before Donald Trump took over the White House. I never thought I would be writing on this subject to this magnitude. In this book, I will be writing about the history of slavery, racism, racist legislation, white supremacy, the Evangelical Churches culpability with it all. In this book I will be writing about the tragic experiences this nation has gone through since I penned the final words on New Year's Eve night; December 31, 2016, in my last book – *"The Spirit of Greed" to be continued ...Stay Tuned!"* Here we are several years later and so much has gone on in our nation that proves that I was on the right path in my last book several years ago. At that time, I was originally writing on the destructive forces of *The Spirit of Greed* in America and had no clue about these two different presidential elections colliding. I had no knowledge that when I wrote the first book that there would be a sequel to it until I penned my last line in the last chapter that very night. I must forewarn you, because of all that has happened from 2016 to 2021 in America, I will not sugar coat or marginalize anything that I will write about in this book. I will be very consciences about what I say or who I am saying it about, but at the same time be truthful and not risk losing the reason I am writing it in the first place. I have been disappointed deeply by the thoughts, attitudes, behaviors, and reality of what is in the hearts of people in America towards racism. It is clear to me that America is a deeply divided nation and mostly that division has to do with race. I have watched and listened to the actions, attitudes, and behavior of many political and spiritual leaders in America in the past five years. What I have witnessed have broken my heart at times. Therefore, it warrants that I do say something about it in this writing. Hear me when I say that Americans have been complicit with racism and the Church is not innocent! I will start off by saying that I am not racist. What I am is super serious in what I am saying in this book to get the attention of all Americans, believers, and non-believers. This book is about something that has become so obvious in our nation that we need to stop denying its truth. The demonic forces of *The Spirit of Greed* through racism have now raised up its ugly head to where there is no shame, guilt, embarrassment, or fear of consequences for what one does or says. People do not care who it hurts as longs as they get what they want. We should be better than this in this nation. Life in America has come down to simply who is going to control and influence power at all costs. Unfortunately, this greed for power, control, and influence through one race is a historical sin in our country that needs to be addressed finally. Therefore, let us stop pretending that it is not there. I have intentionally watched Christian constitutional leaders in the White House, Congress, Senate, Media, and the Evangelical Church be either quiet, complicit, culpable, or naïve to the obvious division that has come between the races in this country when Obama took office. Instead of these leaders loathing the division that has come about - it is like they reveled in its agenda. We have all seen people who should know better fan the flames of racism, bigotry, prejudice, division, and white nationalism in this country. All of these have challenged our democracy in the past few years. They have done it under the umbrella of patriotism or holding to traditional and biblical values. That kind of mess must be called out and stop. I am a follower of the Church of Jesus Christ and have been since I was 20 years old. I also am prior military with the Air Force. The mess I have seen in this country for the past 12 years had nothing to do with patriotism, Christianity, or biblical values. It had everything to do with power, greed, selfishness, racism, and people being blinded by their own individual experiences. Unfortunately, I have seen a lot of our political and spiritual leaders abdicate their independent role and responsibility. They have shown their true colors by fighting for what keeps their race in power. Christian politicians' words and actions have shown that they are not interested in the lives of all people, winning souls for Christ, helping the poor, fight unequal justice and inequality. We have been awakened that it has been about their race's ability to maintain *power, control, and political* influence. They have shown the world that they had no intentions to call those out who divide this nation with prejudice agendas in their hearts. The conduct, behavior, and actions of many in Washington DC, various State Governments and in the Christian pulpits across America have been deplorable. Once again, very few of the leaders have any shame, guilt, or fear of consequences for not speaking out against the lack of character, integrity, race bating, divisiveness, and immoral conduct of the former President. They have said nothing about his agitating racial division, refused to call him into account on his lack of character and integrity flaws. Let us look at the things that some of his key leaders have said about his character after working for him for some time: The Former White House Chief of Staff, retired Marine Gen. John Kelly, has said that *"President Trump is the most flawed person he's ever known, CNN reported. The depth of his dishonesty is just astounding to me. The dishonesty, the transactional nature of every relationship, though it's more pathetic than anything else. He is the most flawed person I have ever met in my life, Kelly told friends, the outlet reported."* His former Secretary of State, Rex Tillerson said *"Trump is pretty undisciplined, doesn't like to read and repeatedly attempted to do illegal things."* His former Secretary of Defense, Retired Marine Gen. James Mattis said *"When I joined the military some 50 years ago, I swore an oath to support and defend the Constitution. Never did I dream that troops taking that same oath would be ordered under any circumstance to violate the Constitutional rights of their fellow citizens...Donald Trump is the first President in my lifetime who does not try to unite the American people – does not even pretend to try instead, he tries to divide us. We are witnessing the consequences of four years without mature leadership. We can unite without him, drawing on the strengths inherent in our civil society. This will not be easy, as the past few days have shown, but we owe it to our fellow citizens; to past generations that bled to defend our promise; and to our children."* While at the same time, many of us have watched on social media a numerous amount of our prominent spiritual leaders *all-of-a-sudden* forget the Word of God *(due to their political expediency)* become mute, blind, culpable, tolerant or at minimum *racially insensitive* to what has happened in America. For them I will quote former Editor Mark Galli of Christianity Today Magazine who said to them, *"We believe the impeachment hearings have made it absolutely clear, in a way the Mueller investigation did not, that President Trump has abused his authority for personal gain (Greed) and betrayed his constitutional oath."* Mark also said in the magazine that, *"Eighty-one percent of self-described white, born-again or evangelical Christians voted for Trump in 2016, and 78 percent said they approved of his job performance as of March 2019, according to the Pew Research Center."* The magazine addressed those evangelicals in its editorial: *"To the many evangelicals who continue to support Mr. Trump in spite of his blackened moral record, we might say this: Remember who you are and whom you serve."* Too bad that they did not listen to Mark's warning. The man knew what he was seeing come out of the Evangelical Right before he resigned as editor of Christianity Today Magazine in 2019.

Nevertheless, the formal investigations made it clear in the beginning that the former President ran his 2016 campaign on appealing to the grievances and rage of many white voters who thought they were losing this nation as their own. When you look at where the former President Donald Trump won most of his votes, 95% where in white republican districts. This man had little to no reach into Black and Brown communities. What does that tell you? Again, In America nothing was said about his behavior, character, or lack of integrity from political leaders or our conservative evangelical self-righteous pulpits for four years. Unfortunately, because none of our conservative politicians or Pastors did not hold him accountable, the end of the matter turned into violence at our nation Capitol on January 6, 2021, and five people are now dead. This will be a stain on America's history and our world influence for many years to come. What has already been said in *Ecclesiastes 7:8* kept me focused during his tenure. It says *"The end of a matter is better than the beginning, and patience is better than pride. Do not be quickly provoked in your spirit, for anger resides in the lap of fools."* I am no fool. I knew years ago that this was going to end badly but no one on the Conservative Evangelical Right was saying anything about it. Also, I knew it was making The Church at large look bad with people. Once again, no one on the Right could see that too. Thank God his presidency ended four years later in 2020. Can you imagine how bad it would be for the people in Ukraine if he remained president? If there is anything that stirs and wakes up the God in me is to see people who should know better between right and wrong ignore it and say nothing about it! To watch and hear who I thought were reasonable minded God-fearing people doubling down to support this man blindly and not be able to see afar off where it was heading this nation was overwhelming. The Apostle Peter said this about those who cannot see afar off and are near-sighted and blind: *"And beside this, giving all diligence, add to your faith virtue; and to virtue knowledge; And to knowledge temperance; and to temperance patience; and to patience godliness; And to godliness brotherly kindness; and to brotherly kindness charity. For if these things be in you, and abound, they make you that ye shall neither be barren nor unfruitful in the knowledge of our Lord Jesus Christ. But he that lacked these things is near-sighted and blind, and cannot see afar off, and hath forgotten that he was purged from his old sins (2 Peter 1:5-9)."* I refuse to be near sighted, blind, and complicit with the racism that has been happening in our nation. What

American's will have to realize is just because someone say's they are *"Pro-Life,"* and they have conservative Christian values, promises to install conservative judges on the bench across the nation, defend religious rights and is a friend to Israel, it does not mean that they are from God. The Church was seduced into believing this man and they ate up everything he said. I learned not to do this very quickly growing up in the inner-city as a kid. It taught me a lot about a lying tongue and how people will tell you what you want to hear to get you to do what they want you to do. We termed them as someone who was *'slick at the mouth,'* you cannot trust them or what they say. Here is what the bible says about those who speaks warmly to you... *"Your enemy shakes hands and greets you like an old friend, all the while plotting against you. When he speaks warmly to you, don't believe him for a minute; he's just waiting for the chance to rip you off. No matter how shrewdly he conceals his malice, eventually his evil will be exposed in public. Malice backfires; spite boomerangs. Liars hate their victims, flatterers sabotage trust (Proverbs 26:24-28).* Therefore, as a mature adult I learned to exercise the spiritual principle of discernment and more importantly do what Jesus said, *"judge a tree by the fruit it bears (Matthew 7: 16-20)."* There was nothing coming off that man's tree that was fruitful and should have ever been tagged as godly. One would think that our political and spiritual leaders would understand this as well, but obviously for four years they showed that they did not have any discernment. They could not judge the tree by its fruit and was caught up in his lying rhetoric. People who say what you want to hear are not always in your best interest. Proverbs 26:23 says, *"Smooth talk from an evil hear is like glaze on cracked pottery."* One can find themself in bed with a snake and that is what happened to many conservative politicians, people, and preachers in our nation. The former President smooth talked all of them for their support and they ended up with buyer's remorse. They found themselves having to live with the stain that this man brought on America's soil because they outwardly with no shame supported him vehemently. Now they must do damage control and try to change their stripes. Unfortunately, because of it, their careers, reputations, and ministries are suffering. Can these people restore their careers, reputations and repair the damage done to their influence over the next few years? Only God knows, but what I will say is that for the next several years they are going to feel the repercussions as to what they have said and not said...what they have done and not done to eradicate racism. The reason is that Americans having been watching them closely and are not stupid. There are Black and white Americans alike not happy with the entire attitude and behavior of the conservative republican party and the evangelical right church. The problem in America is that white nationalist too often think that they can be offensive, nasty, and do whatever they want regardless of who it hurts. They think that everyone should look past what they have said or done as the right thing and move on. Not so! No more moving on because the conservative right said for us to do so. Here is the reality; I tell all my children, relatives, and friends this truth whether they realize it or not *"Words Hurt, Words Cost and Words Last!"* One will pay the consequences for the words that come out of their mouth. The reality is that Black and Brown voices have been suppressed for too long in America and everyone with half a brain knows it. We have been listening to these men control the narrative and tell us what they want for hundreds of years and to move on. One would think that our spiritual and political leaders would understand the impact of the racial bias. Unfortunately, it has been a waste of time. We must attack these issues ourselves even when others do not understand and may judge us for doing so. We are the ones that look around our homes, families and communities and see what it does to people, not them. For hundreds of years in America we had no Black and Brown representation in congress, the senate, in the White House, in the courts and we just got our first Black female Ketanji Brown-Jackson appointed to the Supreme Court justice after 233 years of its establishment. Her appointment has been surreal to so many African Americans. The first black that was appointed to the Supreme Court Justice was Thurgood Marshall in 1967. He motivated many of young Black men and women to become lawyers and they did so. Clarence Thomas would come later as the second black appointed to the Supreme Court in 1991 and that's all I am going to say about him. God has given Black and Brown people a voice just like others and we must use it for good and not evil. I know it is difficult for a lot of Caucasian men and women to wrap their brain around it especially when they have been taught their whole lives that they are *superior, elite, and first compared to all races*. My two brothers, sister and I grew up as children during the *'Jim Crow"* error. We have seen the ugliness of racism as early as three, four, five, six years old. We know what it is like growing up to watch white kids be given special privileges, protections and treated first over Black people by schoolteachers, police officers and other adults. All my siblings including myself have served in our nation's military. Are we not patriots? We all followed the footsteps of our grandfather William Kenneth Bordeaux who served in General Patton's Army as a Technical Sergeant in the infamous trucking unit called the *"Red Ball Express,"* was he too not a patriot? Did he not deserve representation in government and the highest court? He died in 1961 when it was still illegal for him to vote but dangerous to the point of death for him and other Black people to serve in the war. He served at a time when the sadistic signage of *Jim Crow Law* sanctioned by the government, he fought for against the evil Nazi axis. That same government legislation made it illegal for him to ride in the seat of his choice on a public bus in the south. *Jim Crow* made it illegal for him to eat in certain restaurants and drink from highlighted *"whites only"* water fountains. Until you have lived this you have no idea why a slogan like *"Black Lives Matters"* makes a whole lot of sense to people who have seen different growing up. The truth of the matter is that there is no race that is elite, first, or superior to others. God has made all people of the earth from *"One Blood" (Acts 17:26).* No one has ever had to create the slogan *"White Lives Matter"* simply because they have always mattered in this country for four hundred years. Let us just be real and stop trying to make a mess of a group of people who are trying to bring attention to the injustice done to Black lives in this country for so long. The days and attitude of many Caucasians telling Black people to: *"Shut up, listen to me, I am talking first, I am in charge here"* is over and going to stop! We have been listening to you for four hundred years and we are still in many ways in the same spot concerning racism in this nation. I know this reality will be uncomfortable for many of the hardened racially insensitive, bigoted, and white nationalist. Moving forward the pathway has been set. Black and Brown people all over this country is starting to raise their voices in many ways in what they think to make this nation better. It is about time! The lack of empathy towards the plight of Black and Brown people has gone on for far too long. We must use the voice that God gave us and understand that we can do this as believers and not miss heaven. If God's children do not speak up what will the ungodly do? Trust me when I say speaking up will not dilute your purpose in Christ. To open your mouth as a believer to condemn racism, passiveness in the church and racial inequality is okay. Do not let other make you feel like you are being distracted and can lose your salvation behind it. It is all nonsense! Black and Brown believers in this nation is going to have to learn how to walk and chew gum at the same time. They are going to have to know the very bible that others love to use against them. They must stop waiting for clergymen and women to speak up on their behalf when injustice is being done in this nation to people of color. We all have a voice, use it! God, Jesus, The Holy Spirit, and the Angles will get behind it especially when others act like they cannot see for looking. We have seen for four years what most of our brother and sisters in the Evangelical Church will or will not say to our congregations on this subject…Crickets! But we have seen their desire to preach what they want in effort to put all of us in check and move on as if there is not a big elephant of racial turmoil in the room. I cannot begin telling you how many churches was guilty of this during the Trump era. I know this because I have watched many services on-line since COVID-19 broke out in March 2020. About every church had to have services on-line because they could not have more than fifty people in the sanctuary. It is not only Black and Brown people who was disturbed by the Church's silence on racism, but many of my white brothers and sisters in Christ was sick of it as well. We forget as people that there are consequences for your words. It is a part of life. When you endorse lies, racism, false prophecies, white nationalism, and prejudice, there will be consequences. If not now, then later. Satan has always been a liar! He has been lying since the beginning *(John 8:44)*. He is the father of lies. A liar knows how to appeal to your emotions better than anybody to get you to support their mess. The facts are starting to come out that one of our own Supreme Court Justice's wives was even behind the *"Big Lie"* that divided this nation. She was urging via text messages the former White House Chief of Staff Mark Meadows to aggressively overturn the results of the 2020 election by the American people. The only thing that I can say about that is *"Wow!"* For many years, our high-profiled spiritual leaders across this nation who have taught us on television, radio and from their pulpits about Faith in God, Integrity, Excellence, Morality and Character unfortunately have not shown much of that themselves when it comes to racism and social injustice towards people of color in America. They want the microphone and the platforms to teach us about God but do not want to do all what His word tells us when it comes to *injustice, mercy, and faithfulness* to all men. We have watched them turn *deaf, mute, and blind* to the racist's rhetoric during the Trump Administration. For four years we have watched them show no interest in correcting the former President's immoral, hateful, racially insensitive speech in Washington. They just let him slide by with it as much as he liked. They took no measures in calming the racial divide that he would stoke up repeatedly. To the point it impacted our churches. We have seen the lack of *honesty, integrity, character, truthfulness, impartiality, wisdom, fairness and plain ole common-sense* when it comes to how you treat all people in America. Therefore, God had to raise up Joe Biden and put an adult in the White House just to calm this nation down from turning against each other or having another Civil War. Joe Biden had to change his mind about not running for President after he saw how our former President childishly oversaw the white nationalist incident in the Charlottesville, NC that killed a young woman, Heather Heyer. I still get incredibly sad about her death when I think about it. Heather had been protesting racism, unequal justice, and white supremacy in this nation with a group of friends. I cannot believe how many of our Churches leaders said nothing about her death and treated it as though it did not matter. A young woman was dead fighting against social injustice and the Church said nothing. She was plowed down by a car while in a crowd of protester by a white nationalist. Preachers all over this country walked into their pulpits the next Sunday and ignored the elephant in the room. Our former President downplayed the incident once it hit national news and said that *"there were very fine people on both sides."* Once again, nothing but Crickets on the subject from the Church. This kind of nonsense breaks people hearts when we do not acknowledge the *"disease of racism"* and the destruction that it brings. White nationalist is sad news to our nation when they go un-checked. The Church should have condemned that incident all over this nation, but it did not. My prayers are for Heather's family and friends who lost her so tragically. What a terrible way to lose someone protesting hate and the preachers remain silent. Shame on them! Thankfully, that the *Chairman of the Joint Chiefs of Staff* General Mark Miley did say something about these people in the book *"I Alone Can Fix It"* he said, '*These guys are Nazis, they're Boogaloo Boys, they're Proud Boys. These are the same people we fought in World War II."* The Church did not realize it at the time. But Heather Heyer's death would be the turning point in this nation that would make Joe Biden decide to run again for President. The Church and Christian Right republican politicians chose to keep their mouth shut and it was the wrong thing to do. They once again, blew an opportunity to stand up for righteousness and did not do so. Instead, they both chose to be *right and not righteous*. It was despicable! My question is what would make these prominent spiritual and political leaders stay quiet when they see these racist acts, immigrants separated from their children at our borders, militia groups parading in the streets, police shooting young Black men and women without discretion...etc.? What would make our prominent spiritual and political voices remain mute when the world watches and hears the Access Hollywood tape that went viral that clearly unveils the former presidential candidate character and how he treats women sexually? I could not believe how the preachers in this country said absolutely nothing! What would make our pastors and leaders go quiet about a President who is immoral and fans the flames of racial division in America? A man who refused to denounce those who were clearly white nationalist in Charlottesville, NC but once again call them *"very fine people"*? What makes them embrace someone who has been on record demonizing Blacks saying things like we are lazy, only good at sex, thefts, called black athletes bastards and SOBs for kneeling during the national anthem, Latinos are criminals, Veterans are losers, certain women's faces as ugly, mocking where a woman bleeds, tells the police how to roughly treat black people, to not protect their heads when putting them in the patrol car, calling black countries *"Sh*t Hole Nations,"* treat Muslims/immigrants as the enemy of the United States and constantly rabble rousing racist division in this country? What President should ever behave like this? I tell you; these so-called godly leaders have sowed the seeds of disrespect and discord to people of color that we will never forget. I thought these people were called the *"Moral Majority"* but have in four years watched them become the *"Immoral Minority."* Once again, I am not racist! I have love in my heart for everyone. What I am not is dumb. I am very much aware of the actions, excuses and behaviors of our conservative politicians and Christian leaders. I have been a part of the Church that Christ has built *(Matthew 16:18)* since I was 20 years old. I have been ashamed of how quiet and complicit the Church has been on these cultural issues. I am admittedly a believing *activist against the institution of racism and hatred towards Black and Brown people in this nation* and will not be quiet about what is wrong in America even if it includes the Church. Conservatives talk a lot about our 'American values and traditions being challenged by liberal thinkers, but when it comes time for them speak up for the poor, racism, the weak and social injustice, only a few of them can be found in their pulpits or television programs standing against it. My questions have always been: what are our American values and traditions? Who developed them? Did anyone ask Black and Brown people what they think our values and traditions should be? Does anyone ask Black and Brown people anything what they think is right or wrong in the nation? The answer to the last two questions would clearly be no! People of color are never asked anything about their thoughts on matters like these. The Church does the talking for us and do not ask us anything. The halls of justice do not us ask us anything and neither do our legislators. Nevertheless, no matter what conservatives say about President Obama, I have never heard him make racist statements in the Oval Office, on the White House lawn, in the Situation Room, at the Rose Garden on Facebook or on Twitter about anyone. He had too much class, integrity, and dignity to do such a thing, regardless of how liberal one felt he was on American policy. I say it again, the man had class which was certainly missing with Donald Trump that 80 percent of our conservative evangelicals chose to worship. The real issue that most of these conservatives had with President Obama is that he was a Black man that reflected what they thought a President should be in terms of his leadership, character, integrity, fatherhood, a husband, and they were jealous. Jealously is an evil monster that all of us must deal with at one time or another in our lives, but it does not mean that it is right. These conservatives did not understand how could he achieve such prominent position when Black men were never considered superior, elite, or first in this nation? Based on these facts you would think that the conservatives would of saw his rise to power more of a *move of God* than Mr. Trump since he was the one that had the deck stacked against him. Not so, the conservatives thought Mr. Trump's rise to the oval office was a *move of God* and that Barrack Obama's election was of *Satan*. These are the same people that tell us in the Church that we are supposed to pray for all our leaders. I sure did not hear that promoted when Barrack Obama was President of the United States from our Christian leaders across this nation. The answer to this question is that Barrack Obama was never trying to be superior, elite, or first towards any man. As Barrack Obama said in one of his speeches, *"The Presidency doesn't change who you are, it reveals who you are."* The man became a notable leader in this nation in the presence of the conservatives, evangelical right, and they despised it. The President that the conservative evangelicals praised highly and supported vehemently was Donald Trump. It was Donald Trump's presidency that revealed who he was, but our Christian Evangelicals did not mind it at all. The one they believed in contradicted for four years the very words of our nations Pledge of Allegiance that states that we are *"one nation under God indivisible with liberty and justice for all."* He was everything but be *indivisible and did not promote justice for all* during his term. What would make conservative Christians turn a deaf ear and blind eye to what his former National Security Advisor, Chief of Staff, Secretary of Defense and Secretary of State said about his *"incompetence, lack of character, being a loose cannon, unfit to be Commander-In-Chief, having no desire to read the intelligence reports and had no ethics?"* What made them do this when it looked like the former president abused his power in the White House by trying to weaponize the Department of Justice, The Attorney General and the Senate to his favor while weakening the influence of the FBI, CIA, NSA, and other intelligence offices? The need for integrity, leadership and character has always been the main emphasis that evangelicals preach to men in their churches. Where were the need for these prerequisites when it came to this man? I have attended countless evangelical Men's Meetings, Breakfasts, Conferences and went to some of the first Promise Keepers meetings *(which is a Christian Men's Ministry established out of Boulder, CO in 1990)* in our nation. I know what the evangelicals preach and hold Christian men accountable to. When it came to Donald Trump it was like the evangelical leaders forgot

27

who they serve and gave him a pass for some reason. What would make them want a man like this in the highest office in the world? I will tell you what made them want it, the need to put a conservative white man back in charge of this country and he had the following and the others did not. I know very few will admit to this, but that was exactly why so many gave him a pass despite all his faults. He looked and sounded like to them who they thought who should be running this nation. Despite how intelligent, classy, and articulate Obama and his wife was in their presence, he did not fit the role because his skin was black. Nevertheless, on Donald Trump's behalf the evangelical right tried to sell his Presidency from their pulpits, conferences, publications, talk radio shows and television stations to the people. The problem was is that most people were not buying what they were preaching because the man was too flawed. Don't forget that he lost his first race to Hillary Clinton in the popular vote by 20 million. It was the electoral numbers that came in from different states that got him over the top. The Evangelicals tried to promote his administration in line with *righteousness, godliness, holiness, law, and order*. It was not working at all. I also learned to be careful about those who preach law, order, and godliness from reading about the Pharisees and Sadducees in the bible. They were the most law-abiding and orderly people that ever lived and was an absolute mess. Jesus said that they, *"strain out a gnat and swallow a camel"* in Matthew 23:24. It does not mean that they will always do it themselves. They use the law to create a platform for who and what they want to control. When it is men who have established the laws since the beginning of the nation, it will be the same men who change the laws in their favor when they are not benefitting from it any longer. The law of this land is not righteous, it has always been used for a certain group of people to maintain control. Therefore, that is why we are starting to see new voter suppression laws come into play or what we call Jim Crow 2.0. Jim Crow laws were designed to keep Black people on the bottom. These laws in mostly red states that want to:" *restrict early voting, restrict absentee ballots, prohibit ballot drop boxes and drive-through voting centers, ban after-hours voting, make it illegal for election officials to send applications to people to vote by mail who did not request one and mandate all weekday early voting take place between 6am and 9pm."* Therefore, hearing conservatives amplify these law means extraordinarily little to Black and Brown people for we have seen the law controlled by them for their own benefit for hundreds of years. The Pharisees and Sadducees preached the law in Jesus' day and eventually sought to have him executed using the law against him. Jesus of Nazareth had done nothing to offend these law-abiding and pious prelates other than speak the truth to them as to who they were. If I learned anything in my tenor as a believer is that the holier than thou, self-righteous can-not stand it when you tell them the truth about themselves. They will quickly become offended and want to marginalize or get rid of you. The reason they get offended in this country is because millions of Black and white people stood up to marched against social injustice. They were upset because they been controlling the narrative about everything in America for four hundred years and now, they saw people that looked like them protesting in the streets. The Evangelicals Christians are not used to listening to the thoughts of people that do not look like them. That has always brought fear and desperation to them in this country. Therefore, if you are finding yourself getting offended in what I have said so far, you may be the self-righteous, controlling, and holier than thou about which I am writing. It is still early in the book. This is only the introduction. The truth of the matter is that the points that I will make only get worse. Nevertheless, after four years into the conservative's favorite Presidential administration, the evangelical right did not learn to stop making excuses for him whenever he made dumb statements about other countries, women, judges, different races, or COVID-19 without discretion. It reminds me of a quote by the infamous Will Rogers that says' *"A fool and his money is soon elected!"* In case you did not know, Will Rogers was an actor who died on August 15, 1935. The question is, was he just an actor or a prophet? He seemed to know more about his people better than most preachers. He could not have been talking about Black people would do this at that time for Blacks were not able to vote in 1935. He was talking about his own people. The problem in this country is that we have common everyday people who have had more prophetic insight as to what is happening in our nation than a lot of our church leaders. Unfortunately, we do not take racism and social injustice serious as Pastors, Teachers, Apostles, and Evangelist in America. What the prophet Jeremiah said about these preachers in chapter 8:10-12 is true: *"All are greedy for gain; prophets and priests alike, all practice deceit. They dress the wounds (racism and injustice) of my people as though it was not serious. Peace, Peace they say when there is no peace. Are they not ashamed of their detestable conduct? No, they have no shame at all, they do not even know how to blush."* Black and Brown people are the ones that have suffered the deep wounds of racism and social injustice in this country. Their wounds have not been taken seriously by the Church. You can tell how lightly it is taken just by how much it is preached against in the pulpits if addressed at all. It is unfortunate that many of our spiritual leaders have never taken this work seriously, but it profoundly serious to God. They showed no guilt, shame and did not even blush when the former president spoke loosely about people of color without wisdom. Therefore, I will display wisdom and discretion in drafting this book to expose their duplicity. Hopefully by the time you finish reading you will see why *so-called* godly men go silent when racism is running rapid in America. We will see why these leaders are insensitive to matters that do not impact them as longs as there 401k, Pension, Real Estate, and lifestyle is not affected. In other words, you will see why man can be bought regardless of how long they say they have served the Lord. We will see why the bible say's all are greedy for gain, prophets, and priest alike. You will see why very few clergy chose to stand for up righteousness, justice, equality, mercy, faithfulness, and truth for all men with people like Dr. Martin Luther King. Elvis Presley *(who never called himself as a spiritual man)* spoke these brief words that has a lot of merit, *"Truth is like the Sun. You can shut it out for a while, but it isn't going away!"* The African American Novelist James Baldwin said it this way, *"Not everything that is faced can be changed, but nothing can be changed unless it is faced!"* Therefore, strap in with me and let us face some history that I believe is very much responsible for the racism and division in this nation. Maybe there can be a chance for change, at least for our children and grandchildren.

Chapter One

Back To the Spirit of Greed

"What Made Americans Greedy Again"

W.M.A.G.A

Greed Within Our Government Leaders

This is what the Lord says: "Cursed is the one who trusts in man, who draws strength from mere flesh and whose heart turns away from the Lord. That person will be like a bush in the wastelands; they will not see prosperity when it comes."

Jeremiah 17:5-6

To open this book, I would like to first take the time to write about all the greed that is inside our nation's government. As you read you may want to remember the scripture above as you go along. Understand that greed and faith in a man comes with a curse. It is not a cheap price to pay for those who get caught up in these things. Likewise, when a nation's top government officials become possessed with greed and idolatry, the effects of it can be devastating for all of us. I left off in the closing chapter of my previous book *"The Spirit of Greed"* talking about *Greed, Jealousy, and Government.* I was dealing with what was going on during the time of transition of the new Presidential Candidate Donald Trump who was elected on November 8, 2016. That last chapter was about everything that was going on in the country while he was being set to take the oval office on January 17, 2017. Since that time until now a conglomerate of issues has happened in our nation with former top government officials of that administration that I would like to remind you about. We have seen: 1) the controversial firing of the FBI Director, 2) the firing of the #2 person in the FBI, 3) the firing and conviction of the National Security Advisor, 4) the firing of the Secretary of State, 5) the firing of the Attorney General because he recused himself from protecting the President, 6) the firing of a female high profile political aide and then she writes a book in protest, 7) the indictment and conviction of the Presidents former campaign manager, 8) the indictment and conviction of the Presidents former personal lawyer,

9) the indictment and conviction of the Presidents former political consultant, 10) the indictment and conviction of one the President's male aides, 11) the indictment and conviction of a conspiracy theorist close to the President, 12) the FBI televised raid, arrest and conviction of a long-time friend of the President, 13) a political consultant who helped steer foreign money into the President's Inauguration plead guilty and put on three year probation, 14) the pulling of White House Press passes of several well-known journalist, 15) the pulling of the security clearances of several former military Generals that assist in our nation in Foreign Affairs by the President, 16) two Impeachment trials of the President, 17) the former National Security Advisor willing to testify against the President's actions in the White House against Ukraine. The release of his book that reveals all what happened during his time as National Security Advisor, 18) The insurrection at our Nation's Capital on January 6, 2021, and countless more that I will mention later. If I did not know better, I would have thought I was watching a reality TV show from 2016 to 2021. The conservative leaders in the House and Senate have for five years looked the other way to protect a man who they blindly believed in and obviously drew their strength. It has made me wonder who is really working for us Americans on Capitol Hill? Who are these people? Maybe that is the problem, they are not working for the people but for themselves. I have no idea how these people can honor their oath of office, ignore the facts, refuse to get down to the truth and have no shame. How can they lead Americans and cover-up so much wrong? Many of us still have question after this administration has gone due to many clergy politicians chose to put on blinders when it came to the obvious misconduct, temperament, behavior, and illegal actions coming out of the White House. No matter how much we heal and work to get past much that has happened in our country, there will always be questions in our hearts about the people who are so zealous to lead us as law makers. By the time you finish reading this book you will know the difference between a leader and an opportunist. I recognize that many of you reading this book do not have the platform that others have through television, radio, social media, public speaking, and church pulpits. Nevertheless, that does not mean that you should have to stay quiet about the corruption in our want to be leaders. It seems like the real people of influence in America have been afraid to speak out against such attitudes, behavior, and misconduct that we all witnessed from the White House for so long. Thank God for Senator Mitt Romney of Utah, who appears to be a deeply spiritual man, could not stomach it anymore to ignore the evidence put before him as a juror for the senate and voted to impeach him with his conscious. He chose not to disregard

the constitution and its statutes for political purposes. He clearly demonstrated some strength as a man with moral conviction that was far above many within his Republican Party. Only people of conviction can do impartial justice. I think about Liz Cheney a woman who put her entire career on the line by speaking up against the January 6th Capitol Insurrection and calling her party members out on their marginalization of the seriousness of that attempt to overthrow our democracy. When we have people with real faith, hope, trust, and their allegiance is in God and not man, that is when we can see true leadership in this nation. The problem that we have with many of our American leaders is that they have no conviction to do what's right on behalf of all people in this nation. They rather worship an idol in which I will talk about much later in this book. How can we trust what leaders say to us when their actions and behaviors are led with duplicity? How can they expect to lead us into change for the better when they are *compromised, corrupt, hypocritical, and greedy* themselves?

Our leaders are elected to office to represent all the people in their constituent. Expecting our nation's government official to have good character, faithfulness, truthfulness, righteousness, and lawfulness are the minimum that anyone should expect from their elected officials. What we have seen in our nation's government leaders during the Trump Administration was not even close to that during those years. Where are we going with this kind of marginalization of what we expect out of all those who represent us in government? Why are we now tolerating lies, cheating, lawlessness, bigotry, hatefulness, insensitivity, recklessness, unfaithfulness, and outright betrayal towards the government? The taking of a solemn oath by raising a right hand *"so help me God"* now means nothing. Government leaders are breaking their oaths to office every-day, making excuses for it, marginalizing what others have done and become complicit with their actions. Why is all this happening? It is because there is *a spirit of Greed in our government.* It is about POWER and not the people. It is about selfish gain and how many leaders *(not all)* can monetize their positions to make a better life for themselves. The greed we have seen in our American government is about who controls and dictates to everyone else. It is about who will control policymaking, money, rules, judge or make decisions. Greed in government can be about if the rules do not help you win, then you can have the power to change or amend them so that you can. That is why I say that the goal post for right and wrong keeps moving. This is something that I have noticed as an African American man for many years. The rules only apply when certain people are winning, when they are not, the rules are changed. We saw at the Capital Building in Washington a room full of one hundred lawyers that suddenly cannot figure out what is a fair and comprehensive trial during the former President's Impeachment hearings. They did not know if they should allow witnesses or not during an impeachment trial, but all of them went to law school and have been law makers for years. Can you believe it, law and policy makers could not figure out if they should have any witnesses during the impeachment trials? All of them rushing to get ahead to finish law school so they can dictate and manipulate policy to their benefit but cannot follow or interpret the law when the nation is depending on it. I have thought of law school for myself many times when I was much younger, but now I am so glad I did not because what I have seen with lawyers in Washington, D.C. Once again, greed in our nation's government is not about what is or is not legal, it is about who has the power to change or reinterpret what is and is not legal when it is convenient for them to do so. Unfortunately, this greed in government is not just happening in the United States. It is happening in governments all over the world. I have a friend who is from another nation recently told me how the president of their nation has conspired to buy votes and change the citizenship rules to ensure his re-election. This greed in government is happening all over the world. It is a spirit, a spirit that has no boundaries, it goes all over to find where it can control. The White House and government agencies all over Washington, DC are not off limits to its temptations. Unfortunately, we have had a lot of people run for political office, but what are their constituents getting out of it? For example, the first person that was given the National Security Advisor position in the 2017 administration buttered up to the President and his children to get his wish and tried to use it to better his own personal lifestyle. He was charged with a felony and plead guilty for "willfully and knowingly making materially false statements and omissions to the Federal Bureau of Investigation." It comes out that at the same time he was advising the presidential candidate, he was working for the Turkish government and concealing the nature of that arrangement. So here we have a former highly decorated military general positioning himself for top public office. The position should be about serving the nation and people by protecting our national security. We find that he is not wanting that position for those reasons at all. It was about putting himself in a place where he could use that prestigious position to make deals for himself while working directly for the President of the United States. I mean you cannot make this stuff up. He was previously a military intelligence chief in Afghanistan and director of the Defense Intelligence Agency. What is going on? If we cannot trust our highly decorated military leaders to be faithful to this nation, then who can we trust? It is like this guy did not have our national security of greatest importance on his mind, but only how he could enlarge his personal profit because of his close relationship with the President and his family. His rise to prominence would not last long, one month later February 13, 2017, he would have to resign from his prominent position as National Security Advisor following the news and reports of his illegal communications with a Russian Ambassador. He lied to the Vice President about those communications. What do we have here? I say, an act of greed and double dipping. To go into details, while getting paid as a government official, he tried to conduct business as a private consultant to an autocratic government. In fact, there has been several officials accused of gaining financially while in public office. I do not think it was coincidence what I saw while visiting the Washington D.C area in 2018. I went to introduce my then fiancée to friends in the area. While out sight-seeing one day downtown. I tripped while stepping off a street corner only to gain my balance and looking up at a sign on my left. It was a huge hotel with the President's name on it. I thought to myself, that was not there when I lived here many years ago. How did he get that building? The hotel had been reported to bring in millions of dollars just at the bar each week before COVID-19 hit. The Robert Mueller report would uncover and indict so many for a vast number of wrongdoings that I can be writing this chapter for months if I tried to list them all. Greed in government is on an all-time high. There has been nothing but absolute corruption in Washington, DC during the years of that administration. The framer's that established the constitution were supposed to be men of sound mind who established our government. They purposely created checks and balances in it against government officials who would abuse their power. I will tell you that the constitution is real, it is not some poster on a wall or writing in a pamphlet. It is a real document securely kept in the basement of the National Archives building in Washington, DC. Most people have never seen it, but I have laid eyes on it several times while servicing in the Air Force Presidential Honor Guard. Every year on the 4th of July, it is brought up from the basement for a few minutes every hour on the hour for people to see. I have personally performed that protocol function standing guard right next to it with other Joint Service Honor Guard personnel. Thousands of people come from all over the country to lay eyes on it. This greed in our nation's government has gone too far. So many lawyers, politicians, militia groups, people and clergy have put their trust in a man as I mentioned when I started this chapter instead of God. When we put our trust in a man or draw our strength from flesh nothing good can come out of it. This is the reason we saw so much chaos in our country from 2016 to 2021. I never seen the vast amount of people put their hopes and dreams in one man in this country. It was the dumbest thing that they could have ever done. What we must understand that the greed and racism must be destroyed in America and there are things that our government can do to eradicate this disease from our nation. I will say up front, if our local, state, and federal government do not get involved in ridding our nation of racism and greed for those who are prejudice to stay in power, it will never leave. Unfortunately, it is in our government where demonic forces has a foot-hole on our country. Historically the devil has infiltrated our city, state and federal agencies with some wicked people who do not care about anything but power. How many of us have ever done study on the history of the development of the cities in which we live and found that many of those early leaders participated in Witchcraft, Gothicism, or the Ku-Klux-Klan? Unfortunately, many cities in America were established by people who were into these things. It was their intent to control these cities through this kind of wickedness. We must understand that the devil is very territorial. It is his aim to influence people to control territories he claims for his purpose. Many of these people have been mayors, judges, district attorneys, secretary of state, state supreme court judges, city council members, county commissioners, chief investigators, state senate, house senate and chief of police. If you do not believe me; here is an article that I found about the city of Denver, Colorado where I live and how it was controlled by the Ku Klux Klan not so long ago. Let us look at it below:

WHEN THE KKK RULED COLORADO: NOT SO LONG AGO

by NOEL *on June 19, 2013*

Governor Clarence Morley

Ku Klux Klan in Colorado

Ku Klux Klan in Denver

Mayor Ben Stapleton

Archives

Western History Collection

The Ku Klux Klan had no presence in Colorado in 1920. By 1925, Klan members and sponsored candidates controlled the Colorado State House and Senate, the office of Secretary of State, a state Supreme Court judgeship, seven benches on Denver District Court, and city councils in some Colorado towns. Mayor Ben Stapleton of Denver and Governor Clarence Morley of Colorado were also Klansmen. The Klan was stronger in Colorado than any other state. How did the Klan gain power so quickly and absolutely?

William Joseph Simmons of Georgia called for the resurrection of the Klan in 1915. By 1920, only 5,000 or so members had joined in Alabama and Georgia. Clearly, the old organizing prejudices weren't enough to mobilize a respectable membership. The Klan developed a new recruiting message focused more on the menace that Catholics and Jews posed to the "nation's Protestant ideals" than on Blacks. According to the excellent history Hooded Empire: The Ku Klux Klan in Colorado by Robert Goldberg, the KKK posed as saviors of "Old Time Religion" and Americanism. As adherents to the Pope and their "polytheistic" religion of saints, Catholics were seen as completely excluded from such Americanism. Colorado was predominantly Protestant, and this message played well here. Conspiracy theories about a secret Catholic government of overlords abounded, much as such stories about Jews make the circuit today. The Klan also stood for fair elections, for law and order against the backdrop of Prohibition bootlegging and rampant crime, and against the loosening of morals brought by new music, new dances, and Hollywood, things the general public could get behind.

While Catholics, Jews and Blacks spoke out against the Klan in newspapers such as *Denver Express*, Denver's major papers were silent or neutral. The Klan infiltrated both political parties. Local Klan chapters preyed on local prejudices and divisions. Business owners proudly displayed Klan stickers, and protestant elites and working people, men, and women, were quick to join. Barring a few exceptions, such as Denver District Attorney Philip Van Case, a fierce Klan opponent, few politicians or Protestants spoke out against the Klan, allowing them to consolidate influence and power rapidly.

Strangely, part of the Klan's appeal was that it functioned as a social outing for many Protestants. In fact, members in Grand Junction flocked to the KKK not so much from prejudice, but because they thought of it as another Elks lodge, except with hoods and weird cross burning ceremonies out in the desert. Even Dalton Trumbo tried to join because it was the hot "thing to do." In Denver, the Klan held picnics (one drew 100,000 people), auto races (a Catholic won. See photo) and had many other events. Of course, the old Klan sometimes reared its ugly head, driving Blacks from white neighborhoods and discriminating against Italians and Mexicans. Beginning in 1925, the Klan's power in Colorado waned. The Colorado Grand Dragon was investigated for tax evasion, and corruption scandals rocked Klan office holders. But for those few short years, the Klan ruled Colorado. For more information on the Klan in Colorado, visit Western History. Search our Digital Photos to see more pictures of the Klan in Colorado.

This is the reason it is so important to study history on your own and don't depend on our school systems to teach you everything worth knowing. Racism and greed for prejudice power has for hundreds of years been a stronghold on many of our cities across this nation. These types of people make it their point to hold positions of authority and power to control policy. If they can hold office, then they can create/modify policy that keeps people of color down and their people up. Therefore, we need to stop looking up in the sky as believers when we read the scripture Ephesians 6:12 *For we wrestle not against flesh and blood, but against principalities, against powers, against the rulers of darkness of this world, against spiritual wickedness in high places.* The high places that these principalities and powers reign are in positions of authority in our city, state, and federal government. We need to understand that the Apostle Paul is talking about people in government authority that are in high places of influenced by spiritual wickedness and darkness. One would not have to look much past all the dictators and autocrats who have ran nations to figure that one out. My God just look at Vladimir Putin in Russia and Kim Jong-un in North, Korea. If you think about it the Apostle Paul, Jesus and the other disciples had more trouble with the people in high places of government and religious authority than anyone else in the bible. Therefore, we need to start thinking twice about who we elect in office and in positions of authority. Keeping your head down and not getting involved in the peace of our nation is not kingdom. It only makes matters worse. We must vote wicked people out of office! I was speaking to one of my Pastor friends who is from South

Africa, and he told me something about this issue of wicked people being in high places of authority that made so much sense, especially within government. He said to me: Ken, *"Wherever you go, there you are."* He said it twice and it made me think how true that is. The point he was making is that you can go anywhere you want but unless you are changed from the inside-out... there you will be with all your ungodly ways. In other words, we take our mess with us wherever we go when we do not fix ourselves. Likewise, it does not matter if you are in public office for the congress, senate, law enforcement, city council, mayorship, legal system, clergy, military, or the White House...'*Wherever you go, there you are."* Positions of authority only reveal who we are they do not change who we are. Barrack Obama said, *"The Presidency doesn't' change who you are, it reveals who you are."* I find it interesting that the six House Republican Representatives that were found out by the January 6th House Committee to have helped Mark Meadows, the former Chief of Staff try to help keep Donald Trump in power. I noticed that these were all men who were born in the 1950s and 1960s. Why do I mention the time of these men's birth? I have found if you ask yourself where and when people were born it can lead you into how they may have been influenced socially. Men born in the 1950s and 60s is a generation that I am remarkably familiar with their attitudes and belief system. I grew up as a kid dealing with them in Upstate New York. This was the error of the *Jim Crow* mentality which was prejudice to the bone. I have firsthand experience with these people. Unfortunately, they are old now and have high positions in our local, state, and federal government. This is that "Baby Boomer" generation that you hear so much about. A lot of them were taught to be prejudice by their parents and grandparents. Trust me when I say that I know who they are. I went to school with their kids and brought items from their stores in our neighborhoods. These were some of the meanest, nastiest, and racist people I ever met in my life, and they are still around. They just got older in their ways. Things have changed for the better over time, but this era was not a good one in the United States. Unfortunately, these baby boomers brought that same spirit to our nation's capital as lawmakers in the 21st Century and need to be voted out. Remember what my Pastor friend from South Africa said above just in case you missed it: *"Wherever you go, there you are."* Well, they have worked there themselves to power Washington, DC. That is the reason it is so important to exercise your voting rights. Get these people out of Washington and out of your local and state authority. Here is another article that I found on the internet that proves what my friend from South Africa said above is true. Once again, you cannot make this stuff up. Let us look at what was written about several Conservative

White Republican lawmakers and others in Donald Trump's circle who planned to pass on false rumors of election fraud in *The New York Times on December 15, 2021, written by Katie Benner, Catie Edmondson, Luke Broadwater and Alan Feuer.* The article reads:

WASHINGTON — Two days after Christmas last year, Richard P. Donoghue, a top Justice Department official in the waning days of the Trump administration, saw an unknown number appear on his phone.

Mr. Donoghue had spent weeks fielding calls, emails and in-person requests from President Donald J. Trump and his allies, all of whom asked the Justice Department to declare, falsely, that the election was corrupt. The lame-duck president had surrounded himself with a crew of unscrupulous lawyers, conspiracy theorists, even the chief executive of My Pillow — and they were stoking his election lies.

Mr. Trump had been handing out Mr. Donoghue's cellphone number so that people could pass on rumors of election fraud. Who could be calling him now?

It turned out to be a member of Congress: Representative Scott Perry, Republican of Pennsylvania, who began pressing the president's case. Mr. Perry said he had compiled a dossier of voter fraud allegations that the department needed to vet. Jeffrey Clark, a Justice Department lawyer who had found favor with Mr. Trump, could "do something" about the president's claims, Mr. Perry said, even if others in the department would not. The message was delivered by an obscure lawmaker who was doing Mr. Trump's bidding. Justice Department officials viewed it as outrageous political pressure from a White House that had become consumed by conspiracy theories.

It was also one example of how a half-dozen right-wing members of Congress became key foot soldiers in Mr. Trump's effort to overturn the election, according to dozens of interviews and a review of hundreds of pages of congressional testimony about the attack on the Capitol on Jan. 6. The lawmakers — all of them members of the ultraconservative House Freedom Caucus — worked closely with the White House chief of staff, Mark Meadows, whose central role in Mr. Trump's efforts to overturn a democratic election is coming into focus as the congressional investigation into Jan. 6 gains traction.

The men were not alone in their efforts — most Republican lawmakers fell in line behind Mr. Trump's false claims of fraud, at least rhetorically — but this circle moved well beyond words and into action. They bombarded the Justice Department with dubious claims of voting irregularities. They pressured members of state legislatures to conduct audits that would cast doubt on the election results. They plotted to disrupt the certification on Jan. 6 of Joseph R. Biden Jr.'s victory. There was Representative Jim Jordan of Ohio, the pugnacious former wrestler who bolstered his national profile by defending Mr. Trump on cable television; Representative Andy Biggs of Arizona, whose political ascent was padded by a $10 million sweepstakes win; and Representative Paul Goslar, an Arizona dentist who trafficked in conspiracy theories, spoke at a white nationalist rally and posted an animated video that depicted him killing Representative Alexandria Ocasio-Cortez, Democrat of New York. They were joined by Representative Louie Gohmert of Texas, who was known for fiery speeches delivered to an empty House chamber and unsuccessfully sued Vice President Mike Pence over his refusal to interfere in the election certification; and Representative Mo Brooks of Alabama, a lawyer who rode the Tea Party wave to Congress and was later sued by a Democratic congressman for inciting the Jan. 6 riot.

Mr. Perry, a former Army helicopter pilot who is close to Mr. Jordan and Mr. Meadows, acted as a de facto sergeant. He coordinated many of the efforts to keep Mr. Trump in office, including a plan to replace the acting attorney general with a more compliant official. His colleagues call him General Perry.

Mr. Meadows, a former congressman from North Carolina who co-founded the Freedom Caucus in 2015, knew the six lawmakers well. His role as Mr. Trump's right-hand man helped to remarkably empower the group in the president's final, chaotic weeks in office.

In his book, "The Chief's Chief," Mr. Meadows insisted that he and Mr. Trump were simply trying to unfurl serious claims of election fraud. "All he wanted was time to get to the bottom of what really happened and get a fair count," Mr. Meadows wrote. Congressional Republicans have fought the Jan. 6 committee's investigation at every turn, but it is increasingly clear that Mr. Trump relied on the lawmakers to help his attempts to retain power. When Justice Department officials said they could not find evidence of widespread fraud, Mr. Trump was unconcerned: "Just say that the election was corrupt + leave the rest to me and the R. Congressmen," he said, according to Mr. Donoghue's notes of the call. On Nov. 9, two days after The Associated Press called the race for Mr. Biden, crisis meetings were underway at Trump campaign headquarters in Arlington, Va. Mr. Perry and Mr. Jordan huddled with senior White House officials, including Mr. Meadows; Stephen Miller, a top Trump adviser; Bill Stephen, the campaign manager; and Kayleigh McEnaney, the White House press secretary.

According to two people familiar with the meetings, which have not been previously reported, the group settled on a strategy that would become a blueprint for Mr. Trump's supporters in Congress: Hammer home the idea that the election was tainted, announce legal actions being taken by the campaign, and bolster the case with allegations of fraud.

At a news conference later that day, Ms. McEnaney delivered the message.

"This election is not over," she said. "Far from it." Mr. Jordan's spokesman said that the meeting was to discuss media strategy, not to overturn the election.

On cable television and radio shows and at rallies, the lawmakers used unproved fraud claims to promote the idea that the election had been stolen. Mr. Brooks said he would never vote to certify Mr. Trump's loss. Mr. Jordan told Fox News that ballots were counted in Pennsylvania after the election, contrary to state law. Mr. Gohmert claimed in Philadelphia that there was "rampant" voter fraud and later said on YouTube that the U.S. military had seized computer servers in Germany used to flip American votes. Mr. Goslar pressed Doug Ducey, the Republican governor of Arizona, to investigate voting equipment made by Dominion Voting Systems, a company at the heart of several false conspiracy theories that Mr. Trump and his allies spread. Mr. Goslar embraced the fraud claims so closely that his chief of staff, Tom Van Flein, rushed to an airplane hangar parking lot in Phoenix after a conspiracy theory began circulating that a suspicious jet carrying ballots from South Korea was about to land, perhaps in a bid to steal the election from Mr. Trump, according to court documents filed by one of the participants. The claim turned out to be baseless.

Mr. Van Flein did not respond to detailed questions about the episode.

Even as the fraud claims grew increasingly outlandish, Attorney General William P. Barr authorized federal prosecutors to look into "substantial allegations" of voting irregularities. Critics inside and outside the Justice Department slammed the move, saying it went against years of the department's norms and chipped away at its credibility. But Mr. Barr privately told advisers that ignoring the allegations — no matter how implausible — would undermine faith in the election, according to Mr. Donoghue's testimony.

And in any event, administration officials and lawmakers believed the claims would have little effect on the peaceful transfer of power to Mr. Biden from Mr. Trump, according to multiple former officials.

Mainstream Republicans like Senator Mitch McConnell of Kentucky, the majority leader, said on Nov. 9 that Mr. Trump had a right to investigate allegations of irregularities, "A few legal inquiries from the president do not exactly spell the end of the Republic," Mr. McConnell said. On Dec. 1, 2020, Mr. Barr said publicly what he knew to be true: The Justice Department had found no evidence of widespread election fraud. Mr. Biden was the lawful winner. The attorney general's declaration seemed only to energize the six lawmakers. Mr. Gohmert suggested that the F.B.I. in Washington could not be trusted to investigate election fraud. Mr. Biggs said that Mr. Trump's allies needed "the imprimatur, quite frankly of the D.O.J.," to win their lawsuits claiming fraud.

They turned their attention to Jan. 6, when Mr. Pence was to officially certify Mr. Biden's victory. Mr. Jordan, asked if the president should concede, replied, "No way."

The lawmakers started drumming up support to derail the transfer of power. Mr. Gohmert sued Mr. Pence in an attempt to force him to nullify the results of the election. Mr. Perry circulated a letter written by Pennsylvania state legislators to Mr. McConnell and Representative Kevin McCarthy of California, the House Republican leader, asking Congress to delay certification. "I'm obliged to concur," Mr. Perry wrote.

Mr. Meadows remained the key leader. When disputes broke out among organizers of the pro-Trump "Stop the Steal" rallies, he stepped in to mediate, according to two organizers, Dustin Stockton and Jennifer Lynn Lawrence.

In one case, Mr. Meadows helped settle a feud about whether to have one or two rallies on Jan. 6. The organizers decided that Mr. Trump would make what amounted to an opening statement about election fraud during his speech at the Ellipse, then the lawmakers would rise in succession during the congressional proceeding and present evidence they had gathered of purported fraud.

(That plan was ultimately derailed by the attack on Congress, Mr. Stockton said.)

On Dec. 21, Mr. Trump met with members of the Freedom Caucus to discuss their plans. Mr. Jordan, Mr. Goslar, Mr. Biggs, Mr. Brooks and Mr. Meadows were there.

"This sedition will be stopped," Mr. Goslar wrote on Twitter.

Asked about such meetings, Mr. Goslar's chief of staff said the congressman and his colleagues "have and had every right to attend rallies and speeches."

"None of the members could have anticipated what occurred (on Jan. 6)," Mr. Van Flein added.

Mr. Perry was finding ways to exert pressure on the Justice Department. He introduced Mr. Trump to Mr. Clark, the acting head of the department's civil division who became one of the Stop the Steal movement's most ardent supporters.

Then, after Christmas, Mr. Perry called Mr. Donoghue to share his voter fraud dossier, which focused on unfounded election fraud claims in

Pennsylvania.

"I had never heard of him before that day," Mr. Donoghue would later testify to Senate investigators. He assumed that Mr. Trump had given Mr. Perry his personal cellphone number, as the president had done with others who were eager to pressure Justice Department officials to support the false idea of a rigged election. Mr. Donoghue passed the dossier on to Scott Brady, the U.S. attorney for the Western District of Pennsylvania, with a note saying, "for whatever it may be worth."

Mr. Brady determined the allegations "were not well founded," like so much of the flimsy evidence that the Trump campaign had dug up. On Jan. 5, Mr. Jordan was still pushing.

That day, he forwarded Mr. Meadows a text message he had received from a lawyer and former Pentagon inspector general outlining a legal strategy to overturn the election.

"On January 6, 2021, Vice President Mike Pence, as President of the Senate, should call out all the electoral votes that he believes are unconstitutional as no electoral votes at all — in accordance with guidance from founding father Alexander Hamilton and judicial precedence," the text read.

On Jan. 6, Washington was overcast and breezy as thousands of people gathered at the Ellipse to hear Mr. Trump and his allies spread a lie that has become a rallying cry in the months since: that the election was stolen from them in plain view.

Mr. Brooks, wearing body armor, took the stage in the morning, saying he was speaking at the behest of the White House. The crowd began to swell.

"Today is the day American patriots start taking down names and kicking ass," Mr. Brooks said. "Are you willing to do what it takes to fight for America?"

Just before noon, Mr. Pence released a letter that said he would not block certification. The power to choose the president, he said, belonged "to the American people, and to them alone." Mr. Trump approached the dais soon after and said the vice president did not have "the courage to do what should have been done to protect our country and our Constitution."

"We will never give up," Mr. Trump said. "We will never concede."

Roaring their approval, many in the crowd began the walk down Pennsylvania Avenue toward the Capitol, where the certification proceeding was underway. Amped up by the speakers at the rally, the crowd taunted the officers who guarded the Capitol and pushed toward the building's staircases and entry points, eventually breaching security along the perimeter just after 1 p.m.

By this point, the six lawmakers were inside the Capitol, ready to protest the certification. Mr. Goslar was speaking at 2:16 p.m. when security forces entered the chamber because rioters were in the building. As the melee erupted, Senator Mitt Romney, Republican of Utah, yelled to his colleagues who were planning to challenge the election: "This is what you've gotten, guys."

When Mr. Jordan tried to help Representative Liz Cheney, Republican of Wyoming, move to safety, she smacked his hand away, according to a congressional aide briefed on the exchange.

"Get away from me," she told him. "You #ucking did this."

A spokesman for Mr. Jordan disputed parts of the account, saying that Ms. Cheney did not curse at the congressman or slap him.

The back-and-forth was reported earlier by the Washington Post reporters Carol Leunig and Philip Rucker in their book "I Alone Can Fix It." Of the six lawmakers, only Mr. Gosar and Mr. Jordan responded to requests for comment for this article, through their spokespeople. Mr. Perry was recently elected leader of the Freedom Caucus, elevating him to an influential leadership post as Republicans could regain control of the House in 2022. The stolen election claim is now a litmus test for the party, with Mr. Trump and his allies working to oust those who refuse to back it.

All six lawmakers are poised to be key supporters should Mr. Trump maintain his political clout before the midterm and general elections. Mr. Brooks is running for Senate in Alabama, and Mr. Gohmert is running for Texas attorney general.

Some, like Mr. Jordan, are in line to become committee chairs if Republicans take back the House. After Jan. 6, Mr. Jordan has claimed that he never said the election was stolen.

In many ways, they have tried to rewrite history. Several of the men have argued that the Jan. 6 attack was akin to a tourist visit to the Capitol. Mr. Gosar cast the attackers as "peaceful patriots across the country" who were harassed by federal prosecutors. A Pew research poll found that nearly two-thirds of Republicans said their party should not accept elected officials who criticize Mr. Trump.

Still, the House select committee investigating the Capitol attack appears to be picking up steam, voting this week to recommend that Mr. Meadows be charged with criminal contempt of Congress after he shifted from partly participating in the inquiry to waging a full-blown legal fight against the committee. His fight is in line with Mr. Trump's directive to stonewall the inquiry.

But the committee has signaled that it will investigate the role of members of Congress.

According to one prominent witness who was interviewed by the committee, investigators are interested in the relationship between Freedom Caucus after the election.

Representative Bennie Thompson, Democrat of Mississippi, and the chairman of the committee, said the panel would follow the facts wherever they led, including to members of Congress. "Nobody," he said, "is off-limits."

Lastly, I will end this chapter with this statement. Denzel Washington a fabulous actor in the movie '*American Gangster*' was sitting in a diner talking to his brothers and said these words: "*See, you are what you are in this world. Either you are somebody or you are nobody at all*" People are who they are in this world no matter wherever they go. Racist, bigoted, and power-hungry folks that want freedom for themselves are the real nobodies in our nation. They have been plaguing this nation since its beginning. Those of us who will leave this world as somebody are those who work to bring change. Those of us who learn to listen to what others experience before trying to argue a position that makes them wrong. It is the 21st century, we must be different. Life is changing right before our eyes. Technology is advancing, the internet is here to stay, women are more a part of our financial ecosystem and children know how to use a I-Phone before they enter grade school. There must be change especially for those of us who lead, run for public office, represent those in the court, sit on the judicial benches, administer school boards, carry a badge, present the news, govern cities, states or run for election to the Oval Office. Greed, Racism and Bigotry in our government can no longer exist in modern America. It will not be tolerated by a younger and more conscious minded generation. These millennials are different, much different from their Baby Boomers race baiting parents and grandparents. It is time for change. As Edwin Cole said in his book Maximized Manhood; *"Change is Not Change until it Changes!"*

Chapter Two

"What Made Americans Greedy Again"

W.M.A.G.A

Legislators, Church, and Police Officials against Blacks

"You shall do no injustice in court. You shall not be partial to the poor or defer to the great, but in righteousness shall you judge your neighbor"

Leviticus 19:15

When trying to figure out the pieces as to how we got here in America with so much hate, anger, and racism towards Black people one would have to investigate our history that goes back to the 1600s. The truth of the matter is that there have been countless legislators, Christian leaders and people who carry the badge that has made things difficult for Black people for an exceedingly long time. Even when you investigate the Gospel of Jesus Christ one could see how Evangelical preachers had perverted it to help subjugate Black people so they can feel comfortable with being submissive to their slave masters in the south. In this chapter you will see how as early as 1664, American law makers wrote laws that pushed people of color down and raised up the European class…and the Church said nothing. One of the first laws that was written to make Black people inferior to whites in America were anti-miscegenation laws. Anti-miscegenation laws are laws that enforce racial segregation at the level of marriage, intimate relationships by criminalizing interracial marriage and sometimes also sex between members of different races. These laws were written by the British ruling elite who were here because there was a belief by them that Black people were inferior to European people. The British believed if they allowed black blood to mix with British/European blood that they would be allowing an inferior race to be developed. Therefore, these anti-miscegenation laws were written in the 1600s and enforced in states like Maryland and Virginia but then spread like wildfire from state to state. Even though in the early days of this nation it was common for African men to take European wives that came over here to work as indentured servants, the British Elite had a big problem with Black people and whites being in intimate relationships. They especially had a problem with Black men with white women sexually. The laws they created in the Maryland and Virginia colonies were to protect themselves and to keep a pure white race. Before I get into these laws that were written in the beginning against Black people in America, let me share with you how these anti-miscegenation laws *(forbidding blacks and whites to marry or be in intimate relationship)* have affected the thoughts of many Church Leaders in our modern-day. One would think that modern day preachers would know better than this and how it creates division, but the article that I found on-line shows differently. The bible teaches us this principal, *"out of the abundance of the heart, the mouth speaks (Matthew 12:34)."* Unbelievably, here is an article I read that involved two very well-known American preachers. One was black and the other is white. They had an embroiled dispute about marriage between the different races in the 1990s. Here is the article written on March 28,1998 by the Los Angeles Times Religion writer; John Dart entitled:

Issues of Racism Breaks Ties That Bound Two Churches:

The Rev. Fred Price, pastor of the predominantly black Crenshaw Christian Center in Los Angeles, has severed long-standing ties to a leading white Pentecostal ministry in Oklahoma over the issue of interracial dating and marriage. During a series of sermons on racism that were broadcast last winter on his nationally syndicated TV program, Price played excerpts from a taped sermon by a minister who said that young white Christians should not date people of other races. Price did not identify the speaker on the tape, but next month's issue of Charisma magazine, a Pentecostal monthly published in Lake Mary, Fla., identifies the minister as the Rev. Kenneth Hagin Jr. of Tulsa, Okla. Hagin's father, the Rev. Kenneth Hagin Sr., is prominent among Pentecostal ministers and has been a mentor to Price. He is an exponent of what critics refer to as a "prosperity Gospel" that emphasizes that prayer can lead to health and material wealth.

Price received the tape in question about six years ago but did not decide to break with Hagin until recently. According to Charisma, Price wrote to Hagin Sr. about his son's statements but did not get a satisfactory response. After another letter met with no response, Price told his 16,000-member church and his television audience that he was forced to break his fellowship with the minister, whom he still declined to name publicly. "Principle means more to me than friendship," Price said. Although the younger Hagin refused to be interviewed by Charisma, the publication said Hagin Jr. has replied to supporters of his Rhema Bible Church in Tulsa who inquired about the controversy. In one letter, Hagin Jr. said he has apologized to his church and tried to apologize to Price. "If I could take the words back, I would . . . but I can't," he wrote, the magazine said. In response to inquiries this week from The Times, Price and Hagin Jr. declined to comment. In the same April issue of Charisma, editor-publisher Stephen Strang praised Price for "using his considerable influence to shine the spotlight on the passive racism that permeates the church." Strang added: "There is only one race--the human race. To me, the question of interracial marriage is a nonissue. The Bible only forbids Christians to marry unbelievers." Charisma also reported that the Georgia-based publishers of the Dake Annotated Reference Bible apologized in a Feb. 18 letter to Price about, among other things, notes that listed 30 reasons that God intended the races to live separately. The commentaries, written by the late F. J. Dake about 50 years ago, remained in the printed Bibles until the 1997 edition. Dake Publishing wrote to Price after hearing that he planned to cite the older editions on television as an example of racism.

Just so you know, Finis Jennings Dake was an American Pentecostal minister and evangelist who was born in Miller County, Missouri *(a former slave state)*. He was known primarily for his writings about Pentecostal Evangelical Christian spirituality and premillennial dispensationalism. His most well-known work was the Dake Annotated Reference Bible. Finis like many Caucasian ministers back then controlled a lot of the narrative on Christianity, Pentecostalism and Evangelism in America. Therefore, he had a lot of influence on the American Protestant Church. It was his Dake's Bible notes that listed 30 reasons God intended the races to live separately and prominent ministers all the way up to the early 2000s felt the same as he did in our Churches. Can you believe it? I want you all to know that I listened to the eight-minute tape that caused the dispute between these two ministers in detail back in 1997. The tape-recorded Kenneth Hagin, Jr message about the separation of the races in dating and marriage and the late Pastor Fredrick K.C. Price got ahold of the tape, disagreed with it, and decided to do a preaching series on *"Race, Religion and Racism."* A lot of ministers were upset with Pastor Price for doing the national television preaching series, but to Pastor Price's defense and his issue that he had with Kenneth Hagin, Jr., he did an expert job of proving his debate. I listened back then thoroughly along with one of my close Christian female friends and we both were astonished at the facts that Pastor Price brought out about racism in the Church. Dr. Price took his time and proved that the only marriage in the bible that God told believers to abstain from was marrying an unbeliever. He showed that God never told believers in the New Testament to abstain by race. Dr. Price also clearly made all his points from scripture about *race, racism, and religion.* Before he was done with long series, Kenneth Hagin, Jr knew he was wrong for what he was recorded as saying about the problems with mixed relationships for whites and Black people to abstain from dating/ marrying in the Church. Kenneth Hagin, Jr wished that he could have taken his words back, but it was too late, for it had already hurt many people and impacted the two churches long term relationship. It was like letting tooth paste out of the tube. Once it was out you could not put it back in. This is what happens when one race feels like they are chosen to control the narrative and interpretation of the bible. Historically, many white men have systematically used the bible and its interpretation against Black people. As early as 1830 there were few restrictions on teaching slaves to read and write. After the slave revolt led by Nat Turner in 1831, all slave states except Maryland, Kentucky and Tennessee passed laws against teaching slaves to read and write. Gratefully, we are no longer in those times and Black people can read/interpret the bible for themselves. Unfortunately, for these two churches and their long-term relationship, it was too late for *"out of the abundance of the heart, the mouth speaks."* The toothpaste was out of the tube on audio tape for anyone to hear and those two ministers no longer had any relations or church fellowship with each other. I shared this article with you so you can see how these racist beliefs, attitudes and prejudices are still engrained in the minds of men even in our modern-day Churches. There are preachers and Christians to this very day that will have a fit if one of their children married outside of their race. Therefore, this is one of the reasons why prominent voices in the church historically never said anything or stood up against racism in their pulpits. They too do not believe that the races should mix in dating or marriage. Personally, I do not care what race a person decides to marry. That is their business and if they love each other, that is all that matters to me. I have one more article for you to read on this subject. The bible say's in 2 Corinthians 13:1 *"In the mouth of two or three witnesses, let every word be established."* Here is my second witness of how a famous Evangelical Preachers felt about the separation of the races for years in this nation. Quoting from the article written by Gabriel Sherman on January 24, 2022, in Vanity Fair he mentions this about Jerry Falwell

Sr a pioneer of the Evangelical Moral Majority movement. The writer said, *"When you think of Jerry Falwell Sr., chances are you remember him as the Falstaffian televangelist who never refused an opportunity to say something outrageously offensive on camera. Falwell's back catalog of homophobic, racist, and misogynistic comments is as thick as the King James Bible. In a 1958 sermon, Falwell inveighed against the Supreme Court's* Brown v. Board of Education *decision that, on paper, integrated public schools:* Falwell said; *"The facilities should be separate. When God has drawn a line of distinction, we should not attempt to cross that line," Falwell said. During a 1976 service, Falwell preached: "The idea [that] religion and politics don't mix was invented by the Devil to prevent Christians from running their own country." In the mid-1990s, Falwell promoted* The Clinton Chronicles *($43), a right-wing propaganda video that accused the Clintons of a raft of crimes up to and including murder. And days after 9/11, Falwell went on television and blamed the terrorist attacks on gays, lesbians, feminists, abortion doctors, and the ACLU. "I point the finger in their faces and say, 'You helped this happen,'" Falwell said."* If that do not make the hair on the back of your neck stand up, I do not know what will. Now let us get into more unjust laws that stood up in court that were written against Black people. They were written by believing British Colonial legislators and echoed by Christian ministers for hundreds of years.

British Colonial legislators wrote the first Anti-miscegenation laws punishing any *"British or other Free Born Women who marry any enslaved negro men."* The British legislator began to impose even harsher laws against people of African descent. They created legislation that prohibited free Black people from purchasing land, possessing a gun, testifying against a white person or being able to vote. If you are ever going to solve a problem with racism, you cannot shy away from how it got started. We must be willing to look at the root of the problem and why it developed. The objective is to get rid of those prejudices, biases, attitudes, and mindsets that created the turmoil in the first place. Our problem in America is that when there are strides to move forward from the ugly history of racism, we keep ignoring the obvious that divide us and resurrect its' ugly head all over again. By the time I was born in 1963, this was already a 300-year-old problem in our country. Therefore, by me authoring this book I am not starting any problems speaking on it. It was here waiting on me before I was in my father's loins and my mother's womb. I grew up with it as a child and to see us constantly reverting to its hatefulness as an adult makes my heart sick. It tells me that we have not learned a darn thing about the destructive disease of racism, not as legislators, preachers, or Christians. Legislation written to hurt any of us for another race to succeed eventually will impact all of us. It affects our economy because it affects our workplace. When people know that they cannot thrive based on the color of their skin, then those people will not give a 110% of themselves to a company's mission. Fairness, justice, and inclusiveness is what makes people work hard. If we are not giving our full effort in a competitive world market, then the American economy suffers at large because we are not committed. Racism may make one race feel a little better about themselves but how many people can live comfortably knowing that they lived a lie and ignored so many others that did not have their same opportunities? How much longer can we go on living in this country without asking people of color, how do you feel about this or what do you think about that? As we can see the laws written in 1664 and amended in 1681 are indicative that these Christian lawmakers could care less about how people of color felt or thought about anything. Unfortunately, many of these legislators are still making that same mistake in the 21st Century. When Black people where picking tobacco, fruits, vegetables, and cotton in the south that exploded the American economy these Christian legislators were satisfied. We can see that these laws and other laws like them such as *"Jim Crow"* did not only put Black people and people of color in a bad position, but they elevated European folk to power. Whites were described in these laws as *"Christian, Free-Born, deserving of rights and freedoms."* The term *'white'* was used to describe them and distinguish them from people of color. For the record, the first naturalization law was written by Colonial Maryland legislators in 1790 that stated to become a naturalize citizen one had to be *'white',* and this law stayed on the books until 1952 *(11 years before I was born).* These naturalization laws meant that if you are not a U.S. Citizen *(not white),* you cannot vote and if you cannot vote, you have no rights to voice your political needs, concerns, or desires. So once again, Black people and people of color were doomed by these laws written and enforced by faith filled men of God *(Church folk).* If you do not believe me, let me ask you this question. Have you ever heard of the infamous *Dred Scott* case? If you had not here would be a good place to read about it. It was a Supreme Court decision in 1857 that has great historical reference as to how a lot of these faith filled believers *(Church folk)* viewed Black people and citizenship in America. I saw this biography on PBS but found a writing on-line that will get you caught up on the case. It reads: *"In March of 1857, the United States Supreme Court, led by Chief Justice Roger B. Taney, declared that all blacks -- slaves as well as free -- were not and could never become citizens of the United States. The court also declared the 1820 Missouri Compromise unconstitutional, thus permitting slavery in all the country's territories. The case before the court was that of Dred Scott v. Sanford. Dred Scott, a slave who had lived in the free state of Illinois and the free territory of Wisconsin before moving back to the slave state of Missouri, had appealed to the Supreme Court in hopes of being granted his freedom. Referring to the language in the Declaration of Independence that includes the phrase, "all men are created equal," Taney reasoned that "it is too clear for dispute, that the enslaved African race were not intended to be included and formed no part of the people who framed and adopted this declaration." Abolitionists were incensed. Although disappointed, Frederick Douglass, found a bright side to the decision and announced, "my hopes were never brighter than now." For Douglass, the decision would bring slavery to the attention of the nation and was a step toward slavery's ultimate destruction."* Now that you have read this you can only guess where I am going next. Once again to prove that these were faith filled Church going Christians that made and enforced these kinds of laws against Black people, Chief Supreme Court Justice Roger B. Taney was the first Catholic ever to serve on the Supreme Court. He was born into a wealthy; slave owning family in Calvert County Maryland and was nominated by Andrew Jackson (who also owned 100 slaves by the time he was President and was a Presbyterian Christian). Once again, you cannot make this stuff up. The history is all there for one to research and see that many of our Christian leaders back then were not for Black people and very racist. The problem is that modern times is that our evangelical leaders have not learn to not follow them. They have not learned to not show even a hint of it in their walk with God. Therefore, where do we go from here? It is a spirit of greed when a people can only relate or be empathetic to their freedoms and are blinded to the need of freedom for others. Do not even waste your time arguing with people like this for they are delusional and intoxicated with oneself. For those that like to minimize slavery, racism, and injustice towards Black and Brown people in America, I will list the unjust laws that was written against us as early as the 1600s. After you have read them think to yourself if it was the other way around would these laws have had an impact on you and your ancestor's opportunity for freedom and success. Remarkably interesting list of legislation. It is a Study Aide: Slavery and the Law in the Seventeenth Century Virginia. It can be found online at: <u>Study Aid: Slavery and the Law in Seventeenth-Century Virginia | Gilder Lehrman Institute of American History</u>

1662

General Assembly determines "Negro women's children to serve according to the condition of the mother."

1667

General Assembly passes "An act declaring the baptisme of slaves doth not exempt them from bondage."

1669

Virginia passes an act regarding the casual killing of slaves: "If any slave resists his master (or other by his master's order correcting him) and by the extremity of the correction should chance to die, that his death shall not be accompted felony."

1670

Assembly determined that "Noe Negroes nor Indians to buy Christian servants."

1672

"An act for the apprehension and suppression of runaways, Negroes and slaves" states: "If any Negroe, mulatto, Indian slave, or servant for life, runaway and shall be pursued by the warrant or hue and cry, it shall and may be lawful for any person who shall endeavour to take them, upon the resistance of such Negro, mulatto, Indian slave, or servant for life, to kill or wound him or them so resisting. . . . And if it happens that such Negroe, mulatto, Indian slave, or servants for life doe dye of any wound in such their resistance received the master or owner of such shall receive satisfaction from the public."

1680

General Assembly passes "An act for preventing Negroes' Insurrections": "Whereas the frequent meeting of considerable numbers of Negroe slaves under pretence of feasts and burials is judged of dangerous consequence . . . it shall not be lawful for any Negroe or other slave to carry or arm himself with any club, staff, gun, sword, or any other weapon of defense or offense, not to goe or depart from his master's ground without a certificate from his master . . . and such permission not to be granted but upon particular and necessary operations; and every Negroe or slave so offending not having a certificate . . . [will receive] twenty lashes on his bare back well laid. . . . If any Negroe or other slave shall absent himself from his master's service and lie hid and lurking in obscure places . . . it shall be lawful . . . to kill the said Negroe or slave."

1682

Virginia passes "An additional act for the better preventing insurrections by Negroes": "No master or overseer knowingly permit or suffer . . . any Negroe or slave not properly belonging to him or them, to remain or be upon his or their plantation above the space of four hours at any one time."

1691

Virginia votes to banish any white man or woman who marries a black, mulatto, or Indian. Any white woman who gives birth to a mulatto child is required to pay a heavy fine or be sold for a five-year term of servitude.

In fact, if you really want to know where that spirit came from that makes law enforcement feel that they can kill black/brown men and women without penalty, look at the laws above. It was a spirit that was passed down to them legislatively by their ancestors and they do not realize how much it influences their decisions today. Here is another article worth reading that explains why we had these problems again several years ago with white police officers killing Black men. It too is online and entitled: On Oct 20, 1669: Colonial Virginia Authorizes Enslavers to Kill "Rebellious Slaves": *"Colonial Virginia Authorizes Enslavers to kill 'Rebellious Slaves:'" On October 20, 1669, the Virginia Colonial Assembly enacted a law that removed criminal penalties for enslavers who killed enslaved people resisting authority. The assembly justified the law on the grounds that "the obstinacy of many [enslaved people] cannot be suppressed by other than violent means." The law provided that an enslaver's killing of an enslaved person could not constitute murder because the "premeditated malice" element of murder could not be formed against one's own property. In subsequent years, Virginia continued to reduce legal protections for enslaved people. In 1723, the assembly removed all penalties for the killing of enslaved people during "correction," meaning that an enslaved person could be killed for an "offense" as minor as picking bad tobacco. The willful or malicious killing of an enslaved person could constitute murder, in theory, but the law excused the killing of an enslaved person if the killing was in any way provoked. In effect, enslavers could kill enslaved people with impunity in colonial-era Virginia, and the situation was similar in most other colonial territories. Following the American Revolution, many states created penalties for killing enslaved people—but the loophole permitting the killing of an enslaved person during "correction" or to prevent "resistance" remained. As a result, throughout the course of slavery in this country's history, enslavers were rarely punished for killing enslaved people.* Now you can see how these laws of the past had a lot to do with modern day legislation that needed to be amended to keep police from killing Black people without cause. Let us see what happened in more modern times when it came to legislation that was written against Black people. When we look at the 1950s and 1960s. The Civil Rights movement that went on across this country was all about legislation for equal rights, jobs, and fair wages for people of color. The conservative politicians or the high-profile Evangelical ministers did not support the movement. If I am wrong or missing it, I apologize up front, but I cannot remember any of the high-profiled evangelical ministers helping to take on this fight back then as a kid. I think I would have remembered their faces and names if they had done so since we did have a black and white television. I am very much aware that yes, there were white ministers that did get involved, marched in the civil rights movement to bring change, including my wife's parents who adopted her at age two. They both were doing the work of the Lord through the Lutheran Church back then but were not the well-known high-profiled national ministers that I am speaking about. They were a young married Christian couple that had a conscience towards unfair treatment, unequal justice, and racism in America. The ministers that I am talking about is the big-name influential preachers across America back in those days who never said a word. Where were their voices on these issues of Civil Rights legislation in the 1950 and 1960? I tell you where they were, they were mute! This is the way it had historically been in this country for hundreds of years. Back then, all the well named high-profile preachers/evangelist all claimed to have the Holy Spirit, which is the very power of God. Well, if they all had the power of God, it looks like when it came to *courage/boldness* to speak up against racism *(which is a by-product of the Holy Spirit)*, many of them did not get that gift at all. What it looks like is what we had back then were weak Church leaders at a time of great significant social storms just like we saw a few years ago. History always repeats itself! What a missed opportunity for high-profile Preachers and the Body of Christ in America to set a racial standard of zero tolerance. They missed it back then in the 1950s, 60s, 70s and missed it again in 2016, 2017, 2018, 2019 and 2020. I personally do not care anymore to hear Christian Leaders brag about how powerful the Church has been in the past years, especially when I see today these leaders shut their mouths when a social injustice fight is right outside their doors. If the Civil Rights Movement was not enough for you to speak up against racism as a believer in those days, then where was your real conviction? How about the incident at the 16th Street Baptist Church bombing that killed four little Black girls on September 15, 1963 (15 days after I was born)? Where were the Christian politicians and high-profile Gospel Prelates on that day? Did they condemn that racist act? Church pulpits across America should have been set ablaze with denouncement of hatred and racism towards Black people in America, but they were not. That act happened right on the Church doorsteps, killed little children and the Evangelical Church still did not put racism down. If we let all the profound preachers tell it. They all were filled with the Holy Spirit in those days, but what did that do for the Black people at that time to stop the hate? No, what they did was temporize the situation instead of speaking up against it. But what has temporizing racial acts of violence or discrimination historically done for anyone in this nation? It only put us in a position where we must write, sing, protest and talk about it on cable news in the 21st Century to condemn it. How about the days when we had Dr. Martin Luther King, a Baptist preacher assassinated in 1968 by racist, law-abiding, God-fearing people in Memphis, Tennessee? Still not much was done to change the climate of racism in America by believing politicians and clergy. No, what was done after his death is that lawmakers in the 1970s systemically designed deindustrialization of black cities and the closing down of factories that were employing black communities to impoverish blacks. Christian politicians went on to plan and designed the deindustrialization of the inner-city High Schools that also happened during the 1970s that removed programs that taught black kids a trade in plumbing, auto repair, carpentry, welding, machinery, and masonry. My father Arthur C. Williams was a by-product of that program at his high school in Tuscaloosa, Alabama. That is what got him started in the work force at age 18 after graduating high school. He would retire from General Motors as a foreman after working for them for 31 years. In other words, another attempt to make sure Black people could never be employable, self-sufficient, and financially independent. Again, all this done by legislators to impoverish our Black communities. To add insult to injury, in the 1980s *"Crack Cocaine"* was populated in all the black inner cities by our own government to fund a war in Nicaragua, producing a generation of crack addicts and babies to deal with for years. Again, another piece under handed legislation to find a way to finance a war. Because we did not learn any lessons from the police brutality of the 1960s towards Black people. The 1990s once again brought in another influx of police brutality crimes on Black men across the nation. In 1991 the world was shocked to see the video tape of *Rodney King* being tortured and beaten by a police mob in Los Angeles, CA which sparked the LA riots. Again, tighter legislation written to fund and protect the police from facing any criminal charges. Which only created a barrage of police violence towards Blacks in the subsequent years. In 1997, police officers in Brooklyn, New York took Haitian immigrant *Abner Louima* in custody after pulling down his pants to a precinct and with a broken broomstick sexually assaulted the man while in handcuffs. In

1999, *Amadu Dialo* a New York immigrant was shot and killed by four New York City plain clothed police officers who had mistaken him for a rape suspect from one year earlier. The four police officers were all acquitted. In the 2000s, police brutality and murders would only escalate in America. To name a few: In 2006, *Sean Bell* was leaving a club with a few friends as a part of his bachelor party the night before he was to get married when New York Police fired fifty shots in total with fewer than half hitting their intended targets. Bell was struck in the neck and arm and pronounced dead on arrival to the hospital. Many of us never heard about in 2009, in the early morning of New Year's Day a transportation police officer responding to reports of a fight on a crowded Bay Area Rapid Transit train detained *Oscar Grant*, kneed him in the head and forced him to lie face down on the platform. The police officer pulled his weapon, shot Oscar, and killed him. This one a lot of us do remember, in 2014, *Eric Garner* of New York, a father of six, was approached by NYPD after a call came where he had broken up a fight. One of the police officers arriving to the scene approached Eric for illegally selling cigarettes. While he was in police custody, he was put in an illegal choke hold. Garner repeatedly told the police officer, *"I Can't Breathe,"* and dies after losing consciousness at the hands of the police. Within hours a video of the incident begins to spark outrage across the country. It is previous incidents like these that has set the stage for all the mayhem we saw in the Summer of 2020. There is more to write about. How many of you remember what happened to *Michael Brown* in 2014? Michael was an unarmed Black teenager *(18 years old)* who was shot and killed by a police officer in Ferguson, MO. The police officer saw Michael walking in the street with a friend and demanding that they get out of the street and onto the sidewalk. A confrontation started between Michael and the police officer through his SUV window. The officer got out of his vehicle and fired twice killing Michael. Michael and his friend tried to leave, when the police officer exited his vehicle and Michael turned to face the police officer who then fired twelve shots in which six hit him. Twelve shots fired on an unarmed teenager created protests and riots in Ferguson that soon spread across the nation. This officer was not indicted.

Let us not forget the 17-year-old *Laquan McDonald* of Chicago who was shot and killed by a police officer in 2014. Laquan was reported to be walking down the street behaving erratically and refusing to put down a knife at the police command. The internal police report described the same and leading to a judgement of the police shooting judged as justifiable. Therefore, the police officer was not charged at that time. A year later when the court ordered the police video dash-cam to be released and made public, everyone could see that Laquan was walking away from the police officers when he was shot sixteen times. This too led to protest and demonstrations against the Chicago Police Dept across the country. The officer was later charged with sixteen counts of aggravated battery with a firearm and second-degree murder. The Department of Justice opened a Civil Rights investigation in Laquan's death and the activities of the Chicago Police Department. It found the police as having *"excessive violence,"* especially against minority suspects, and having poor training and supervision. The officer involved in Laquan's death would go to jail and he would be released after serving 39 months of his 81-month sentence. Things started getting worse in America with police brutality as time went on. In 2015, a 25-year-old man by the name of *Freddie Gray, Jr* was arrested in Baltimore by six police officers for possessing a knife. While being transported in a police van, Freddie sustained injuries to his spinal cord and later died from those injuries a week later. All six officers denied any claim to the cause of his death. A medical examiner's report concluded that Grays death could not be ruled an accident and was instead a homicide. Then on February 23, 2020, three white men chased down 25-year-old *Ahmaud Arbery* while he was jogging and shot him several times point blank range with a shot gun. The three men suspected him to have done some robberies in their South Georgia neighborhood. Two of the men had former positions working with the police. As the video of this incident went public protest heated up around the country. Legislators got involved and argued about private citizens and their right to detain people who they believe to be breaking the law. These rights in Georgia were spelled out in a controversial Civil War-era statue that was significantly weakened by state lawmakers in direct response to the outrage over the death of Ahmaud. Those three men would be later indicted, charged and sentence to life imprisonment. The very next month on March 13, 2020, *Breonna Taylor* at 26-year-old woman was riddled with bullets in her apartment by Louisville, Kentucky police. Three officers conducted a forced entry into the apartment at 12:40am as part of an investigation into drug dealing operations. Breonna's boyfriend was at the apartment and thought the plain clothed officers where intruders and fired a warning shot at them in which one of the officers was hit in the leg. The officers returned thirty-two shots in the apartment in which six bullets hit Breonna as she was hiding behind her boyfriend. According to police, Breonna's home was never searched. This shooting led to numerous protests that added to those across the United States against police brutality towards blacks and racism. What the country did not know at the time which would come out later September 1, 2020. On March 23, 2020, the death of Daniel Prude of Rochester, NY while in police custody. Then, on May 25, 2020; the forgetful incident that would capture the world's attention and protest. The video released that showed *George Floyd* of Minneapolis killed while three police officers pinning him down to the ground and one officer's knee on his neck. The world stood still and watched him while he cried out for his mother and saying, *"I Can't Breathe!"* This incident was the final limit for everyone to see. Millions of people across the world rose to take to the streets about racism in America and everywhere. After a summer of protest all around the country, on August 23, 2020, *Jacob Blake*, a 29-year-old Black man, was shot and seriously injured by police officers in the back. He was shot seven times when he opened the door to get into his SUV with his three little children in the back seat. The reason I list these incidents and facts about the killing of Black men and women by police for many years in this country is because there are people out there that deny the truth. We got here because we have historically had terrible legislation that allows this to happen towards Black people The people that deny the truth ignore the facts and change the narrative. It is pitiful when we have lawmakers and police officers that deny the truth. But it is even more deplorable when Church leaders, ministers of the Gospel do the same and function as if they cannot see, read, or hear. They go on preaching in their pulpits as if nothing happened and there is a big ole' elephant in the room. Unfortunately, these ministers show no regard to what is affecting our society and their parishioners of color in the pews. They marginalize what has happened, attack the very people who are the victims and talk about what they do not understand about Black life in America. As you can see from the lengthy list of deaths of Black people in modern times at the hands of police officers is really a spirit that came out of the South that they have inherited from their ancestors from terrible legislation. For the Church ministers that just winks at this mess and always have something negative to say. I will end this chapter quoting what the writer's say's in the book of Jude Chapter 1:10-13; *"Yet these people slander whatever they do not understand, and they very things they do understand by instinct as irrational animals do will destroy them. Woe to them! They have taken the way of Cain; they have rushed for profit into Balaam's error; they have been destroyed in Korah's rebellion. These people are blemishes at your love feasts, eating with you without the slightest qualm – shepherds who feed only themselves. They are clouds without rain, blown along by the wind; autumn trees, without fruit and uprooted-twice dead. They are wild waves of the sea, foaming up their shame; wandering stars, for whom blackest darkness has been reserved forever."*

Chapter Three

Back To the Spirit of Greed

"What Made Americans Greedy Again"

W.M.A.G.A

"Greed In Racism and White Supremacy"

"And hath made of one blood all nations of men for to dwell on all the face of the earth, and hath determined the times before appointed, and the bounds of their habitation"

Acts 17:26

The worse pandemic that has ever attacked America was not the Corona Virus, but the *disease of Racism.* Racism has claimed the lives of millions of Black people in America for over four hundred years. It has been like a massive outbreak in our country that gets worse and worse. In the year 2020 it exploded! Unfortunately, as we read in the previous chapter, America has a rich history within the states that created laws that progressed this nation under the mantle of slavery. Once again, there was a belief by whites that Black people were inferior, and it was God's will for man to enslave them. Dr. Martin Luther King was clear in his speeches in the 1960s about the *disease of racism* in America that needed to be eradicated out of our country by the leadership of our government. He spoke about how that racism began with slavery and put Black people in a very unfortunate and painful position even though slavery was abolished in 1863. Dr. Martin Luther King said, *"if you free a people from slavery but in return do not give them any land, property, rights or respect to get started then you did not free them at all but only introduced them to extreme poverty."* In Dr. Martin Luther King's speech, the biproduct of racism is poverty. People of color, especially Black people have been wrestling with systemic, overt, covert racism and poverty for hundred's years in America. Until the death of George

Floyd we have not fought together as a nation in 50 years to end the disease of racism in America. Why? Because we think that racism only hurts people of color. We Americans fight hard together to find the cure for cancer, leukemia, Alzheimer's, COVID-19...etc. The reason we do this is because these diseases affect us all. They take the lives of everyone without discrimination. These diseases do not care about race, finances, or class. We work hard together to solve the problems that affect all of us and got a vaccine for COVID-19 within one year. Nevertheless, when it comes to the *disease of racism in America,* we do not fight as hard together to eradicate it from our soil. Thankfully because of this young generation of white and black millennials 20 to 40 years of age we are starting to see differently. This generation sees how racism affects us all and have participated in protest all over this nation against it. I personally got to experience one of these protest with these young millennials while drafting this book. Ironically, I was downtown Rochester in a courthouse early September 2020, right next to the courthouse where the video cam recorder would come out that day about Daniel Prude's death. He was in the custody of Rochester Police officers earlier that year and died. I was not aware of this at all, but Daniel had died in March 2020 before the whole Ahmaud Arbrey, Brianna Taylor and George Floyd craziness had happened that same year. The Rochester police approached him with weapons drawn and told him to lay down on the cold grown. He was completely naked. He had told the police he had COVID-19 and they put a spit bag over his head and kept him on the cold ground for a period and he went brain dead. Daniel's death was covered up to the citizens of Rochester by the police for almost six months. The community knew about his death but never got the information on what really happened early hours of that morning. When the body cam video came out to the public at the courthouse, I just so happened to be right next door at another courthouse next to it. Unfortunately, the Sheriffs had to rush me and a few others out of the court building because of the protesters were right outside. I did not understand what was really going on since I was only home on vacation for a visit. Later that evening I watched the news, and it became clear to me what was going on. The deputies in the court building made me leave for they could not take any risk of us to be in their building for they were concerned that some of us could have been a part of the protest. Later that day I got caught up on what was happening in my hometown and was able to go with a close high school friend to the vigil and rally for Daniel Prude the next day. I was shocked that it was held in my old neighborhood. I knew nothing about it at all. To these young millennials credit, I will say that I never saw so many White kids in my former neighborhood which is still a Black community. I will testify, that these young protestors are not who the media and church leaders make them out to be. I saw young kids very respectful of the sensitivity of the death of Daniel Prude, his family, and the community he lived in. I also noticed that these kids were serious. They were ready to protest racism and police brutality against Black people. These kids had on their bicycle helmets, armed with leaf blowers, water-bottles, eye goggles, umbrellas and trash can top to protect themselves from rubber bullets and tear gas. None of them were disrespectful to Black people, the community or property in my old neighborhood. Never once did I see any of them appearing to try to control the narrative or take over the protest. They were organized and stood in solidarity with Black protesters, their family members and community. I noticed that it was just as many of them than people of color at this rally and vigil. It was surreal! I saw young whites trying to sing old Negro spiritual songs lead by black protestors. Songs that has gotten our ancestors through some of the hardest times in America. I saw these kids who I did not know at the time that some of them where the children of some of my high school classmates. As I recorded the rally/vigil live taking place close to where a lived as a teenager my cell phone started pinging one after another with comments. The young protesters participated in every *chant, song and prayers* lead by young Black people in the community. I will say that night, going home felt so different. It had more meaning and significance than ever before. I felt like I needed to be there to see what was really going on in our nation with these protest and God allowed me to see it in my old neighborhood. I left Rochester right after high school when I was 18 years after joining the United States Air Force. Here I was that night in my mid-fifties watching the community come together for one cause with whites and Black people, mostly young people who were not even born when I left. I was so proud and touched by what I was seeing. I saw that we can come together and fight for the same cause, against social injustice, and police brutality if we must. There were no news media present, only a few police drones flying above us watching from a distance what was going on. I was proud of the kid's courage, behavior and respect for a human soul that allegedly had been killed right where we were standing while in police custody. Community leaders clapped, sung, made speeches, and prayed before they lined up in squads to march a few miles to protest the Rochester Police department downtown. If that were not enough to blow my mind, I noticed that the white kids placed themselves in front of the Black protesters. This was to send a message to the police that they will have to shoot at them first before they could harm the Black protestors. That just made me ask myself, what have we created in this country? The people that that tried to decimate Black people we now have their grandchildren and great-grandchildren wanting to protect us. To make this even more real, as I was getting ready to leave the vigil/rally I then saw several cars pull up and a bunch of elderly white men and women (in their late 60s and 70s) got out. They too were getting ready to line up and march with the young people. I asked someone in the crowd, who are these people and one of the young protestors said, *"these are the elders."* I was shocked! These White elders *(male and female)* had on their jackets, baseball caps, and sneakers ready to take on the long march downtown. They were acting as a buffer between all the young people. They would lead the march. Talk about something that made your heart sink. I knew that this would be dangerous for these senior citizens, not only the lengthy march but the chance of them getting shot with rubber bullets, tear gas, knocked over or hit with police batons and shields. The irony about it is that I could tell in their faces that these elders had done this before. I then realized that these elders where some of the young people that marched with Black people back in the 1960s during the civil rights movement. This made me think right away of my *mother-in-law* who was safely in her home in Colorado. She told me how she marched with her late husband during the Civil Rights Movement when they were in their early twenties. I noticed that all these elders getting out of their cars and lining up looked her age. I personalized it and knew right away that I would not want her getting out of a car to go on the long march and potentially dangerous protest. That is what made this whole thing very real to me. It was starting to hit at home even more. I was saddened that we had come to this point in America that elderly White people were taking this kind of risk. The elderly supposed to be safe at home enjoying their late years, not at protest dealing with police. Once again, I thought to myself, who is reporting on these facts? What has this country come to that our seniors cannot rest in their homes but feel that they must accept the cross of protest to protect kids that were young enough to be their grandchildren and great grandchildren? Therefore, I would like to say to all the critical preachers that had no problem with putting their mouth on the protesters across this nation. Let me give you a little insight as to what Jesus said earlier. Straining out a gnat and swallowing a camel simply means that the self-righteous tends *"to exaggerate or put too much focus on minor issues and make it seem like a major one."* In this case, the minor issue is the kid's protesting. To many of these young people's defense, I have heard many Church ministers criticize these kids without going to see what was going on themselves. It was the preachers and media that exaggerated what was minor, which was the protest and took the focus off what was major, which was the police killing of Black men without cause. If any of these preachers ever wanted to know where their mouths can be most useful, it would be at these vigils/rallies when the kids are not in front of police rubber bullets and tear gas. They can use your words, thoughts, and prayers before they go protest. The ministers of God need to stop sitting in their seat of judgement and get out in the streets, go lay hands and pray for someone's 14,15,16,19,20,25, 30-year old's safety before we see another Heather Heyer situation. I say again, this millennial generation is different, they want their lives to be significant and do things that Matter! Social injustice matters to them and that means that you will probably see your children and grandchildren out protesting if you do not change your attitude. That night I saw no clergy out at this vigil. The young people ran it themselves. To be honest with you, I saw more faith and courage in those kids that night than in the Church in all of 2020 on these issues. Once again, no national media attention only the cell phones of many people like myself and one of my best friends from high school reporting the issue on Live on Facebook. I thought to myself, who was telling these kids story? No one was telling it. Therefore, since I realized that I was already nine months into drafting this book, I decided at that moment that I would tell their story myself since I was there. I'm a journalist and writer too. I was the one amid all these young protestors and seniors on the behalf of Daniel Prude, therefore I will tell it. I saw that year how protestors got so much negative press from conservative politicians and self-righteous church ministers who major on the minor and what is major gets lost. Jesus called them *"Blind Guides,"* in Matthew 23:24. The conservative press constantly shows the public on television what the *opportunist, looters and rioters* are doing, but not what is really going on at a protest. I also later learn the next day that one of kids who was protesting that night was the son of my first and closest white friend I had in Rochester growing up. We played Pop Warner football together at age 10, 11 and 12. His sister called me and told me that her nephew was there and he had been tear gassed by the police the night before at a protest. I was not surprised when I learned of this for this kid's grandfather and grandmother used to allow me to stay the weekend to play with their son back in the 1970s in an all-white neighborhood. His grandparents where very much aware of the racial issues in the city back then but did not care what others thought. They knew that their son and I were best of friends and that is all they cared about. Shout out right here to Mr. and the late Mrs. Denning who taught me by their example when I was ten that being racist is a waste of time. When we see protestors stand up in their own way against racism…understand that protest does not necessarily mean *rebelliousness, disobedience, and lawlessness.* What these young protestors today have done for democracy in America in two years is more than what the Church and Christian Politicians has done to fight against injustice and racism in America in four hundred years. Yet we hear preachers from their pulpits and live video chats label them as *lawless, lost, disobedient, violent, and rebellious.* I would say, what have the clergy of this nation done to fight against racism and social injustice? Have these self-righteous prelates even much opened their parking lots, let alone their churches to pray for these young kids' safety before they take off and protest the police? The answer is No! I have not seen any of them do it because they are too busy doing what the church has historically done… which is nothing! If the Church is ever going to be the salt and light of the world it is going to have to learn to stop sitting on its behind judging young kids who protest wrong. When injustice is being done, people will always protest. We need to stop labeling them as *rebellious and a lawless* generation just because they stand up against police brutality.

The self-righteous, fault-finding spirit that Church leaders have projected towards them is no different than what the *Jews, Pharisees, and Sadducees* did in Jesus' day. Jesus told them, *"Woe to you, teachers of the law and Pharisees, you hypocrites! You give tenth of your spices, mint, dill, and cumin. But you have neglected the more important matters of the law-justice, mercy, and faithfulness. You should have practiced the latter, without neglecting the former (Matthew 23:23)."* The Church needs to see that these kids are putting their lives on the line to solve a historical social problem in this nation. None of them are old enough to understand how it even got started, but their ancestors know. That is how old the problem is in America. To address that issue, I found a documentary on-line that will give you a quick synopsis of how all this racism, bigotry and injustice got started. Unfortunately, our schools or educational system will not take the time to teach our kids this history so we can all learn from it and not repeat it. Personally, I believe that every child; *(white, brown, or black)* should be educated on the history of racism in America and how it got started before they finish the eighth grade. Since the teachers cannot do it, here is something that I think all the kids should understand. Therefore, I will display it:

In 1619, Virginia was an isolated British settlement on the Chesapeake Bay sparsely populated by men trying to make the colony profitable for England. But the colonist was devasted by hunger, disease, and raids by Native Americans. So, when the White Lion, a badly damaged Dutch slave ship carrying 20 kidnapped Africans the colonist bartered food and services for the human cargo. The colonist had no model for slavery. The Africans joined poor white Europeans as indentured servants they would earn land and freedom for exchange of seven years of hard labor. The colonies prospered and as exports grew more profitable the colonist where reluctant to lose their labor. Unlike their European counterparts who held citizenship in their own countries Africans were not subject to English common law, they were workers without rights. In 1641 slavery was legalized. Africans became chattel personal property that could be owned for life. Slave labor enabled the colonies to become so profitable that in 1660 England's King Charles II established the royal African company to transport humans they called "Black Gold" from Africa to the Americas. When England finally outlawed its slave trade in 1807 America relied on its own internal slave trade. By 1860 a million humans were being moved and sold in the colonies. Families were torn apart; traders marched their chattel from the east coast to the southern plantations. Along the way slaves were herded like animals into crowed pens, yards, and warehouses. Traders and owners wanted a self-reproducing labor force and the labels the used reflects the degradations of slavery. Bucks and Breeding-Wenches were sold at auctions along with prime hands to work the fields and Fancy-Girls (the graceful light skinned women who were sold into prostitution or to be mistresses to their Masters). The enslaved population was controlled by legally authorized violence, whippings, and public floggings. Owners were fined if they did not punish recaptured runaway slaves. But slavery had always had its critics in America. As the slave trade grew so did opposition and eventually American became a country divided against itself.

As we can see from this information above in how all this got started. The greed from the colonist that was reluctant to lose their free labor with the Black indentured servants because their colonies were prospering because of it. Instead of letting the Black indentured servants go free after seven years of labor, the colonist chose to make slavery for life and legalized it in 1641. That is where they went wrong. Not even God in the bible, if they were using it as their reference point permitted slavery past seven years. Let us take a quick look. In Jeremiah 34:12-14 it says, *"Then the word of the Lord came to Jeremiah: 'This is what the Lord God of Israel says: I made a covenant with your ancestors when I brought them out of Egypt, out of the land of slavery. I said, 'every seventh year each of you must free any fellow Hebrews who have sold themselves to you. After they have served you six years, you must let them go."* In the book of Exodus Chapter 21:2-3 it says, *"If you buy a Hebrew servant, he is to serve you six years. But in the seventh year he is to go free without paying anything. If he comes alone, he goes free alone; but if he has a wife when he comes, she is to go with him.* Deuteronomy 15:12-15 says it this way: *"If any of your people Hebrew men or women sell themselves to you and serve you six years, in the seventh year you must let them go free. And when you release them, do not send them away empty handed. Supply them liberally from your flock, your threshing floors and winepress. Give them as the Lord God blessed you. Remember that you were slaves in Egypt and the Lord your God redeemed you."* Slavery even if you try to defend it was never to be a permanent situation for no one. The people back then could sell themselves into slavery for work, which only lasted six years. The colonist in Virginia wanted to make it permanent because of greed. These are the facts that our children need to know that our schools will not teach. Also, notice that it says above *"Traders and owners wanted a self-reproducing labor force and the labels they used reflects the degradations of slavery. Bucks and Breeding-Wenches were sold at auctions along with prime hands to work the fields and Fancy-Girls."* It has always been about what greedy men want in this nation that gets legalized. The bible say's in Matthew 18:16 *"that in the mouth of two or three witnesses every word may be established."* Here is my second witness how all this hatred got started. Let us now to look at the deep roots of racism in America by listening to a lecture given by a U.S. Historian PhD, by the name of Ms. Jacqueline Battalora; in 2014. I was really impressed by her speech and what she says. She speaks out about race in a speech she entitled, *"The Birth of a White Nation":*

" White people did not exist before 1681. Again, white people did not exist on planet earth until 1681! Number two any claim that this group called 'White People' that this group is rooted in biology or derived from genes of biology or is innate or is from nature is a LIE! Third and final point, as a matter of foundational law, actually let me say it this way: WHITE SUPREMACY HAS BEEN EMBEDDED in the United States of America from its founding as a matter of law. I don't expect you to buy all that, to get all that or to believe all that. At least not now, but my job is to share with you the legal history that proves each of those three claims that I begin with. So, let's go, let's get started. We would have to begin this conversation in colonial north America specifically with two British colonies – Maryland and Virginia in the early 1600s. Both were British Colonies, and both shared in particular characteristics. First, their economies were both rooted (foundational) in tobacco farming. If you know very much about tobacco farming, it requires tremendous human labor. Lots and lots of workers. Therefore, those who owned large plantations constantly needed laborers to do the work to grow the tobacco. In addition to sharing an economic base, both colonies had an incredible gender imbalance, roughly 10 men for every woman. Let understand a little bit about the folks that constitutes the people in these two colonies. There was a population boom in England in the early 17th century and there were lots of poor British people in dire straight for work. They could not find a way to make a living, they could not feed themselves. Therefore, the King of England (King James) was quite happy to have them sign a contract of indenture to then go work in the British Colonies both enslaves and indentured people, according to historian Edmond Morgan, both enslave, and indentured people were sold and traded like cattle. But of course, not all laborers stand equal in

terms of their labor agreement or lack thereof. Those who came under a term of indenture worked for a term of years and presumably this indenture was an agreement that they chose to enter in to. The terms of indenture were largely protected by British Law. Although the terms that took form in Colonial North America were quite different than those that existed in England. For example: In England, indentured servants could marry because that was the way that viewed to produce the next group of workers. In this country, indentured servants were prohibited from marrying and if women fortunate enough to get pregnant during their term of indenture, they added usually about seven to nine years onto their term of indenture and one year to the father. Slavery, of course of was a status that came with life. Work for life! There was neither British Law or International Law to prohibit or restrict slavery. What we do know is at this time period in Colonial North America there were free persons of African descent. We know that land holders freed slaves by doing so in Wills, by allowing them to purchase their own freedom or the freedom of a family member. The vast majority of laborers/workers in Colonial North America at this time were British Men. The vast majority! There were some women, Europeans laborers from Portuguese, Dutch, Ireland, and Scotland are all revealed in the records. But the vast majority were British Men. There were small numbers of persons of African descent and even smaller numbers of person of native tribes. The land holding elite in today's terms, which was the one percent. The vast majority of the persons who were in the colonies were laborers, they were British, Europeans, Africans and members of Native descent. Here is what I find that folks have the most difficult time with – we tend to really struggle with getting a good picture of social life, the social context at this juncture. We're very good at understanding the social relations that exists later. But pre-Baker's Rebellion society in something that we generally in this country struggle to grasp. I will do my best to paint a broad stroke picture of this time period.

What we know is that British and African laborers worked, ate and slept together! Furthermore, the evidence from this period which covers the first ¾ of the 17th century. That the antidotal evidence reveals that they lived under similar conditions and faced the same opportunities and chances to make it once one was free of their term of service. Whether free of enslavement or free of indentured. Let's review this: British laborers constituted the vast majority of the populations in both Colonial Maryland and Colonial Virginia. All men, because of the law of coverture, which is derived from British Common law, and it structures *marriage. This is how Barrister Blackstone, famously described marriage for that time: In marriage, the man and the woman become one and the one is the man. Women didn't have the right to retain their own wages, they couldn't create estate planning or wills of trust without the approval of a man. So, all men who were free of enslavement and indentured faced the same opportunities in these colonies as a matter of law. For example: free men of African descent could own servants or slaves and they did so. They could vote and they did. They could marry persons of the opposite sex regardless of national origin. In fact, marriages between men of African descent and women primarily of British descent were not uncommon at all. In one county, one-half of the freemen of African Descent were married a European woman. There was a challenge to these marriages, but it did not come from the masses, it came from elites. The Colonial law makers in Maryland passed a law in 1664 punishing British and other free born woman who marry enslaved negro men. The punishment for entering into these marriages was that the woman herself would be enslaved for her husband's life and any children they have would be enslaved until their 20s. Imagine that you are a plantation owner; hmm...now imagine that you are a plantation owner, that's not a bad deal, I get more property! I like that and that is exactly what happened. Rather than deter these marriages which is the expressed intent of the law of 1664, these marriages were encouraged by property owners because that in fact such a marriage increased their property value. This law of 1664 represents if not the first, certainly the precursor to anti-miscegenation law. These are laws that punish or prohibited marriage (notice that the term white people did not exist yet in 1664, at-least as referenced in that law) most generally speaking anti-miscegenation law prohibit and punished marriages between a white person and a specific non-white person or person(s). Let me be really clear, I read all the time in history book in academic text, and I hear anti-miscegenation law described as prohibiting interracial marriage. That's not correct! For example, a person of a Native Tribe could marry a person of Chinese descent both were understood as racially distinct but never did anti-miscegenation law prohibit such kinds of marriages. The only marriages that anti-miscegenation law prohibited where those between a white person and always a person of African descent and sometimes various other groups. So just we are really clear about anti-miscegenation law and its link to Whiteness. A couple of other things to know about anti-miscegenation law it's not derived from British Law. Anytime we look at law and study history and you see a break from British Common Law you always want to pay attention because it tells us something about the needs and desires of those who wielded power in the colonial context. Anti-miscegenation law was one of these laws, they were passed colony by colony and then state by state. It's a really important area of law for a number of reasons, its where this human category called "White" first appears on planet earth the first time. In addition, anti-miscegenation law is important because it lasted more than 300 years. These anti-miscegenation laws literally shaped the faces of this group of more than 2,000 X number of people that I'm looking at today. The Maryland legislators sought to correct for the encouragement of marriages that they described in that previous law of 1664 as "a disgrace to the British people." As an indication that "British or Free Born Woman must be forgetful of her status as Free." So, they passed the law of 1681 and, in this law, it made it illegal for British and other "White" women from marrying a negro slave. Furthermore, the law punished any land holder who encouraged the marriages any religious authority who performed it. This law equals the invention of the human category "White." Did these group of labors some of whom were from Portugal, from Holland, Ireland and Scotland, did they have a little genetic transformation that occurred right after the general assembly in Maryland met, creating a genetic sludge that we can now call "White?" Virginia passed its first anti-miscegenation law in 1691. In Virginia, the law prohibited both white men and white women from marrying a person of African descent or a member of a native tribe. But less I leave you thinking that gender equality was being created in this law, let me quickly dispel that. Studies of Antibel and Courts reveal that in fact anti-miscegenation law was at least in the language of the law prohibited these marriages for white men and white women. But here is what we know from Antibel and Court cases: We know that plenty of white men married or engaged in intimate sexual relations with prohibited women. However, very rarely were they brought to court and punished under the anti-miscegenation law, very rarely. So here, pay attention to this, this law in its enforcement is largely focused on controlling the relationality and sexuality of white women and non-white men. Furthermore, think about the enforcement practices that come out of this particular law. What's the result? Who becomes more available for who? We see a further step in locating patriarchal power squarely among and within white men. We've talked about the law of 1664 and the amendment to that law in 1681. And we noted that the key difference between those two is the reference to the group of concern, the language has shifted from British and other Free Born to British and other White Women, in that particular law. So, the question is, what the heck happened between 1664 and 1681? And the answer is Bacon's Rebellion in 1676. This was a massive revolt in the colony of*

Virginia that lasted more than a year. Let's talk about some of the seeds of this rebellion that gives rise to this violent outburst. Those who were enslaved, I don't think it's hard to imagine by definition of their status were disgruntle laborers. Remember that pool of readily available workers from England who were poor and happily sent off in the guts of ships? Well, they dried up, that population surge had ended and there was no longer a pool of laborers from Britain available to handle the work on the plantations in the colonies. The result is they began to impose harsher punishments on indentured servants who were already here, so that relatively minor infractions would result in significant extensions to their years of service. Those who completed their term of indenture or who were released from their status as enslaved were frustrated. They were frustrated because the King of England gave almost all the farmable land to his buddies. Even if they could find land to grow tobacco on, prices dropped, and taxes went up. So, land and other opportunities became much more limited. So, this guy Nathaniel Bacon, he didn't have to search very far for disgruntle laborers. Both those who were enslaved or indentured faced worse treatment and those freed face less ability to make a future for themselves. Persons of European and African descent fought in the first phase of Bacon's Rebellion against members of native tribes. Then in the second phase of Bacon's Rebellion, against the British Ruling Elite. Nathaniel Bacon ultimately died from wounds that he received in a battle and England sent troops into the colony and that eventually squashed the rebellion. But not without having made a significant impression upon those who wielded authority and were threatened by this rebellion. Remember, this rebellion lasted over a year and records from lawmakers in Virginia to the legal oversight authority in England revealed that over 30 percent of the population were in support of the rebellion. Here were the lessons from Bacon's Rebellion: A united labor force is a threat to the form of capitalism taking hold within the colonies. Virginia law makers wrote letters to the oversight authority in London explaining that they intended to pursue a divide and conquer strategy in order to prevent a future rebellion. Its' only after Bacon's Rebellion that we see the emergence of White People as a group of humanity. Lets' think about this for a minute, 1681 some lawmakers invent a new label for a group of people. Imagine that I am a lawmaker and I just pass a law claiming that ¾ of you in this room are "Cronchies" and the other ¼ of you are not. Who gives a damn? Who would care? Some silly lawmaker came up with a label for you. Its' really unlikely that it would mean much but let's say I follow it with this: Those who are "Cronchies" you can pay no more than $25 dollars a night for that hotel, no more. Those who are" Cronchies" are the first to come in any room at this conference and the first to leave. The first in line at the bathroom at lunch at any other line that forms and the first to get to leave. And that these privileges and advantages that come by virtue of this label that asserted upon you as a lawmaker continues when you walk out these doors. That it shapes how you are treated and what you get to do for years and years to come. Imagine if you are one of the "Cronchies." Imagine how you might start to feel? Wow, I must be special. Imagine you are not a "Cronchie." Wow, what's wrong with me? This is not fair! Let's return to the divide and conquer strategy. Laborers prior and through Bacon's Rebellion were united. They lived the same darn lives, they faced the same opportunities, rights and privileges once they were freed from enslavement or freed from indenture. That's about to change, a slew of laws was passed in the decades after Bacon's Rebellion and continued to get passed into the first quarter of the next century. The first slew of laws including the prohibition of Free Blacks from holding public office, the prohibition of Blacks and Native Tribes from marrying Whites, the requirements that Whites upon the completion of their terms of service be paid good including guns and gun powder and the prohibition of Free Blacks from possessing a weapon we are going to come back to that) the prohibition of Blacks testifying against Whites. These laws began to give different meaning to these labels that prior to this moment just referenced where your nation of origin was, not anymore. I want to return quickly to a law that prohibited Free Blacks from possessing a weapon. What this law did was essentially strip Free Black men of their ability to hold patriarchal power. Because look, under the law of coverture here's how things worked. Men were in control, controlled women their spouse controlled their children and had legal authority to do so including severe beatings, all financial assets and land. The man had the control, but the exchange was that in exchange for that authority, he protects. That's the tradeoff for patriarchal power. Stripped made impossible by virtue of this law. And then let's look at this law the prohibited Blacks from testifying against Whites. We will see that throughout US history. Mexicans prohibited from testifying against Whites. Chinese prohibited from testifying against Whites and then it just becomes mongrels to include people of Japanese descent and the like. So that's a law that we see throughout US history. When you look at these laws, what's the message to White people? Each one of these laws has a message to these new group of people called White folks on the one hand and a message to those who it denies or restricts on the other, each one of them. This package of laws first passed after Bacon's Rebellion did something extraordinary. Let's imagine this light up there represents the one *percent, the land holding elite, and this represents the socio-economic ladder in the colony. And so, this hand over here represents this new group of laborers called 'White Ones' and this hand over here represents laborers of African descents and members of Native Tribes. Before Bacon's Rebellion and through it, these two laborers had the same lives, faced the same opportunities and that changed. But when you look at these laws that passed that created this change, it divided and created different meaning for this group and this group, but it didn't do a whole lot to lift the economic status of White People closer to that of the White Elites. Very little movement up. What it did do is that it plummeted the bottom and created a new bottom to colonial society and shoved persons of African descent and made members of Native Tribes there. So, let's look at this group of humanity called 'White People.' We learn from this history that White People were built upon the idea that British had of themselves as white, as Christian, as freeborn, as deserving of rights and privileges from which others can be denied. To this day, White People have not been defined as a matter of law, until this day. This history teaches us that white is the tool by which laborers were divided. Those who shared the same living conditions, the same opportunity now experience us as more connected with Paris Hilton then with our African American neighbor even though our economic status is far more similar to that neighbor than to lives of the one percent. But not only did this new organization of society create a new bottom to it, it created a link that here to for had not existed that connected this new group of laborers called 'White People' with the elite. And what was that connection? The shared status called white embedded with the presumption of its superiority. The other thing to note about the invention of white people and the meaning of white that this history reveals. Is that white constituted the center of patriarchal power and we see that most clearly through anti-miscegenation law and specifically through its enforcement. We are going to move from the 17th century to the 18th century. The American Revolution has taken place and the First Congress of the United States of America will meet for the first time. And when they meet, they will establish laws regarding citizenship in this new country. This is a picture of the building where they met in New York. Here are the men who represented the First Congress. These laws regarding citizenship include an area of law call 'Naturalization Law.' Naturalization Law provides the process in which one who is not born in the country can become a citizen. The First Congress of the United States determined in 1790 that in order to become a naturalized citizen of this new republic called the United States of America, one had to be White. This was valid law in the United States until 1952 (Wow, how do you like those apples?). You had to be white to be a US citizen. And as often the case, laws impacted those who are female then those who are male. No less true with the naturalization law, for example: white women who were citizens, if they dare to marry a man who was ineligible for citizenship via the naturalization law, in other words, he wasn't white. She loses her citizenship; these laws work to make white women most available to white men and frankly all women available to white men. The requirement of whiteness in naturalization law has had a significant impact on various groups of people who have come to the United States of America. In fact, the naturalization law was a significant piece of evidence used in the Plessy vs Ferguson case in 1896 to determine that US citizenship status and therefore protections of the constitution where never intended to be applied to persons of African Descent. Naturalization Law assured that the masses of Chinese laborers Japanese laborers and various other groups of laborers that came to this country would remain cheap – dependent labor! Why? Because even though they were significant in number, especially relevant to their employer and land holders and railroad companies… if you're not white you're not a US citizen and if you are not a US citizen, you don't vote, if you can't vote, you can't voice your political needs and desires. Thereby, reducing these groups of people to dependent cheap labor. In addition, Naturalization Law was used to block persons of Chinese, Japanese and Pilipino, we can go on and on, various groups not only did it result in them getting paid less for doing the same job, but all kinds of taxes got imposed upon them. There was a foreign wage tax, various laws were passed blocked them from being able to work in the public sector, blocked them from being of holding a managerial position. Then of course, alien land laws were passed, these were laws that made it illegal for those ineligibles for naturalization, i.e., not white people, made it illegal for them to own property. So, what's the results of these laws for white people? Right, because were really good about seeing the harm that these laws caused for certain groups. But let's get the flip side of that coin. When I make land, when I make a whole group of people ineligible to purchase land it makes more land and cheaper for me, for White People. When you're the lowest paid worker and prohibited from moving up as a matter of law, then those positions that get paid more or more desirable are more available to white people. So, we see just from this one law, and I can spend another hour with you at least going through these combinations of laws: naturalization law, anti-miscegenation law and immigration policy all that combined in these ways to continue in advantage to give economic value, symbolic value to white people to give us the unearned advantages that we continue to receive today. I have a favor to ask:*

Would yawl close your eyes for a moment? Close your eyes, imagine a society where White Supremacy is not embedded in our institutions. Sit with it! Think of the person complex. Think of our education system. Think of Church on Sunday, Synagogue on Saturday, Temple, Mosque. Think about the organization of neighborhoods. Think about the government of the United States and how assets and resources would be distributed. It looks pretty different, doesn't it? White Supremacy...you can open your eyes if you like... is institutionally embedded in the United States of America as a matter of foundational law. So, what do we do? Whatever image you had of an institution, an example, a relationship that was free of institutionalized and personally held on to against White Supremacy...hold that! Hold on to it, it's a glimpse, it's a tool to tell us where we need to go, where we can go. It offers hope!

As we can see from Jaqueline's speech, America's legislative history has been embedded in racism and white supremacy from its foundation. So, when we see former President Trump attacks Bob Woodward after he questioned him about white privilege in America stating that Mr. Woodward "must *have dranked the Kool-Aid.*" It is clear to me that the former President is inept in America's history. The colonist began racist legislative policy making that were intentionally written against people of color starting with states like Maryland and Virginia. But I guess the former President of the United States did not get that information in his history class in school either. These laws and policy making habits permeated across America down to local and state governments. Not only the letter of these laws was wrong, but the spirit of them were racist in nature. To me it becomes clear who was the one that *"dranked the Kool-Aid"* and it was not Bob Woodward. The *Kool-Aid* was passed down to him from his father, Frederick Christ Trump. He was known to march in Ku Klux Klan rallies in New York. Therefore, we can see that spirit of racism and white supremacy was already in his father. There is a wise saying still to this day that says, *'the apple doesn't fall far from the tree.'* The former president had his father's spirit. He was taught as a child that he was better, that others were below him and worse thing he could ever do is lose. That is why we saw such bizarre behavior from him for four years. I have one question for you all, did anyone notice his father's middle name? I did so. It is *"Christ."* I have noticed that the self-righteous historically love to attach bible names to themselves. What is that all about? Just because you attach a bible name to yourself it does not mean that God is with you. That person can still be a devil. Before I conclude this chapter, I want to say this very clearly that you all may understand. What we are seeing today with these Christian politicians and militia groups is the same *spirit* for white power, supremacy, privilege, and racial bias towards black/brown people that started with the colonist in Virginia and Maryland in the early 1600s. That power was to established control for the European colonist in the early 1600s. We are seeing that same spirit rises its ugly head again today through legislators, politicians, lawmakers, militia groups and notable Church leaders. It is at work in our politics and policies. If you do not believe me, look at how legislators are changing the voter laws in the state of Georgia since Donald Trump lost the re-election and the republicans lost two House seats. It is just another way of streamlining Black and Brown people out of the voting process in racist states. Then you take these local and state legislations from these states and over lay it with Federal Government policies that support a racially insensitive former President. He had a team of Senators, Congressman and Governors that was willing to do anything, including break the law to keep him in office. This is how America catapult backwards more than 50 years in race relations in less than four years during the Trump administration. Unfortunately, many prejudice Americans became Greedy Again for power like the colonist did in the early 1600s. Hear me when I say this: much of the protest that we have seen in the past several years that has happened in our cities like Charlottesville, NC; Minneapolis, MN; Elizabeth, NC; Glenn County, GA; Sanford, FL; Ferguson, MO and your own local town are all steeped in prejudice policies, habits and attitudes that many legislators are not willing to give up even in the 21st century. That is why *"Black Lives Don't Matter"* to them. What our cable news channels, and I-phones are not capturing when reporting these police shootings is how many Black people are living below the poverty line in these areas. We are not seeing the impoverished environments from lack of work, plants closing and the prejudice culture that these police shootings are happening. It is the attitude that these police officers have towards Black people in these communities that does not make them hesitate to kill. Don't get me wrong, I have met and experienced some very good white police officers. It is those bad apples that are among them that has caused so many problems. As I showed earlier that the attitude was developed through legislation out of Virginia written back in the 1600s. We do not see this kind of senseless shootings by police towards those that live in suburban or more affluent neighborhoods. They only do it in the Black and Brown communities. If you have noticed, the police exercise discretion when dealing with white men and women. I watched a YouTube video where a white man called *"Jerry"* fought two police officers to the ground. He took one of their police night sticks, struck both officers with it and then stole their Sheriff vehicle. The man drove off unharmed without one shot was fired at him by either officer who also were white. If that would have been a Black man, one of the officers would have shot him before he could get to their night stick. We must understand that state laws are written to protect the police in case they do dispose of anyone *(just like the ones written in the 1600s if a white person or slave master killed a Negros slave)*. It is no different today. This is how it has been in the past with these laws. Once again, no accountability when a white officer takes a Black life. Legislation has been written to keep policing power and judgement in their control with very few questions asked. There is nothing new under the sun. Until we change the infrastructure of who are our law makers, Prosecuting Attorneys, Judges, and Attorney Generals across this nation that do not care, then we will continue to see the mayhem that we have been witnessing around the country. Everything is based on infrastructure and who is making these decisions of right and wrong. We need Black and Brown Attorney Generals, District Attorney's and Governors for each state that see the problems and do care. The only reason we saw a conviction in the George Floyd case in 2021 is because Minnesota finally got an African American Attorney General in 2019 by the name of *Keith Ellison* who pursued the case. He put together a phenomenal team of lawyers to investigate, fight the police brutality in his state and what was done to George Floyd. Keith and his team have become the blueprint of what we need to see in each of our states to settle these abusive and deadly policing matters. That spirit is now being held accountable and must end in America!!!!!!

Chapter Four

Back To the Spirit of Greed

"What Made Americans Greedy Again"

W.M.A.G.A

"Racism in America and Why the Church Is Not Innocent"

"If anyone says, 'I Love God," yet hates his brother, he is a liar"

1 John 4:20

Anyone reading this book by now could say, 'Wow, Ken," you have sure been hard on the Church with this whole racism thing. One would ask, why so? Well, it is because we have found out in the past few years that we can-not always count on a lot of our *prophets, pastors, and priest* and those who have the access to people through media to speak out against racial bigotry and disparity in this nation. We know that we live in a country that has an overwhelming history of racial bias but very few try to do something about it. Therefore, it is going to take everyday people like you and I who are reading this book to stand up to speak for those who suffer when influential men have no regard for them. The remarkable thing about the bible if you read it is that you get a chance to hear a lot about God's heart through the Old Testament scriptures, prophets, and the letters of the apostles. It has a way of bringing a balance between right, wrong and how we should treat all people. Right before I started drafting this book, I heard God voice speak to me and say, *"We are not second-class citizens (meaning Black people), but first-rate human beings made in the image and likeness of God."* Now, that will preach! We must treat other right because we are all people who have been made *"in his image and after his likeness (Genesis 1:26)."* We must watch how you treat all people. Let me remind the Church to what the Apostle Paul said to the saints in Corinth, *"For it is written: 'I will destroy the wisdom of the wise; the intelligence of the intelligent I will frustrate.' Where is the wise person? Where is the teacher of the law? Where is the philosopher of this age? Has not God made foolish the wisdom of the world? For since in the wisdom of God the world through its wisdom did not know him, God was pleased through the foolishness of what was preached to save those who believe. Jews demand signs and Greeks look for wisdom, but we preach Christ crucified: a stumbling block to Jews and foolishness to Gentiles, but to those whom God has called, both Jews and Greeks, Christ the power of God and the wisdom of God. For the foolishness of God is wiser than human wisdom, and the weakness of God is stronger than human strength. Brothers and Sisters, think of what you were when you were called. Not many of you were wise by human standards; not many were influential; not many were of noble birth. But God chose the foolish things of the world to shame the wise; God chose the weak things of the world to shame the strong. God chose the lowly things of this world and the despised things and the things that are not to nullify the things that are, so that no one may boast before him" (1 Corinthians 1:19-29).* It is obvious that the Evangelical Church in their quest for political power have a huge grievance. One of the constant mistakes that I see the Church does is try to enforce godliness, righteousness, holiness, and the scriptures that the Father is calling his children to live by on the world through legislative policy. When I came to Christ, I did not do it because it was a federal or state law for me to do so. Nor did I do it because the scriptures were federally, stately, or locally enforced. Living for Christ is voluntary after one has come into the knowledge of God, the forgiveness of sins and the need for salvation. I have been telling Church folk for years that you cannot legislate godliness and righteousness. People will never do what is righteous just because you make it law or put all so-called Christians in power. We have many Christians in public office and they themselves cannot treat people fairly. If one's conscience is not convicted by the Word of God or heart is not converted, then chances are they are going to do what they want to do until they learn to do better by God's Word. Instead, the Evangelical Church grievance has made them forget what the Apostle Paul said to the Church over 2,000 years ago. They have taken their grievance too far and put their faith in an ungodly man and made the Church, and its supporters look stupid along the way. Now what we have is very few can even trust in the Church and what it teaches anymore for they saw that the Church people do not treat all men properly themselves. Proverbs 11:7 say's it like this *"Hope placed in mortals die with them; all the promise of their power comes to nothing."* The Church attempting to anoint the former President by controlling the narrative about his character and saying that he was *"God's Man."* We must recognize that the Church Leaders said that about him and not God! The Church said he was God's man. Well, if that were true, we would not have seen so much division during his term in office. Whatever it was that the Evangelicals were trying to push to the Church at large, it will now have to deal the world's not so favorable view of it moving forward. I have never been so disappointed with my brothers and sisters in Christ in all my years as a believer. It was an embarrassment to the Church that Christ has built upon a rock. If the Evangelicals where so in tuned with what God and what He was doing one would think they would know when it comes to *injustice, inequality, imbalances and unfairness,* God has no tolerance for it by anyone. Proverbs 11:1 reads, *"The Lord detests dishonest scales, but accurate weights find favor with him."* Anything or anyone out of balance, unfair or unjust He detests. Therefore, it pays for people to read the Word for yourself. You would think that the Evangelicals would know this when it comes to standing up for what is right and against wrong. They would have known what it says in Proverbs 11: 3 that *"The integrity of the upright guides them, but the unfaithful are destroyed by their duplicity."* You would think that they would know when it comes to who God calls righteous and to lead a people that there would be evidence that follows. Proverbs 11: 10-11, both say it like this: *"When the righteous prosper, the city rejoices; when the wicked perish, there are shouts of joy. Through the blessing of the upright a city is exalted, but by the mouth of the wicked it is destroyed."* There was no evidence of the nation rejoicing when the former President took office, and his mouth almost started another civil war. The city did not rejoice, especially the inner cities of America. There was no evidence of America being exalted in the world to foreign counties when he took office. In fact, when he went to address the United Nations General Assembly, they laughed at him. But there was evidence of our nation's reputation being destroyed and almost destroying one another the entire time he was in the White House. It makes me think that we have given too many Christian people credit for reading and understanding the bible just because they have influence in this nation. I am seeing where many of them did not understand it at all. They are novices when it comes to the Word. Therefore, many Evangelical Churches today is now wrestling with the stress of trying to keep their doors open. Like a zebra who changes its stripes many of them are now trying to change what they believe about race and racism, but it might be too late to retrack their inaction. The Genie is already out of the bottle. One former popular Mega Church in Denver has closed its doors, sold the building and it has been said it will be torn down and new apartments/condominiums will be put up in its place. This is so sad. Americans arc trying move forward to a better world without the influence of the Church because they openly saw its duplicity. They Church should have been taking a stand on race and racism known to the world a long time ago. The truth of the matter is that the Church was too insensitive to the abuses done to *"Black Lives"* by law enforcement in America. They were too busy embracing conspiracy theories that came from the Q' Anon cult instead of standing up for their Black brothers and sisters. It has now caught up to us. These facts are that it caused so much pain, division, and violence in America while the Church watched and said absolutely nothing. If anything, the Church made things worse not better. People saw the sincere heart of our Church leaders and are having a tough time now embracing the institution. The world watched how the Church honored and respected forty-three white Presidents all the way up to George W. Bush, then disrespected the first black President Barrack Obama. The Evangelical Church leaders treated him with contempt, dishonor, disrespect, and disdain for eight years. To add insult to injury the Evangelical Church turned around after his term and had overwhelming support, respect, and appreciation for another white President - #45, Donald Trump. What do you think that said to a people that is paying attention? Were they blind? Are they delusional? You can say what you want and think what you want, but *'perception is reality'* to most people. It is what it is! That is exactly what people of color witnessed in this nation and abroad. But we have those who want Black and Brown people to close their eyes, shut their mouths and say nothing about it. Fortunately, I am not one of them, thank you Jesus! I know what I saw for 12 years, and it was the most bigoted and racist spirit that one could fathom. Not all Black people are blind to the historical racial issues that is in this country like Senator Tim Scott. If you listen to him talk, he basis his view on if America is racist through his own personal experience, which is ridiculous for any Black man to ever do. Senator Tim Scott has not lived all over this country and dealt with everyone in this nation. He has only dealt with the conservatives that accept him if he lives conservative. Let him say anything that is not conservative speech, (for example, wanting band the death penalty) and he will soon find out if America is racist. We should never let our experiences determine if racism exist. It is just your experience. It has extraordinarily little to do what is really going on in the world. There is a thing called *"Miles Law"* as explained by David French of the Atlantic Journalism. It is contained in a single simple sentence: *"Where you stand depends on where you sit."* I too have been treated very well by many whites in my life, but that does not erase the racism that is still in this nation that affect many people. Let us listen to Senator Scott's words in a recent article written: *"Sen. Tim Scott on Wednesday offered up a GOP alternative to President Joe Biden's vision for the country, pushing back on Biden's agenda in a wide-ranging speech that propelled the South Carolina Republican further into the national spotlight. In the official GOP response to Biden's first joint address to Congress, Scott, the only Black Republican in the upper chamber, drew on his own personal experiences to push back on the drastic expansion of government that has defined Biden's first 100 days in office — from his pandemic relief package to the president's proposals on jobs and infrastructure. "We should be expanding options and opportunities for all families — not throwing money at certain issues because Democrats think they know best," Scott said. Scott's racial identity and conservative politics have made him a rarity in Congress, where he hasn't been afraid to lean into both. And Wednesday was no exception. During his speech, Scott reiterated that he has "experienced the pain of discrimination." But he also emphasized that "America is not a racist country" and cautioned that "race is not a political weapon to settle every issue the way one side wants," citing voting rights as an example."* I have heard some Black people in America say the same thing that Senator Tim Scott said in the article. I admonish them to never give that kind of verdict on this nation because of their own personal experience especially when it has hundreds of years of history that says different. One's personal experience has nothing to do with the history of that nation. Some of my friends all the way on the island Dominica that sits in the Caribbean Sea said to me that they noticed the racial difference in how Americans and Christians treated all the previous Presidents in this country verses how they treated first black President Barrack Obama. They saw it a fifteen hundred miles away. They could see that there were no National Prayer Breakfast held by the Evangelical Church for Obama and he too is a Christian. Just in-case you did not know about Dominica it is because our so-called historians and geographers when creating the world map did not want us to know about Black nations and Islands like Dominica… It is located over 1400 by air from Miami, Florida. Dominica is an independent Black nation that broke off from British rule in 1975. It was one of the main islands that slaves were brought to and sold during the Atlantic Slave Trade. Believe it or not, I learned about it myself through a dream that God gave me. By now you are starting to see that some my dreams a very real. I have been there a few times. Forty-Nine (49) percent of the slaves that came from Africa ended up on many of the islands in the Caribbean Sea. My friends on this island explained to me how they saw for themselves that the Evangelical Church in America was well behind all the faith-based initiatives and had multiple prayer breakfasts when George Bush and other Presidents. They saw the bias and how the Evangelical Church was completely silent, isolated from, and disregarded Barrack Obama. They saw no national prayer breakfasts for him by the evangelicals for eight years.

Most of the evangelical pastors would not dare to mention the man's name let alone pray for him and his administration. They noticed when Donald Trump became President that the Evangelical Church rose with voice, support, respect, appreciation, and all kinds of prayers for him. How did they notice it? They have access to BBC News and other cable News channels that reports on everything going on in America. They have access to our Christian radio and TV stations like; Focus on The Family, Moody School of the Bible, 700 Club, Facebook, Twitter…etc. This image of the Church in America is out there to millions around the world. Its' an image that the Church created itself. Unfortunately, many Black and Brown people have seen the Evangelicals honest heart. It is not about the Kingdom as they say. It is not about the Body of Christ as they want us to believe. We have seen that it is still about them and their ability to have power to control everything from the Church to Politics. I agreed with my Christian brothers on this island, for I saw the same things right up close in this nation. All I can say is that when you get to the chapter *"What Can the Church Do"* pay attention to the open letter written by John Pavlovitz, *"White Evangelicals, this is Why People Are Through with You."* It is a powerful letter that I included in the book. Unfortunately, it is the way a lot of evangelicals have managed themselves during the Bush, Obama, and Trump administrations. I will say that the matters that divide our nation have publicly discredited the faith and it only took one man to do it. The former President has not only weakened the Republican Party, but he has hampered the influence of the Evangelical Church in America. How was that done? The Church publicly pronounced and accepted him as I quote *"God's Chosen, God's Man, God's Anointed."* Let me say, God is not the author of confusion, and He despises those that creates discord among the brethren. The bible says that very clearly. There is not one of these Evangelical Church Leaders that can truly stand up and say that the former President did not create confusion and willfully bring discord between the brethren. There was not a Church, Family, Branch of Service or Business that did not have to deal with the impact of his divisive rhetoric for four years. It pays to read your bible so that you are not gullible to swallow everything someone tells you. Unfortunately, this was the problem that the slaves had with the preachers and evangelist in America on the plantations in the South. The narrative was already chosen and controlled by the slave masters. The slaves had no way of reading and knowing any different. They could not be caught reading the bible, so they were dependent on the born-again, spirit-filled preacher's and evangelist interpretation from their controlled pulpits. Do not feel bad, the Catholic Church did the same thing for hundreds of years to their followers with only allowing their Bishops and Popes to own/read and interpret the Bible to their congregations. It was not until Martin Luther busted that whole thing up by posting his 95 Theses condemning the excesses and corruption of the Roman Catholic Church on October 31, 1517, that began the Protestant Reformation. It also pays to study Church history. It gives you an idea of why things are the way they are and if there has been change. The average American citizen have observed the Evangelical Church bias over these three past Presidential Administrations and to their own doing, we have seen their *favoritism, partiality, and culpability towards racial issues.* As I said that I speak with believers all over this nation and other countries who seen the same things that we have seen in this nation and are so done with the *"Church in America!"* Churches are now scrambling feeling the backlash of those who do not trust in their words anymore and trying to change their stipes. Instead of owning up, apologizing, and repenting for their lack of actions some are now playing the victim. I have heard many Pastors now saying how the Church is under attack. These Pastors are starting to feel disrespected and dishonored. Isn't it amazing how the Church leaders are saying that they are under attack when it was them that did not speak up about the racism in America towards young Black men and women? What these pastors who feel like they are under attack do not realize is that this void in their congregations was brought on by their own inaction. People expect their pastors to speak when there is a racial injustice being done to a people. I have heard that during the pandemic tens of thousands of churches in America have completely closed. There were another hundreds of thousands of clergy and church employees that had to get regular jobs. Churches that survived the pandemic had to figure out alternative ways to hold services for they could no longer afford the expenses of how they paid staff. May I remind you what 1 Peter 4:17 says' *"For it is time for judgement to begin at the household of God."* If one wants to say that God is judging America just remember that His judgement will always begin first at the household of God. Why? Because God is a loving father and does not discipline the children down the street. A father disciplines his own children. The Church is His household and if it has been disobedient in how it is functioning or representing Him in the world then there are consequences. He disciplines His household so we can be more like Him. Therefore, what I would say to all the Church Leaders that are putting it out there that the Church is under attack. I would say No, the Church is being exposed and disciplined. Therefore, humble yourselves, take this butt whooping, and become better representatives of Him when racism starts permeating this country again. It has also been said that history always repeats itself. I want to remind you that by the late 1860s, the Black people who were slaves in America were no longer forced to worship or go to church with their masters. Therefore, thousands of Black people during that time abandoned the segregated evangelical churches. In 2020, once again a countless number of Black people left evangelical churches across America because of the racial insensitivity that they saw in our Church leaders. It was not only Black people that left these churches but there were many whites who also left. For many of them did not agree with racial division in America that went unspoken about by a lot of pastors. George Floyd's death on video has caused them to rethink the treatment of Black people in this nation while the Church Pastors remained silent. I have always said, *"People are not stupid, many do pay attention to what is going on in the world and church whether you realize it or not."* I have personally watched the Church as a believer closely for the past 16 years and what I observed all I can say is that *"I am not stupid either!"* The real problem in America is that we do not have enough people with backbone that will exercise their human ability of critical thinking in our church services. We are so gullible that we just eat everything that someone says without question or thought. Hear me when I say this, I do not have a problem with the institution of the Church, God, Jesus, The Body of Christ, Faith, The Holy Spirit, or Salvation. I am a believer and benefactor of all of it. What I do have a problem with is the representatives of all these things and their lack of voice for a man *(George Floyd)* who was publicly lynched right before our eyes in broad daylight. It did not matter if he was a crack-addict, no human being deserves to have the life choked out him like we all saw on cable news. The Evangelical Church act like they had no eyeballs when that was on every cell phone and television. That was a terrible response by our so-called God-Fearing leaders. We all watched the police officer in Minneapolis keep his knee and body weight on George's neck for 9 minutes and 29 seconds until he was dead. The sad part is that many in the Church was not disturbed enough to say anything publicly about it at all. To me that video was the final limit in America. We already had shown in this nation that we could not see the racial hatred in this country when George Zimmerman of Sanford, Florida shot and kill 17-year-old Trayvon Martin. Now Zimmerman is trending on social media signing Confederate Flags and packages of Skittles. Then we get George Floyd's death in front of our eyes and the Church still says nothing. It should have been enough for every pulpit across America to be in outrage against such racist actions. To see a person's civil rights denied while being arrested and treated like he is an animal was uncalled for. To add insult to injury, a few days after his death, I watched several pastors on social media treat their pulpits like any given Sunday and business as usual. They said extraordinarily little or nothing at all that would help heal the hearts and pain of many black, brown, and whites. People were hurting that watched the incident repeatedly that weekend on cable news. I am reminded of what the Lord said to the Israelites when delivering them out of Egypt about how to treat people or immigrants that we in the Church so often forget: *"Do not kill the innocent and the just, because I will not justify the guilty. You must not take a bribe, for a bribe blinds the clear-sighted and corrupts the words of the righteous. You must not oppress a resident alien (immigrants – this is what have we done in America?); you yourselves know how it feels to be a resident alien (immigrant) because you were resident aliens (immigrants) in the land of Egypt"* (Exodus 23:6-9). The Apostle James addressed the believers in his day in an equivalent way. He said in *James 2:1-12 "My brothers and sisters, believers in our glorious Lord Jesus Christ must not show favoritism. Suppose a man comes into your meeting wearing gold ring and fine clothes, and a poor man in filthy old clothes also comes in. If you show special attention to the man wearing fine clothes and say, 'Here's a good seat for you,' but say to the poor man, 'You stand there' or 'Sit on the floor by my feet,' have you not discriminated among yourselves and become judges with evil thoughts? Listen, my dear brothers and sisters: Has God chosen those who are poor in the eyes of the world to be rich in faith and to inherit the kingdom he promised those who love him? But you have dishonored the poor. Is it not the rich who are exploiting you? Are they not the ones who are dragging you into court? Are they not the ones who are blaspheming the noble name of him to whom you belong? If you really keep the royal law found in scripture, 'Love your neighbor as yourself,' you are doing right. But if you show favoritism, you sin and are convicted by the law as lawbreakers. For whoever keeps the whole law and yet stumbles at just one point is guilty of breaking all of it. For he who said, 'You shall not commit adultery, also said, 'You shall not murder.' If you do not commit adultery but do commit murder, you have become a lawbreaker. Speak and act as those who are going to be judged by the law that gives freedom, because judgement without mercy will be shown to anyone who has not been merciful. Mercy triumphs over judgment.* It is worth mentioning here that the word also says, *"Have nothing to do with the fruitless deeds of darkness, but rather expose them.* That is why it says: *'Wake up, sleeper, rise from the dead, and Christ will shine on you* (Ephesians 5:11-14). Unfortunately, when it comes to the elements of greed in America with bad character and divisive speech that goes all the way to the White House, many of our leaders *(natural and spiritual)* are *complicit, asleep, silent, or dead.* They have no intentions of exposing the fruitless deeds of darkness that have divided us and set our nation back more than 50 years. A nation that has a birth defect of slavery with embedded systemic racism can-not afford to wink at *white supremacist, militia, and nationalist* groups. I know this is not something that people like to hear, but the fact of the matter is that racism in the heart of millions of people still exist in our nation. History shows that men went over into Africa from Europe in the 1600s and ripped Black men, women and children from their families, and homeland against their wills. They were put in slave camps in Africa, locked down in the belly of ships, sold on Caribbean Islands, moved on to places like Brazil, Puerto Rico, Cuba and finally to America. These men did everything possible from the time they captured Black people who were human and treated them like animals to break their spirits, wills to make them subjective to all whites. Any resistance was deemed as disobedience and was validation for death. Who were these people to say the African people were disobedient? Where the Black people supposed to let white men abuse them with no resistance at all? This was always arrogant and narcissistic to me. No, the Africans were fighting for survival. Even one of their own top Phycologist shows in his Maslow's Hierarchy of Needs scale that man's most important need are physiological needs that starts with *"air."* The slaves could not breathe (like George Floyd) in the belly of those ships, they were not rebellious. They were suffocating, fighting for air and other physical needs like food, water, and safety. The truth of the matter is that those of us Black people who were born in America are the descendants of those suffering slaves who were treated so badly by whites for hundreds of years. What many of our republican leaders fail to realize is that there are millions of Black people that refuse the very thought of a *society, government, leadership, or Church* that takes us back to those years. I will say that this is not the chronicles of an angry Black man, once again, I am not a racist! I have white members in my family, my grandchildren are mixed and on my grandmother side I am part Irish through a marriage. My great, great, great, great grandmother Nancy from North Carolina was married to a man by the name of Martin O' Neal (changed to Neal) from Virginia whose father was from Dublin, Ireland. The ironic thing about this marriage is that my family and I traced the marriage to have happened in the 1860s right before or after slavery was abolished. To make it doubly confusing is that the state of Virginia where they were married was the birther of Anti-miscegenation laws as early as 1641. These laws were still on the books in many states until overturned on June 12, 1967, by *Loving vs Virginia.* They were still on the books when me and all my siblings were born. Obviously, these laws were not enforced especially when a European man married a Black woman. My great, great, great, great Grandmother Nancy and Grandfather Martin had children. One being my great, great, great Grandmother Martha, who birthed my great, great Grandmother Dora, who birth my great Grandmother Ethel, who birthed my Grandmother Rita, who birth my mother, Carol. As I said, I am not racist but what I am is serious about this subject of the history of racism in America and the Church not being innocent! I have paid close attention to the attitudes, hearts, minds, feelings, behaviors, and emotions of a lot of Caucasian men/women in the political and spiritual sphere since 2008. Trust me, I have watched a lot of it. What I observed during this period was many times mind boggling. It was wrong how President Barrack Obama was isolated by politicians and Evangelical Church leaders that preach that we are to submit to those who are in authority over us. Well, they sure did not submit to Barrack Obama when he was President. But these same evangelicals will push their agenda for people to recognize all the other Presidents' that this country has had and prayed for them. Barrack Obama was not prayed for by the evangelical preachers at all. What does that tell you? Instead of being silent on this issue, I have chosen to write about it and expose the darkness that is in our Churches. Especially towards those Black people who dare to lead this country. The evangelicals will tell you that they did not isolate him because he was black but because they did not like his policies. Enough is Enough! We hear all the time that *"Facts Matter."* I say, heart, minds, conduct, attitudes, and behavior matter even more. It tells you with whom you are dealing. Knowing what is in a person's heart is difficult and I do not claim to know. But if you pay close attention to what they say and do or what they do not say and do, it may lead you close to who they really are deep inside. I am not going to sugar coat anything in this book. It will be clear to anyone who reads it that I believe that we must get our *act together* and *hearts right* in the Church. Once again, people are not stupid! I'll be honest about who I am and how I feel rather than have my readers think that I am someone that I am not. What I am is for what is right and how we treat everyone. The Apostle Luke teaches us that *"for it is out of the abundance of the heart that the mouth speaks"* (Luke 6:45b). It has been through my ability to sit and watch what people do or do not do and say or do not say over these past 16 years that has helped me draft this book. I have seen what was in the hearts of many that is supposed to be the *"Salt of the Earth and Light of the World"* (Matthew 5:13). When you grow up in a household with three siblings, one mother and an uncle that comes to check on you, there is a natural fight to get your mom's and uncle's attention amongst the four children.

If you are the third child (in which I was) you are not going to get the attention of your mom and uncle as much as your two older brothers and younger sister (by default) because she was the only girl. Therefore, I learned at an early age to be silent and watch what people say and do to learn. I do know what is going on in America. I have watched it for 16 years. I have been watching and listening to our *senators, congressperson, governors, mayors, lawyers, journalist, business executives, scholars, college professors, pastors, and presidents.* To be honest with you, it has been very discouraging and disappointing! Therefore, I was more encouraged by listening to two older journalist *(Dan Rathers and Tom Brokaw)* who have covered every major story in America since the 1960s speak up and express the same exact concerns I have as to what has been going on in America over the past years concerning racism. These two legendary journalists made more sense to me than all the so-called present day elite leaders in our government hallways and godly pulpits. These are two older men that have influence and the respect of the American public who in their old age have expressed openly the concerns of the direction of where this nation has been heading with the racial divide for some time. They both know that America is changing and not for the better. It has been sliding backwards and not moving forward away from its racist ugly past. It has been like we have been trying to slide right back into it and not even the Church is alarmed by it. The goal posts of right and wrong keep moving. The rules are constantly changing to the point where right or wrong are only a matter of semantics. If you do not believe me, President Obama when he wanted to appoint a Supreme Court Judge 10 month before an Election Campaign. His nomination never got reviewed by the senate. Likewise, the Republican Senators change the rules when Ruther Bader Ginsberg passed away and was able to fill the empty Supreme Court seat during the 2020 Election Campaign within 30 days. Consider how the after Georgia lost two senates' seats in January 2021. Two months after their loss, the General Senate Assembly that was Republican controlled passed a bill to change voter election laws/rules which included: stricter ID requirements, limited voter drop boxes that can only be inside advance polling places during the hours they are open, setting earlier absentee ballot request deadlines, restrictions on Sunday early voting a tradition mostly held by the Black churches in Georgia to reduce voter turnout. The rules always change when the people that make them are not winning. Unfortunately, in America, what is truth, right and wrong is being changed regularly depending on who is in power. How about our Senators and Congressman on capitol hill who could not determine if our national security had been breached by a foreign government or not? The problem is that many of these Senators and Congressman cannot even admit that the sun is in the sky let alone confess that our nation suffered a national security breach by a foreign government. In 2016, America experienced one the most serious security breaches on our nations soil since its democracy. The tampering of foreign(s) government into our election process with people of high degree who were clearly not concerned about it. I am struck with amazement as one who served honorably 35 years ago in the United States Air Force and had responsibility for our national security working for a subsidiary unit for the Joint Chiefs of Staff and for a Telecommunication Squadron overseas. I also worked at the White House and conducted formal protocol functions at the Pentagon, Arlington Cemetery, U.S. Capital Building, National Archives…etc. I know first-hand the seriousness and gravity of our nation's security. It is nothing to play with and only trusted people should be doing those kinds of jobs. Even General James Robert Clapper said it himself, *"never have I seen and heard so many arguments, excuses, and rhetoric against the evidence that our National Security Agency, Federal Bureau Investigation and Central Intelligence Agency found to be true that Russia did meddle and breach our election system. Never have I seen such derelict of duty by congress and the senate."* If that is not a breach of our national security, I do not know what is. Instead of our nation leaders coming together and sending a strong message to Russia that this can-not and will never happen again, we have heard so many politicians' waters down and marginalize the gravity of what happen since the election turned out the way they wanted it to. How can we be so blind and unconcerned about such breach of security? What is really going on in America and how many of our top officials ignored things like this for they may have been personally involved in the breach of this nation security themselves? Who are these people that lead us and are they really who they say they are? We should all be deeply concerned! It looks like these background checks need to get much deeper into the lives of people. The Apostle Paul teaches us that *"a little leaven leavens the whole lump" (Galatians 5:9).* I ask you, what kind of leaven has breached our Senate, Congress, and White House? The leaven that we are dealing with in America today is lies, deceit, racism, and corruption that is birthed out of greed! The greed to *"Make America Great Again"* and for who? When has America ever been great for people of color, may I ask? That is the most racist slogan that anyone can produce in this country for it only dog whistle to those who want to see things back the way it used to be in this country. This greed for *white power* has travelled from the White House through the Senate, Congress, Department of Justice to government agencies, cities, states, families, universities, churches and all the way to our homes. Leadership everywhere has been infected one way or another to not make a sound about what has been happening in our country. The Church is supposed to be the prophetic voice of God in the world. I always said, either the Church is *prophetic or pathetic.* Unfortunately, the church has spent most of its time being the latter more than the former in this nation. The Church has clearly abandoned its prophetic duty when it comes to issues like: racism, unequal justice and speaking out on police brutality of Black people in this nation. We need more prophetic souls to stand up and call America into account for her historical and continued racist sins that infects the people in this country. In fact, who's responsibility has it always been to correct a people or a king when they are operating un-righteously? It has always been the prophets and the priests, but where have they been in America? I guess sleep. When the prophets and the priests go silent, the people and the government run wild. There has been a vast amount of duplicity in our modern-day leaders: *natural, political, and spiritual.* It has been insulting, demeaning and despicable for the last several years. To see the lack of conduct, character, integrity, sensitivity, and the marginalization of corrupt behavior from those who make decisions on the behalf of millions in this nation was unforgettable. They claim to be Christians but have caused others to question their Christianity and the Church. In this country, attacks from our former President on women, children, Muslims, Latinos, Blacks, Prisoners of War, Handicap, Judges, Dead people, Immigrants, and black nations has gone unchecked. They have been laughed at, ignored, and tolerated by a vast number of Christian leaders. These are the same people that wanted to promote the *"Big Lie."* That the 2020 election was rigged, illegitimate and stolen from Donald Trump. This was the biggest lie that had all kinds of corrosive effects on our democracy. I watched and listened to well named preachers in this nation repeat this lie to his millions of viewers on their broadcast. This showed me that our Christian leadership was culpable to all what was going on in our nation. I realized that the Church could speak up when they want a different turn out than what the people voted for in America. It was the lack of Christian integrity that has caused the division in this nation. When it comes to the needs of others, the Self-Righteous are clearly bias, distracted and do not have the capacity to feel what others experience in this country who are trying to make it. At the least they are utterly *"insensitive."* Greed has a way of making people look at their own situation. The acronym I created for this is *"H.I.S"* meaning they are *"Heartless, Insensitive and Selfish."* Anyone who has infected with *"H.I.S"* only thinks about *his* own, that is why I coined it *"H.I.S."* When the Spirit of Greed gets into the hearts of people it will cause them to ignore the lives of others and make them focus on HIS own welfare. It causes them to forget the lines between right and wrong. In fact, it will justify them to step on top of what is right, wrong, and even cross it when they are gaining from the situation. When people can only point to the achievements of the economy growing stronger, increase of jobs, a record number of conservative judges placed in courts, the wealthy is paying less taxes, a stronger defense of religious liberties and their personal bank accounts have grown, just know that they are not thinking about people in this nation who are looking for equal justice. Issues like racism, white nationalism, unemployment, evictions, inequality, 500,000 COVID-19 deaths *(when there were only 291, 557 total American combat deaths during World War II),* affordable healthcare and police brutality towards Black people are not on their hearts. If their investment accounts are gaining, they can care less about what is going on in the average person's world. They say they do, but they don't. They care about their own. This is what causes people to look the other way from social injustice and pass the potatoes at the dinner table while not talking about significant issues safely in their homes. The stock market went up again, that is their focus. But I am reminded, what does the bible say about greedy people, *their ill-gotten gain and those that disregard the poor*? What does it say about gaining at the expense of others and mistreating them? This too the Church has historically ignored and therefore is not innocent of it results. I will name a few verses to jar your memory:

"My son, if sinners entice you, do not consent. If they say, 'Come with us, let us lie in wait for blood; let us ambush the innocent without reason; like Sheol let us swallow them alive, and whole, like those who go down to the pit; we shall find all precious goods, we shall fill our houses with plunder; throw in your lot among us; we will all have one purse" – my son, do not walk in the way with them; hold back your foot from their paths, for their feet run to evil, and they make haste to shed blood. For in vain is a net spread in the sight of any bird, but these men lie in wait for their own blood; they set an ambush for their own lives. Such are the ways of everyone who is greedy for unjust gain; it takes away the life of its possessors" (Proverbs 1:10-19).

"The person who gathers wealth by unjust means is like the partridge that broods over eggs but does not hatch them. Before his life is half over, he will lose his ill-gotten gains. At the end of his life, it will be clear he was a fool" (Jeremiah 17:11).

"Then they come to you as a group, sit down right in front of you as

if they were my people (so called Christians), hear your words and then they don't do what you say because they're seeking only their own desires, they pursue ill-gotten profits, and they keep following their own self-interests" (Ezekiel 33:31).

While I am at it, what does the bible say about how we are to treat the foreigner, stranger, refugee, and the immigrant? Oh, it talks about that too. I can give you some those as well that the Evangelical Church has seemed to forget:

"When immigrants live in your land with you, you must not cheat them (by the way, black slaves were unwilling immigrants in this nation and if anybody has been cheated, they certainly have been. The only way to right that ship is to pay their predecessors in this nation). Any immigrant who lives with you must be treated as if they were one of your citizens. You must love them as yourself because you were immigrants in the land of Egypt. I am the Lord your God" (Leviticus 19:33-34).

"The Lord proclaims: Do what is just and right, rescue the oppressed from the power of the oppressor. Don't exploit or mistreat the refugee, the orphan, and the widow. Don't spill the blood of the innocent in this place" (Jeremiah 22:3).

Let's not even try to begin to talk about the countless innocent black blood that has been spilled in America by former slave masters, white supremist and prejudice police officers. We would be here all day.

"To the thirsty bring water; meet the fugitive with bread. O inhabitants of the land of Tema" (Isaiah 21:14).

Then we have those who want to make it seem like slavery is fake news and America never had such history. I spoke to a young male during the time I was drafting this book and listened to his defense towards slavery in America. His defense was that he never met one Black person who knew who their slave masters were. Therefore, slavery in this country can't be proven and was *fake news.* When he said that to me, I stopped him right there and said, *"well you just have met your first one"* and he was shocked. Not only did I tell him that I had documents on the people that owned us as Bordeaux slaves, I told him that they came from Grenoble, France. I informed him that I knew and been to the very location in North Carolina that my ancestors served as slaves. I let him know that I still had family living on and near those former plantations.

I let that young man know that I can put him on the phone with some of them. I advised this young man who was too young to even remember the LA riots that started behind the Rodney King beating that he was barking up the wrong tree. I told him that he must know that anytime he tries to correct a Black man about his history in America that he is arguing from a deficit and not a surplus. I informed him that the history of his ancestors in America is available for anyone that researches it. I forewarned him that it is not a particularly good. Nevertheless, I knew it was wise too to not argue with a fool. Therefore, I wouldn't and gave him my own family story and he was ready to end the conversation. Since we are on the subject about my own family history with slavery, below you will read the last will and testament from one of our family's former slave owners. From its writings you can clearly see that he and his family were Christians. This former slave owner, his family members, and siblings all prospered off the slave labor of my ancestors *(men, women, boys, and girls)*. He even praised God for his success and all he was able to accomplish. This man or his brother was the owner of my Great, Great, Great grandfather – Benjamin Bourdeaux *(we now spell our last name Bordeaux. My grandfather William Kenneth Bordeaux changed the spelling in the 1938 while he was in college at Howard University)*. This man and his brother lived, purchased many acres, and prospered off slavery in the same area in North Carolina. There were two Bordeaux Brothers in the area and both owned slaves. The story of the brothers that owned Bordeaux slaves in North Carolina is a known one in Pender County. It is so well known that I ended up talking to a white male a few years ago who had the same last name as mine. He only knew my first name but did not know my last name. I asked him where he was from and he told me Burgaw, North Carolina (which is exactly where my family is from). I told him that was where my family was from as well. I then told him that I had the same last name as him. He immediately got incredibly quiet. I told him that it was okay. It was he who began to tell me the story about the two Bordeaux brother's that owned slave in that area (in which I already knew the story). He knew that he was a descendant from that Bordeaux family and the two slave owner brothers were his ancestors. He immediately knew who I was, and I immediately knew who he was from the facts of our last names and location where our ancestors formerly lived in North Carolina. Can you imagine how strange that conversation felt between the two of us? In fact, my family and I have researched this family online records who were Christians that started slave plantations in the south when they arrived here in1684. That is when the first Mr. Bourdeaux and his wife came by ship from Grenoble, France. They landed in Charlestown, South Carolina and immediately started plantations that same year and they plantations were passed down to their children until slavery was abolished. By reading some of their last wills and testaments, the family did very well through the tobacco and cotton industry in North and South Carolina from the free labor of my ancestors. They did so well, that if our family would have been paid just 20% of what they generated through those industries my family would be doing quite well. As I include this in my writing, I am going to omit certain first names out of the last will and testament I found online so that you can pay more attention to what's in the document that proves that these people were Christians. It reads: *"IN THE NAME OF GOD AMEN, this 20th day of June in the year of our Lord one thousand eight hundred and fifteen, I "D Bourdeaux", of New Hanover County and State of North Carolina being of weak body but of sound mind and memory I therefore calling to mind the morality of my body and knowing that it is appointed for all men to die, do make and ordain my last Will and testament that is to say principally and first of all I commend my soul into hands of Almighty God that gave it and for my body to the earth to be buried in a Christian like manner nothing doubting but a General Resurrection to receive the same from the might power of God, as touching my worldly concerns wherewith it hath pleased Almighty God to help me with in this life. I give, devise, and dispose of the same in the following manner and form. Item: I give and bequeath to my Daughter P Evans, five hundred and eighty acres of Land lying in the fork of Cypress and Bee branch being part of the tract of 640 patented by me. Item 2nd: I give and bequeath to my Son D Bourdeaux the one half of all my back lands lying between the head of Beaver branch and Harpers branch being three parcels containing four hundred acres. Item 3rd: I give and bequeath to my Son M Bourdeaux the other half of the above four hundred acres to be equally divided between him and my Son Danl. Item 4thd: I leave my perishable property consisting of Negros, Stock of all kind, Farming utensils etc to be equally divided between my children, the Negros to be valued*

105

and parceled in equal lotts as near as practicable, care being taken to include in each lott a proper proportion of Small and grown ones and as far as possible, families to go together provided notwithstanding it is my will that my Daughter P Evans shall have thew family Negros. I purchased M. Ritter, Ann and her four children Fan, Jack, Rachael, and Bob, I do further hereby invest the proper right and title of the aforesaid negros together with all and Singular other property which she may inherit of me, in my Said Daughter P Evans and the heirs of her Body. In Witness whereof I have hereunto set my hand and seal the day and year above written. D Bourdeaux (his seal) Witness: J Parrish, J Poitevent. D Bourdeaux will dated 20 June 1815; probated August 1815. ***D Bourdeaux served in American Revolution as a minute man in the North Carolina service. 1790 Census of New Hanover Co, NC lists D Bourdeaux with one male over 16, three males under 16, three females and five slaves.

Finally, if nothing above I have written have convinced you *"Why the Church is Not Innocent,"* then I will leave you with a copy of an online article that was sent to me by one of my cousins written by David French with The Atlantic on March 25, 2022, entitled *"The Worst Ginni Thomas text wasn't from Ginni Thomas."* He says in one article everything I have been saying in this book. It shows just how involved prominent religious leaders and Christian lawyers were at the forefront in trying to keep the 2020 Election from being certified for Joe Biden. Also, included was a list of 73 Influential Evangelicals names in which only four of them were not white men or women who tried to *"Stop the Steal"*. The article reads as such:

"Yesterday evening, *The Washington Post*'s Bob Woodward and Robert Costa broke a rather <u>extraordinary and disturbing story</u>. Ginni Thomas, the wife of Supreme Court Justice Clarence Thomas, sent a series of text messages to Trump White House Chief of Staff Mark Meadows that is best described as utterly unhinged.

In 29 text messages (revealed so far) with Meadows, she repeated and referenced some of the wildest election conspiracy theories of the far right, demanded that Meadows do all he could to overturn the election, and expressed disgust at Vice President Mike Pence, apparently for his failure to do the president's bidding on January 6 and refuse to certify the presidential election.

And when I say she referenced wild conspiracy theories, I mean *wild*. She texted a fringe theory (popular in Q'Anon circles) that the Trump administration had watermarked ballots to trace election fraud, she forwarded a video by a known conspiracy theorist who had claimed that the Sandy Hook school shooting was a "false flag" operation, and she quoted this, from right-wing websites: This is the kind of communication that would make you worry about a family member's connection to reality. When it comes from the wife of a Supreme Court justice who enjoys direct access to the White House chief of staff, it's not just disturbing; it's damaging to the Supreme Court.

No, I don't think we can conclude that Justice Thomas has been corrupted by his wife's activism. We all know that spouses can and do possess their own, independent views. Justice Thomas's jurisprudence is squarely within conservative legal traditions and originalist legal norms. Originalists in particular have long admired the clarity of his writing and the rigor of his thought.

Yet there's no real question that Ginni Thomas's extraordinary extremism (she also attended the January 6 rally but did not storm the Capitol) creates an appearance of fanaticism that is far beyond the norms of political engagement.

It is thus understandable if ordinary Americans wonder whether she's made an impact on her husband, and it's important for Justice Thomas to recuse himself from any future cases that could potentially involve additional disclosures of his wife's communications with the White

House or her involvement in the effort to overturn the election.

But the Ginni Thomas texts were not the most alarming aspect of Woodward and Costa's story. There was a text in the chain that disturbed me more than anything Ginni Thomas wrote. It came from Meadows, and here's what it said:

This is a fight of good versus evil . . . Evil always looks like the victor until the King of Kings triumphs. Do not grow weary in well doing. The fight continues. I have staked my career on it. Well at least my time in DC on it.

One of the most dangerous aspects of the effort to overturn the election was the extent to which it was an explicitly *religious* cause. January 6 insurrectionists stampeded into the Senate chamber with prayers on their lips. Prominent religious leaders and leading Christian lawyers threw themselves into the effort to delay election certification or throw out the election results entirely. In the House and Senate, the congressional leaders of the effort to overturn the election included many of Congress's most public evangelicals.

They didn't just approach the election fight with religious zeal; they approached it with an absolute conviction that they enjoyed divine sanction. The merger of faith and partisanship was damaging enough, but the merger of faith with lawlessness and even outright delusion represented a profound perversion of the role of the Christian in the public square.

All too many Christians, people who are supposed to "act justly" and to reject the "spirit of fear" for, among other things, "sound judgment," panicked about the future of the country and the church and shed any form of critical thinking in favor of embracing the most outlandish of false allegations. And those Christians weren't just the January 6 rioters. They included believers at the pinnacle of American power.

I remember the assurances I received before Donald Trump's election. Trump-supporting Christians told me, "Trust us. If Trump wins, we'll object when he's wrong, but at least we'll have something we'd never have if Hillary Clinton wins—a seat at the table."

A long-time friend and leading member of the Christian conservative legal movement emailed me to explain that Trump will have an "open door" for evangelicals in the White House. Good people will be close to him, he assured me.

And Trump did have an open door for religious conservatives. His administration was stacked with evangelicals and other conservative Christians, and some were able to achieve important policy goals. But along with access came loyalty, and over time that loyalty morphed into a kind of political devotion I've never seen in my adult life.

Yes, I know there are Christians who want Trump's critics to "move on," but Christians aren't supposed to "move on" from sin. They're supposed to repent, and it is notable that precious few have uttered the slightest hint of an apology to the American people for their role in wrongly and recklessly attempting to instigate what could have been the gravest constitutional crisis since 1861—all in service of an obvious lie.

We don't know if Ginni Thomas had the slightest influence over her husband's jurisprudence or the White House's response to the election. But we know Mark Meadows's position, and to see his religious zeal in the pursuit of profound injustice is to remember that Christian power does not always result in Christian ethics, and that Christian moral corruption was and is a sad hallmark of the age of Trump.

Chapter Five

Back To the Spirit of Greed

"What Made Americans Greedy Again"

W.M.A.G.A

"What Would It Take to Despise Racism and Social Injustice?"

"Give justice to the weak and fatherless; maintain the right of the afflicted and the destitute"

Psalms 82:3

In my introduction to this book, I alluded to what would it take for a nation of insensitive privileged folk and leadership to realize that injustice towards anyone will eventually impact everyone. I asked, what would it take for them to realize that their insensitivity towards the poor will put them in a position to only see that they are no better than anyone else? When you read the bible, you will find that injustice towards a people *(Old Testament or New Testament)* has always been a big issue with God. He will step in to have the final word on the matter. Unfortunately, man and his quest for money, power and control has historically troubled others. Some men feel that there will not be any consequences and justify their action in how they treat others. Powerful men everywhere have always bent the rules, policies, and legislation to his/her favor to justify what they do wrongly. Look at the images and atrocities that we have had to witness coming out of Ukraine done by the Russian government. The killing of innocent people in marked theatres with children, apartment buildings, personal vehicles trying to get to safety, and people standing at a train station. What man does not realize is that unprovoked violence, backroom deals, crooked legislation, and bogus contracts will catch up with you. Man does not realize when we make rules, laws, and legislation to fatten our own pockets has never gone unnoticed to God. Man has already been warned about this in Proverbs 1:10-19 were its say's', *My son, if sinful men entice you, do not give in to them. If they say, "Come along with us; let's lie in wait for Innocent blood, let's ambush some harmless soul; let's swallow them alive, like the grave, and whole, like those who go down to the pit; we will get all sorts of valuable things and fill our houses with plunder; cast lots with us; we will all share the loot" – my son, do not go along with them, do not set foot on their paths; for their feet rush into evil, they are swift to shed blood. How useless to spread a net where every bird can see it! These men lie in wait for their own blood; they ambush only themselves. Such are the paths of all who go after ill-gotten gain; it takes away the life of those who get it.* The prophet Jerimiah said it this way in Chapter 17:11 - *Like a partridge that hatches eggs it did not lay are those who gain riches by unjust means. When their lives are half gone, their riches will desert them at the end of his life, it will be clear he was a fool."* I like to say it this way, *"Man may get by, but he never gets-away!"* Take for example the infamous story of how God spoke to Moses on the behalf of the Children of Israel in Exodus Chapter 3:1-10 when they were being enslaved, persecuted and oppressed by the Egyptians: *"Now Moses kept the flock of Jethro his father-in-law, the priest of Midian: and he led the flock to the backside of the desert, and came to the mountain of God, even to Horeb. And the angel of the Lord appeared unto him in a flame of fire out of the midst of a bush: and he looked, and behold, the bush burned with fire, and the bush was not consumed. And Moses said, I will now turn aside, and see this great sight, why the bush is not burnt. And when the Lord saw that he turned aside to see, God called unto him out of the midst of the bush, and said, Moses, Moses. And he said, here am I. And he said, draw not nigh hither: take off your shoes from your feet, for the place where stand is holy ground. Moreover, he said, I am the God of thy father, the God of Abraham, the God of Isaac, and the God of Jacob. And Moses hid his face; for he was afraid to look upon God. And the Lord said, I have surely seen the affliction of my people which are in Egypt and have heard their cry by reason of their taskmasters; for I know their sorrows; And I am come down to deliver them out of the hand of the Egyptians, and to bring them up out of that land into a good land and a large land flowing with milk and honey. Now therefore, behold, the cry of the children of Israel is come unto me: and I have also seen the oppression where the Egyptians oppress them. Come now and I will send you to Pharoah, that you may bring forth my people the Children of Israel out of Egypt."*

Here we see God saying to Moses, that I have heard the children of Israel's cry and call. I have seen their oppression and know the sorrows from their tyrants, and it is wrong. Therefore, God said, *I am come down and sending you to speak on my behalf.* Pharoah had no idea that God had just commissioned Moses. He was getting ready to put a stop to him and his tyrants on the behalf of the Children of Israel. I do not know

111

about you but that seems like an email that I would have liked to have received up front. Know that God does not have to speak to *arrogant, prideful, haughty, violent, hateful, ignorant, or immoral* people. He knows how to go around them to do what is right and just. If Pharoah only knew that God had issues with him and his injustice towards the Children of Israel, he might have reconsidered his ways. But like most people who feel that they are in power, their pride will not allow them to see the error of their ways. Likewise, we have seen such pride, arrogancy, immorality, insensitivity and injustice done to people of color in America for four hundred years. During the Trump years in the White House, the Senate and the Evangelical Church has been no different. The bigoted attitudes, hateful speech, thoughts, feelings, and emotions towards people of color has increased to an all-time high in the United States in 21st Century. The malice and spite that was in their hearts was so evident to see. Likewise, Eighty-Five percent of the Evangelical Church has been culpable of the racial divide. They have supported, remained quiet, been naive or complicit to the racial tensions in this country. The people who you would think would be speaking out against racism, police brutality, defending the weak and the poor from a spiritual standpoint said nothing at all. They waited until things blew up so badly before they started making any statements towards America's issues of division and race. They went on to endorse several well-known preachers' self-righteous rhetoric towards people protesting in the streets who wanted to see change, equal rights, justice, and support for all people in America. Instead of the protesters being prayed for and heralded for courageously standing with their Black brothers and sisters, they were demonized by politicians, journalist, and preachers around the country. These leaders' stance against the protesters has caused Americans to further split apart from one another instead us of coming together. It was like they were quick to take the side of the police officers and not listen to the heart of what people were really protesting about in our streets of America. I did not see any of these self-righteous pre-lates go to the rallies to see what was going on before they judged. For the first three years of Donald Trump's four-year term, all we had seen in Washington, DC is the Republican Right walk around with smirks on their faces, denying every immoral act that came out of the White House. After three years of racial bias and a spring-summer in 2020 with police brutality, social injustice, and civil unrest most people got tired and took the streets. Supernaturally, just like God did for the Children of Israel thousands of years ago in Egypt, in the fourth year of that Administration God heard the cry of the majority and wiped the smirks off the Republican Right faces. The Republican Right got surprised with the COVID-19

Pandemic that knocked America to her knees and put everyone on the same playing field. We all had to social distance and stay at home to protect our lives. The pandemic hit the nation of China in December 2019 and we now know that America had cases as early as January 2020. No leadership from the White House took any real action or made plans to protect American citizens for fear that the stock market would drop, and the economy would crash. The Republican Right was concerned about the economy and a re-election of Donald Trump more than the lives of the American people. We now know that our President at the time was warned by our intelligence agencies as early as January 3, 2020, that the pandemic that started in China was threatening American soil. He knew that it could be detrimental to hundreds of thousands of lives. Still no real action was taken but cutting off flights coming from China to America for the sake of protecting the monetary gains that our country was making at the time. To add insult to injury we now know that there were a *secret closed-door Senator's meetings* on January 24, 2020, and after it several Senators came out of that private meeting and moved millions of dollars out of the stock market that same day. What does that tell you? Still, Americans were not properly warned about this virus attacking our citizens, especially those who are most vulnerable, the elderly in nursing homes and people of color living in poverty. At the time of this writing, COVID-19 had claimed 20.1 million confirmed cases in America with over 347,000 deaths. Over 30 percent of the cases in the world showed up on America's front door, five times as much as anywhere else in the world. Over 20.5 million people in America have filed for unemployment. The jobless rate rocketed to 17%, the worse since the Great Depression. Over 7.5 million small business are at risk of closing, many of them have already closed if not permanently. The reality is that most large companies in America depend on the small business to purchase their products, goods, and services. Due to small businesses going out of business, large business too has suffered. All churches had been ordered to close their doors and do webcasting type services. No meetings or gatherings of more than ten people was in affect for several months. America got hit the worse more than any other country so what does that tell you? The Republican Right can call it the *"Chinese or Wuhan Flu"* all they want, it does not have influence, at the end of the day, America was judged the worse with more cases than any other nation. If we do not realize that God is amid showing the world that we need to trust and depend on Him and Him alone, then you have missed a lot to understand about God. The social injustices towards people of color have gone on too long into American history. We saw the rich, poor, politicians, and preachers sitting isolated in their homes for over a year. Very few were keen enough to figure out *"what the hell was going on?"* I will take something out of the Church play book to enlighten you. It is called *"disobedience"* from the White to the poor house! We were all put on the same playing field. We all were concerned about our own, family, and friends' welfare against COVID-19. I never seen so many people with means lose their wit over their property, businesses, future, and staff. Before COVID-19 people had plenty of time to care less about their neighbors or the greatest commandments that the bible teaches: "*And the second is like unto it, thou shalt love thy neighbor as thyself (Matthew 22:39).* As I said earlier in this book: *"Man may get by, but he never gets away."* How can we claim, especially those of us that should know better that we have loved our neighbor as ourselves when we sit back and watch our top leaders *(natural and spiritual)* make negative remarks towards people of color? How dare we say that we are *"the apple of God's eye"* and *"His treasured possession"* and we cannot utter one word in defense of the minority, poor and vulnerable in this country? Yet instead of defending the weak and vulnerable, we paraded these leaders like they are *"God's Chosen & Anointed."* Really? Give me a break! I have been in Church for the past thirty-seven years of my life and what I saw that was in the White House from 2016 to 2020 was clearly not *"God's Chosen & Anointed."* I do not care what preacher said it. I knew better than 20 days after he was elected. Pastors and spiritual men & women around the country on their TV, Radio and Social Media networks flocked to him. They tried for four years to sell us that lie. Why? Because the market was doing great, their port folios were growing, they were getting their conservative judges, Roe vs Wade would overturn, the U.S. was backing Israel again, a Border wall was going to be built in Mexico, and The Affordable Care Act was going to be overturned. I have watched the Dow Jones drop 10,000 points in America in a matter of weeks due to COVID-19. The very thing that the rich, powerful, privileged, and self-righteous depended on was hanging in the balance. Their money and gains have dropped significantly and then they need the very people in this country that wanted equal justice and rights to go in their stores to buy their products. They needed us to go on to their websites and by their products, to their web-stream churches services and give financial support. Many of them still don't know how we had got in that position. I will tell you; it was the pious attitudes towards the weak, vulnerable, and poor for hundreds of years that put us there. COVID-19 shut down the entire world and the world's economy for months. Unfortunately, the world does not take seriously the second greatest commandment of *"Loving your neighbor as yourself."* We think we can do whatever we want to whomever we want and there is no price to pay. We think we do not have to treat others in a way we want people to treat us and get away with it forever. I got news for you. God keeps record of everything we do until we ask Him for forgiveness. Man does too much degradation for far too long without repenting. It means turning away from it and doing different. I know a whole lot of under privileged folk that is not feeling sorry for what has gone on in this country with the loss of many jobs, businesses, and stock portfolios of privileged people. I will tell you that they are thinking about you just as much as you have been thinking about them. It is so ironic how tables turn. I personally do not want to see anyone's business close, stock drop or lose a loved one. But there are times that God is trying to get our attention and show us ourselves. COVID-19 was doing exactly that work. The scriptures warn us all *"Be not deceived; God is not mocked; for whatsoever a man sows, that shall he also reap" (Galatians 6:7).* In other words, you get back what you put out! Judging from America's legislative leadership since 1607 when the first colonial ship docked the shores of Virginia, there has been a lot put out that been disastrous, destructive, prideful, and racist. I understand that many may not agree with me and would want to argue that what I am saying is not true. But I am reminded of what it says' in Proverbs 26:21 that *"A quarrelsome person in a dispute is like kerosene thrown on a fire."* I do not have time play around with kerosene, just want to state the facts. The history books have been written. Black people have been able to read, write, study and travel in this nation for many years. The history of European ancestors in America is not a good one, especially in the south. In fact, it is amazing what you find out when you travel. So, let us be people about it and figure out how we can solve the problems that are systemically in our institutions against Black people instead of arguing a battle that you cannot win. Again, what is it going to take for man to open his and her eyes to stop walking on top of the weak, vulnerable and the poor? Is it going to have to be COVID-20? I do not know, what I do know is that God will always defend the weak and the poor. Let me ask another question, was it God who shut down all the bigoted M.A.G.A rallies that was traveling across America? They had been tolerated and gone unchecked by so called Christian political and spiritual leaders for four years. It is clear when I looked in those crowds that the people that gathered in those rallies were not a full representation of America. Many of them extremely angry with malice and hate. They were obtuse and do not represent what real American society looks like. Do they not realize that a lot of white people have black/brown folks in their families now through marriages, adoptions and mixed couples having babies? In other words, white mothers are feeling the same fear as Black woman when she knows her mixed son or daughter encounters a police officer in the wrong neighborhood. It can be deadly! This M.A.G.A group had deep racial epithets stoked by a person who cares nothing about them. He only used them to fan the flames of white nationalism, prejudice and division that has been deplorable. Since our preachers and political leaders would not say anything to shut it down, could it now be God? People of all colors rose and went to the voting ballot boxes early with their mail in ballots and defeated the old divisive administration on November 3, 2020. May it send a message to any future republican administrations that if you do not care about Black and Brown Lives in America, you can lose again. We are tired of lip service, and want to see real change with different attitudes, and tangible social justice results from all leaders. We are looking towards the fresh and new! The old will no longer do. You cannot keep putting new wine in old wineskins, it will burst (Matthew 9:17). No one miss seeing the hateful and racist M.A.G.A rallies on television. Americans can say that *"All Lives Matter"* (in which they do) but what we need to see is that Black Lives do too! It is one thing for an administration to say that they are aware of certain things and the systemic racism in our institution. It is another thing for an administration to work to bring actual awareness and change. Watching things is being culpable rather than taking steps to solve them!

Chapter Six

Back To the Spirit of Greed

"What Made Americans Greedy Again"

W.M.A.G.A

"What Can the Church do to solve the problems?"

"I know your deeds; you have a reputation of being alive, but you are dead! Wake up, strengthen what remains and is about to die, for I have found your deeds unfinished in the sight of my God"

Revelation 3:1-2

Revelations chapter three is an interesting book in the bible. It speaks of three diverse types of churches...*The Dead Church, The Faithful Church, and the Luke-Warm Church.* Many of us have heard Pastors preach on all three churches, but the one that gets the most attention for some reason is the *"Luke-Warm Church."* I have heard more messages or references about the Lukewarm Church by ministers in my tenor as believer than the other two types. I constantly hear or am reminded that God is not coming back for a *Luke-Warm* Church. And to that I would say that I agree. The Apostle John on the Island of Patmos gets revelation from God about all three of these churches and God has him write a letter to each. The Dead Church in Sardis, the Faithful Church in Philadelphia, and the Luke-Warm Church in Laodicea, he writes: And to the angel of the church of the Laodiceans writes in verse 14; *'These things say the Amen, the Faithful and True Witness, the Beginning of the creation of God: "I know your works, that you are neither cold nor hot. I could wish you were cold or hot. So then, because you are lukewarm, and neither cold nor hot, I will vomit you out of My mouth. Because you say, 'I am rich, have become wealthy, and have need of nothing'—and do not know that you are wretched, miserable, poor, blind, and naked— I counsel you to buy from Me gold refined in the fire, that you may be rich; and white garments, that you may be clothed, that the shame of your nakedness may not be revealed; and anoint your eyes with eye salve, that you may see. As many as I love, I rebuke and chasten. Therefore, be zealous and repent. Behold, I stand at the door and knock. If anyone hears My voice and opens the door, I will come into him and dine with him, and he with Me. To him who overcomes I will grant to sit with Me on My throne, as I also overcame and sat down with My Father on His throne. "He who has an ear, let him hear what the Spirit says to the churches."* These are some strong words from the Lord and a statement that is worth paying attention to. It makes me think, "what kind of church is it in God's eyes that watches injustices done to people of color and say's nothing?" What kind of church is it to God that is complicit or looks the other way when injustices are being done to people of color or any person? What kind of church was it that was encouraging abusive methods to control slaves and coddled racism in America? In fact, what kind of Church was it that supported wicked legislation towards Black people? Keeping in mind a lot these preachers that talk about the *Luke-Warm* Church today, supported a bigoted President. I did my research on the Church in the United States as early as the 1600s to see what kind of Church has been here since that time.

The Donald Trump Impeachment Trial and 2020 Presidential Election once again revealed the sincere heart of what kind of Evangelical Church is in America. It certainly is not hot! For many believers to ignore the monumental evidence presented before them against the President that we all saw on television, disregard the constitutional statues and rule of law was apparent. Church leaders unveiled their lack of spiritual conviction and requirements they have before God for partisan purpose which is unforgettable. Although the evangelicals claim to be truth bearers, but they showed no righteous back bone from 2016 to 2020. We were living in a climate where so many Evangelicals *(not all)* did not seem to care about the racism showed towards Black and Brown people provoked by the former presidential administration. One spiritually convicted republican Senators Mitt Romney demonstrated when he voted to convict the unrighteous President from office on *Article One.* He showed that his allegiance and trust is in God, not man or a party. The vast majority of the Evangelical Church instead remained, *stiff-necked, mindless, motionless, passive* and shrugged their shoulders to it all. They hoped that Americans would be stupid enough to ignore the mountains of damning evidence against the former president. The Evangelicals has showed were they stand and still refused to criticize the former president for his unfaithful, racist, and divisive behavior. It was clear for four years that this man was only interested in policies and values that benefitted the rich. The evangelicals constantly ignored what he said that was racist and culturally insensitive. Very few dared to call him out on his divisive tweeting and comments. They knew that violent words and hateful rhetoric from any leader can lead to violent action from his followers and it did. The deep seeded racism has infected this nation and has been allowed to fester and grow without eradication. Because of its growth, one must not fear and speak truth to power in this nation. Realize that even powerful men, they too *"Must appear before the judgement seat of Christ, so that each of us may receive what is due us for the things done while in the body, whether good or bad" (2 Corinthian 5:10).* When we have leadership or a group of people that will not show empathy towards people of color who are crying out for justice in America then there is a real problem. Empathy is not rocket science; it is simply being able to feel one's experience even though you were not there. When it comes to racism one has to acknowledge the problem before you can solve it. Its' like an alcoholic that refuses to acknowledge that their alcoholism is causing problems in their families and society. Many *(not all)* in the Evangelical Church refuse to preach, teach, and acknowledge that systemic racism toward Black and Brown people in America. In truth, Black and Brown people do not need their acknowledgement to come against this spirit that has hurt so many people for hundreds of years. The truth is that racism has been a sin that the Church in America has been very culpable of since the inception of this nation. It is the one sin that the Church does not want to discuss when it comes to our national history. The Church does not want to do this because they were very much involved in it and benefitted from it. Ignoring the issue or being ignorant of it does not mean that it does not exist or fixes the problem. The Church like most people love to brush over this sin and would much rather tell the stories of America's independence and its breaking free from British rule in 1776. What they do not realize is that America's diabolical history of slavery and racism does not go anywhere. The truth of the matter is that racism, slavery, and legislative injustice was etched in this country's infrastructure for 170 years before its independence from the British. The American Church refuses to understand that the Independence Day was freedom for white people but still struggle for African, Japanese, Chinese, Mon gruels and Natives in this nation. To prove it let us start by looking at the speech given by the great orator and abolitionist from my own hometown in Rochester, New York, Frederick Douglas on the 5th of July,1852.

On July 5, 1852, Frederick Douglass gave a keynote address at an Independence Day celebration and asked, "What to the Slave is the

Fourth of July?" Douglas was a powerful orator, often traveling six months out of the year to give lectures on abolition. His speech was delivered at an event commemorating the signing of the Declaration of Independence, held at Corinthian Hall in Rochester, New York *(Ironically, the city in which I was raised up as a child)*. It was a scathing speech in which Douglass stated, *"This Fourth of July is yours, not mine, you may rejoice, I must mourn."*

In his speech, Douglass acknowledged the Founding Fathers of America, the architects of the Declaration of Independence, for their commitment to "life, liberty and the pursuit of happiness":

"Fellow Citizens, I am not wanting in respect for the fathers of this republic. The signers of the Declaration of Independence were brave men. They were great men, too, great enough to give frame to a great age. It does not often happen to a nation to raise, at one time, such a number of truly great men. The point from which I am compelled to view them is not, certainly, the most favorable; and yet I cannot contemplate their great deeds with less than admiration. They were statesmen, patriots and heroes, and for the good they did, and the principles they contended for, I will unite with you to honor their memory....

Douglass states that the nation's founders are great men for their ideals for freedom, but in doing so he brings awareness to the hypocrisy of their ideals with the existence of slavery on American soil. Douglass continues to interrogate the meaning of the Declaration of Independence, to enslaved African Americans experiencing grave inequality and injustice:

"...Fellow-citizens, pardon me, allow me to ask, why am I called upon to speak here to-day? What have I, or those I represent, to do with your national independence? Are the great principles of political freedom and of natural justice, embodied in that Declaration of Independence, extended to us? and am I, therefore, called upon to bring our humble offering to the national altar, and to confess the benefits and express

devout gratitude for the blessings resulting from your independence to us? Would to God, both for your sakes and ours, that an affirmative answer could be truthfully returned to these questions! Then would my task be light, and my burden easy and delightful. For whom is there so cold, that a nation's sympathy could not warm him? Who so obdurate and dead to the claims of gratitude, that would not thankfully acknowledge such priceless benefits? Who so stolid and selfish, that would not give his voice to swell the hallelujahs of a nation's jubilee, when the chains of servitude had been torn from his limbs? I am not that man. In a case like that, the dumb might eloquently speak, and the 'lame man leap as a heart.'

But such is not the state of the case. I say it with a sad sense of the disparity between us. I am not included within the pale of glorious anniversary! Your high independence only reveals the immeasurable distance between us. The blessings in which you, this day, rejoice, are not enjoyed in common. The rich inheritance of justice, liberty, prosperity, and independence, bequeathed by your fathers, is shared by you, not by me. The sunlight that brought light and healing to you, has brought stripes and death to me. This Fourth July is yours, not mine. You may rejoice, I must mourn..."

We must understand that in 1852 Frederick Douglas not a citizen and that the naturalization laws established in 1790 by the First Congress in New York were still on the books until 1952. Frederick Douglas would pass away on February 20, 1895. The naturalization laws did not allow him or any other Black person to be considered a natural citizen, give them voting rights or hold any public office. Fredrick Douglas new all this and was speaking from that understanding when he gave the speech above in Rochester, New York. Unfortunately, this is one of the very things that a lot of our European Christian's in America do not seem to understand. They do not realize that many Black people are now educated about the history of our American laws. They do not see why we do not do cartwheels at what is said when they tell their version of American history. There is a reason why we do not jump up and down with excitement. Here are some of the reasons above. If you cannot vote, do not have means, cannot hold public office then you cannot as a people address politically your needs therefore you are not Free. Here is a more recent assessment about these issues by an African American journalist for the New York Times, Nikole Hannah-Jones. She explains our history in a more modern light. Nikole said, *"What if I had told you that the year 1619 is just as important to the American story as the year 1776. What if I told you that America is a country that is born of both an idea and a lie? I read the words by Deron Bennett where he describes these words about the White Lion. This was the ship in 1619 that brings that first group of enslaved Africans to Virginia. 'What seems unusual today that no one sensed how extraordinary she really was, for few ships, before or since have unloaded or more momentous cargo. Like most Americans I was taught very little about the institution of slavery. It of course explained the American presence of my family, all the black people I knew and saw. But like most Americans slavery was always taught as something marginal to the American story. Slavery had to be mentioned in our history books because we had to talk about the Civil War. But outside of that it was just a brief discussion that relegated slavery to the backward south and assured us as a nation that slavery had little to do with how our country developed. We would not be the United States were it not for slavery. When we think about the shear wealth that the forced labor of those who were forced to come here from the continent of Africa produced for the colonies, it was this labor that made the struggling colonies wealthy. It was this labor that allowed these Founding Fathers to both have the wealth and Moxy to believe that they could break off from the most powerful empire in the history of the world, one of them. But certainly, the most powerful at the time and start their own country. We know that the slave grew and picked more cotton anywhere else in the world at the time. Supplying 66% percent of the world's supply at the time. It was the money and the dizzying profits from the enslaved laborer that paid off our war debts after the Revolutionary War. It financed some of our most prestigious Universities. It helped fuel the Industrial Revolution. It was enslaved people that built and laid the railroad tracks that crisscrossed the south. At one time the second richest man in this country was a Rhode Island slave trader who never had to own a single human being but made millions of dollars transporting them across the middle passage. Here in New York, Wall Street was named "Wall Street' because that was the name upon which enslaved people were bought and sold and the very reason why we are the financial capital of the world. Because it is there, the systems of banking, insurance and learning to collateralize rise around the insurance and collateralizing and mortgaging of black human beings. But much important than the material wealth that enslaved people created for this country is that black people have played one of the most vital roles as the perfectors of this democracy. Because you see, when the countries founding documents were written by enslavers, they were FALSE. When a man by the name of Thomas Jefferson wrote 'We hold these truths to be self-evident that all men are created equal, that they are endowed by their creator with certain inalienable rights. That among these are life, liberty and the pursuit of happiness.' These are some of the most famous words in the English language. But as he wrote these words, he owned over 130 human beings that would enjoy none of those rights. At that time 1/5 of this country lived in absolute bondage. We were founded not as a Democracy but a Slaveocracy, a country run and ruled by slaveowners. If this feels uncomfortable, simply imagine the truth that the first ten of our presidents trafficked human and worked them on forced labor camps. But while the founders set up an undecidedly un-democratic constitution that denied the franchise to the majority of its citizens, to women, to native people and to black people. Also deprived absolute rights to 1/5 of the population, black people actually believed and took those words literally. Black people responded to their enslavement and demanding and fighting not just for their own rights but for universal rights. They believed those words that our founders did not. It's time to stop hiding from our sins but rather confront them and in confronting them, make them right."*

To this day you will hear evangelical pastors and leaders refuse to confess the sins of themselves and their ancestors but will proudly remind us of the establishment of this nation's freedom by its founding fathers. They promote it as if the founding fathers helped everyone but fail to realize that freedom back then was only for white people, not Black and Brown folk. They proudly preach how this nation core beliefs are based on Judeo Christian values. Really? Which one's? They want us to believe that America was developed by God-Fearing Christian men that quoted and lived the King James Bible. They preach as if America has a great past and began with godly men like Christopher Columbus, the Pilgrims, the Mayflower, and faith in God. Let me ask this question. Were the Christian colonizers that came here led by the spirit or the flesh? For us to answer this question I must weigh it against what the word say's about the flesh and the spirit. In Romans 8:5-8, it reads *"Those who live as their flesh tells them to, have their minds controlled by what the flesh wants. To be controlled by the flesh results in death; to be controlled by the Spirit results in life and peace. And so, people become enemies of God when they are controlled by their flesh; for they do not obey God's law, and in fact they cannot obey it. Those who obey their flesh cannot please God."* If you consider what you have already read and will continue to read, you will see that America was never established on Judeo Christian values. It was established as a slaveocracy for economic reasons like Nikole Hannah-Jones said above. Therefore, lets' keep it one hundred when we talk about our nation's history! The colonizers were making laws and policy for their own pockets and European people based on their fleshly desires. The historian and author Jon Meacham, who said it so eloquently during the 2020 Democratic National Convention, *"Often we (meaning Caucasian people) like to hear the trumpets rather than face the tragedy."* They continue to boast about the ideas of a free nation and not face the tragedies of our real history. No matter what others think, we must have the discussion of racism and slavery regardless of who it makes uncomfortable. The freedoms that were established as Frederick Douglas spoke at Corinthian Hall on State Street in Rochester, NY *"Is yours, not mine. You may rejoice, I must mourn"* are understood by millions of Black and Brown people in this nation. My question for those who only want to portray the good American history is *"whos' lens are these people looking through when they teach our history so proudly?"* Unfortunately, many of these prelates do not realize that most Americans do know better. We also know that many have been blinded by their own selfish desire to have power and control over the American gospel narrative. This too is Greed! If they would slow down and start asking their black/brown brothers and sisters in Christ questions about racism, they would realize that their narrative is not what they should be preaching. The reason they do not ask us is that a lot of them do not want to hear what we think and feel. They fear that they can lose control of the narrative. This notion of selfishness has infected America for far too long. It is the reason there is still much division and ignorance amongst us when it comes to our historical past. This ignorance has even showed up at our major and most prestigious colleges/universities. I have personally been told by a Christian College Dean/Professor when I was in college *"that I needed to expand my Christian paradigm"* This was because I did not come in agreement with his analysis of a discussion on Rahab the Prostitute in a Situational Ethics class. Well, I have done just that. I have expanded it to drafting books that brings out the facts. I was told by another professor while attending a Seminary School taking Church history classes that *"I needed to be at a local traditional College University, but not at a Seminary. That I wasn't ecumenical enough."* I thought that was very racist, nevertheless this happened because I did not come in agreement with her analysis and discussion on a same sex marriage scenario that we had to review in a Pastoral Counseling class. I thought ecumenicism was the idea of accepting and representing several different Christian views and Churches. This is what happens when you do not come in agreement with religious men and women who do not want you to think for yourself. Nevertheless, in both schools I had my own views, experience, and facts for drafting my papers in the way that I did. I saw how in both schools that the other students' views, and opinions were accepted but not mines. I was the only Black person in each class. What does that tell you? We do know that there is ignorance in our college universities about Black history especially when you can watch the television game show *"Jeopardy"* and it is the Grand Champion College game. When you look at the board you can see all the categories on the board empty except the category listed under *"Black History."* Not even some of the brightest college kids from top universities know much about Black History in America. The Church in America has been one of the entities that has historically tried to shape the minds of people like these kids when it comes to God and country in America. Unfortunately, the Church perception of America has not been the reality that Black people have experienced in this nation. It does not understand that there are Black people that would wait for hell to freeze over before we would go back to the days of only white men making decisions for us. Therefore, when any European man or women says, *"Let's Make America Great Again,"* they need to know how that may ring in some Black people's ears. It will always make the hair on the back of our neck stand up. Why can't these people just say, *"Let's Make America Greater?"* They could have easily said that but that would not dog whistle the prejudice groups of people that they wanted following the party. They did not want to say it that way because that would mean that we would have to work together to *eradicate racism, injustice, inequality, and division* in this nation. In fact, racism according to the Apostle Paul in the early church should never be tolerated. I was reading where the Apostle Paul rebuked the Apostle Peter in front of everyone because of his racist cowardly behavior towards his Gentile brethren when the Jewish believers were around. In Galatians 2:11-14 it reads, *"But when Peter came to Antioch, I opposed him in public, because he was clearly wrong. Before some men who had been sent by James arrived there, Peter had been eating with the Gentile believers. But after these men arrived, he drew back and would not eat with the Gentiles, because he was afraid of those who were in favor of circumcising them. The other Jewish believers also started acting like cowards along with Peter; and even Barnabas was swept along by their cowardly action. When I saw that they were not walking a straight path in line with the truth of the gospel, I said to Peter in front of them all, "You are a Jew, yet you have been living like a Gentile, not like a Jew. How, then, can you try to force Gentiles to live like Jews?"* You can read the rest of the chapter on your own, but as we can see the Apostle Paul stood against Peter's fear in not wanting the Jewish Christians to know that he was living like a Gentile believer and even ate with them in their homes. He began to distance himself from them when the Jews were around, and Paul called him out with a public rebuke for his cowardly avoidance of his Gentile brothers. You must ask yourself *"Why did the Apostle Paul do this openly and publicly?"* He did it openly and publicly because he knew that it was spreading to others to behave in the same way. We must understand that racism is a spirit that spreads and not only affects the person that is bound by it, but others who are in their circle. Nevertheless, our God inspired preachers will constantly marginalize racism in America, speak passively about it when it is in plain view of everyone, minimize the significant issues of our past, change the narrative, or reduce it to America has its *problems, issues, and troubles.* They can never admit that our real problems were established in a slaveocracy that produced *injustice, racism, bigotry, greed, and white supremacy.* We must obliterate the very idea that this country foundation was built upon Godly principles and stop lying about the truth. Once again, just because one tags *God's Name* to something and what they are doing, it does not mean that God is for it! In fact, these so-called preachers could not much utter the words racism, slavery, injustice, or white nationalism in their sermons. That tells you that they do not have the capacity to solve the problem in our nation. That is why it is still here in 21st Century. It is an uncomfortable topic for most because much of it has to do with them and their ancestors. America was not built upon Judeo Christian values like many of them would want us to believe. It was built upon on a slaveocracy and greed! This nation was instituted by European men who *raped, enslaved, beat, burned, and viciously murdered* Black men, women, and children in America with no accountability. They created a free labor force and financial system for themselves. They prospered from the free-labor and the Church was a benefactor by preaching a gospel that did not convict the people in their hearts for their evil ways. In fact, much of the Church's wealth in the denominations as we know them came from slave labor. Here is one of the articles from my uncle that he sent to me for you to read. It can be found on-line at it is entitled: Churches played an active role in slavery and segregation. Some want to make amends. (nbcnews.com). It was written on the NBC News page by Michela Moscufo on April 3, 2022. It says:

"Two and a half years ago, Episcopal Bishop of New York Andrew M.L. Dietsche reminded a group of clergies of the ugly history of their diocese.

Not only was slavery deeply embedded in the life and economy of colonial New York, but Episcopal churches across the state often participated in it. Church founders, churchgoers and even churches themselves had enslaved people. The abolitionist Sojourner Truth had once been enslaved by a church in the diocese.

"The Diocese of New York played a significant, and genuinely evil, part in American slavery," Dietsche said during his November 2019 address. "We must make, where we can, repair."

After his speech at the diocese's annual convention, the clergy unanimously voted to set aside $1.1 million of the diocese's endowment for a reparations fund, marking the beginning of what the diocese referred to as "The Year of Reparation."

The year has become years. Churches across the state have been engaging in a variety of activities to attempt to make amends for this past: putting up plaques acknowledging that their wealth was created by enslaved labor, staging plays about the role their congregation had in the slave trade and committing parts of their endowments to reparations funds.

This comes more than a decade after a 2006 resolution by the General Convention in which the national leadership of the Episcopal Church — which is 90 percent white — called on churches to study how they benefited from slavery. Since then, Episcopal dioceses in Georgia, Texas, Maryland, and Virginia have begun similar programs.

Other predominantly white denominations, including the Presbyterian Church and the Evangelical Lutheran Church, also passed resolutions (in 2004 and 2019, respectively) to study the denominations' role in slavery and have begun the process of determining how to make reparations.

Together with the United Church of Christ and the National Council of Churches — as well as Network Lobby for Catholic Social Justice, the Religious Action Center of Reform Judaism and the Samuel DeWitt Proctor Conference — Black leadership in these denominations have formed a faith-based coalition to lobby for HR 40, federal legislation that would create a commission to study how the United States could make reparations for slavery and its aftermath.

They've also been holding monthly webinars and creating educational resources for their congregations.

"We want to have grounded learning, both biblically and theologically, around why reparations are due," the Rev. Velda Love, minister for racial justice at the United Church of Christ, said. "It is not just writing a check from churches."

These efforts are thought to constitute the most sustained church activism since Black churches were on the front lines of the civil rights movement.

"Our faith requires us to do something," the Rev. Sekinah Hamlin, minister for economic justice at the United Church of Christ, said. "This is what God calls us to do."

How churches benefited from slavery

Georgetown University, a Jesuit institution, voted in 2019 to create a reparations program as a way of atoning for its sale of 272 enslaved people in 1838. Since then, Virginia Theological Seminary, Union Presbyterian Seminary and Princeton Theological Seminary have followed suit.

While Baptists in the South played the most vocal role in defending the institution of slavery before the Civil War, other denominations — including the Presbyterian Church, the Episcopal Church, the Lutheran Church in America and the Catholic Church — and other religious educational institutions all benefited from enslaved labor in some way. Whether it was members of the clergy or the churches themselves owning enslaved people, or the churches receiving taxes from congregants in the form of tobacco farmed by enslaved people, the wealth of the churches was deeply intertwined with the slave trade.

Well into the 20th century, churches and their clergy also played an active role in advocating policies of segregation and redlining.

"Every time you open a book, you find another story," said the Rev. Grey Maggiano, the rector of the Memorial Episcopal Church in Baltimore, which began a reparations process last year.

Memorial Episcopal Church is one of a dozen churches across the country that have begun their own reparations programs, independent of the organizing happening at a national level.

Memorial Episcopal was built in the early 1860s with profits from Hampton Plantation, where hundreds of enslaved people worked at the founding rector's family estate. One of the parish's deacons, Natalie Conway, discovered that her great-great-grandmother, Hattie Cromwell, was enslaved at Hampton Plantation by the church's founding rectors.

"It hits you between the eyes," Conway said. "Somebody actually took the shackles and put them on my great-great-grandmother and -grandfather, and the children were taken away. How do you do that? It becomes so hurtful personally. And even now, it's still hard to fathom."

Conway said she considered leaving Memorial Episcopal Church.

"I said, 'God, what am I supposed to do now?' And God said, 'Why do you think you're at Memorial?'" she recalled.

Since it began a reparations process, Memorial Episcopal Church has taken down the plaques memorializing the church's founders. The congregation also set up a $500,000 reparations fund and formed a reparations committee to determine where the money will go.

"This is a chance to do what we were charged with in our baptismal covenant," Conway, who attends the reparations committee meetings, said. "To respect the dignity of all people."

The Church was notorious at attaching God's name to everything that they were doing. The did this for justification so that their conscious could be clear on Sunday morning when they went to worship. In other words, they could profit off indefinite slave labor, brutalize Black people all week in the fields, hang them on Saturday and praise God on Sunday mornings while they sung out of their hymnals with no conviction. The Denominational Churches as we know them were a hot mess. These people never felt guilty or the need to repent of what they were doing because they controlled the narrative and the interpretation of the scriptures. Therefore, writing a false history that included God's name but not having anything to do with God, was no more than committing the sin of, *bearing false witness.* By attaching God's name to their pilgrimage to this country it gave the appearance that God was endorsing their voyage and what they were doing along the way. They praised men like Christopher Columbus in our history books who was a highly esteemed Christian by European believers and the Catholic Church. Christopher Columbus was also known for his duplicity. He was known to reward his lieutenants with female natives to do as they pleased with them during his expeditions. He sailed across to the Americas with two Christian flags billowing at the top of his ship called the Mayflower. But let the church tell it, Christopher Columbus was a godly man that deserves a national holiday celebration. Think about it: If I put a Nike logo on the front cover of this book, it looks like that corporation is sponsoring what I write. The problem is that corporation would have nothing to do with me at all. They do not know me, and I do not know them. I may buy some of their products but doing such thing could land me in jail with hefty fines. Likewise, these so-called Christians did the same thing with God's Name, Jesus Name and His Logo which is the cross. Any novice lawyer would know that this would be called fraud! That is why I put a picture of myself on the front of this book because it is written and endorsed by me the writer. If others come along and purchase it, that is great. This is what the colonizers did in the past and committed fraud towards God. Nevertheless, God did not know them. How can you ever establish something in God's name and do not reflect *his ways, behavior, and character?* Likewise, European Evangelical Christian has been putting God's name, word, and crosses on everything that they do since the establishment of this nation. Heck, they even showed up in *"Jesus Name"* at our nation's Capital and broke into the place on January 6, 2021. They stood in the chambers and offered up prayers and petitions while trying to halt the certification of the 2020 Presidential Election for Joe Biden. As I watched it live on television, I could not help but notice all the crosses and Jesus banners. I do not want to bust anyone's bubble, but I do not think Jesus was with you that day breaking into the Capitol. The evangelicals are still doing the same thing this very day to make people think who study history believe that God was at the epicenter of what they have been doing. Once again, if you research the history of the establishment of this nation, it did not start in 1776 in which so many Christians proudly reference. It started in the early 1600s and there was nothing godly about the core thoughts of these British European colonizers that came to establish America. If anything, the men that came to America in God's name where like the leaders of the house of Jacob that God said to the prophet Isaiah in Chapter 29:9-16:

"Stop and be astonished; blind yourselves and be blind! They are drunk, but not with wine; they stagger, but not with beer. For the Lord has poured out on you an overwhelming urge to sleep; he has shut your

eyes (the prophets) and covered your heads (the seers). For you, the entire vision will be like the words of a sealed document. If it is given to one who can read and he is asked to read it, he will say 'I can't read it, because it is sealed.' And if the document is given to one who cannot read and he is asked to read it, he will say, 'I can't read' (They clearly did not understand the Word of God when they read it.) "The Lord said: These people approach me with their speeches to honor me with lip service – yet their hearts are far from me, and human rules direct their worship of me. Therefore, I will again confound these people with wonder after wonder. The wisdom of their wise will vanish and the perception of their perceptive will be hidden. Woe to those who go to great lengths to hide their plans from the Lord. They do their works in the dark, and say, 'Who sees us? Who knows us?' You have turned things around as if the potter were the same as the clay." How can what is made say about its maker, 'He didn't make me'? How can what is formed say about to the one who formed say about the one who formed it, 'He doesn't understand what he's doing.?

The book of Isaiah Chapter 58 has never been so relevant for us in America which says: *"Cry out loudly, don't hold back! Raise your voice like a trumpet. Tell my people their transgression and the house of Jacob (The Church) their sins.* That is exactly what I am doing in this book. I am telling the Church its historical culpable sin towards God's Black and Brown people. It is much their fault that America has been on fire with racial issues. Now their children and children's-children are wondering what in the *heck* is going on. We saw them marching in the streets, protesting racism, being shot at with rubber bullets and chanting that *Black Lives Matter*! Why? Because their deaf, dumb, and blind parents, grand-parents, great grandparents in the Church would not stand up against its years ago for righteousness' sake. If the Church would have had as much zeal for standing against racism and injustice for people of color as they have displayed against *partial birth abortion, same sex marriages and conservative judges on our benches and overturning Roe vs Wade* we would not have had to see their children at risk protesting in the streets. Their children *(the millennials, who won't stay silent)* are willing to go in the streets and put their lives at risk with the National Guard, Military, State and Local Police for something that is humanly right for all people in America. The millennials want to live a life that is significant and do things that matter like fight against social injustice, Global Warming, polluting our environment and making everything Green.

I have been saying since the late nineties that these young millennials *(who were teenagers back then)* were different from their parents, grand-parents, and ancestors, but no one believed me back then. They realize that the people that established this nation were weak, closed minded, passive, and racist. These young millennials we are seeing today are strong, courageous, and love fighting for the truth. They are a generation that want to live for a cause. I noticed that the church cannot say anything good about them. Right now, it is a different time for the church in America. I am sure it is embarrassing as a nation to know that the entire world see's our dirty laundry while we hypocritically try to be the example of freedom to other nations. I am sure at a lot of dinner tables there was a lot of explaining that whites had to do with their children/ grandchildren during all the Black Live Matters protest. I hated to have to explain the racism, slavery, and police brutality to my children. Instead, I apologized to my kids that it has gone on so long and that we tried but didn't fix it during my generation. Obviously, our Baby Boomer efforts were not good enough. But, as the Lord said to the prophet Isaiah in Chapter 58:2 about these believers, *"They seek me day after day and delight to know my ways, like a nation (America) that does what is right and does not abandon the justice of their God (They have acted like they have done nothing wrong for 400 years). They ask me for righteous judgments (understanding); they delight in the nearness of God (400 years of fasting, church services, revivals, conferences, and meetings in America)." "Why have we fasted, but you have not seen? We have denied ourselves, but YOU haven't noticed!" Look, you do as you please on the day of your fast and oppress all your workers (slaves and foreigners). You fast with contention and strife to strike viciously with your fist.* **You cannot fast as you do today, hoping to make your voice heard on high.** *Will the fast I choose to be like this: A Day for a person to deny himself to bow his head like a reed and to spread out sackcloth and ashes? Will you call this a fast and a day acceptable to the Lord? Isn't this the fast I choose: To break the chains of wickedness (slavery, racism, and injustice), to untie the ropes of the yoke, to set the oppressed free and to tear off every yoke? Is it not to share your bread with the hungry, to bring the poor and homeless into your house, to clothe the naked when you see him and not to ignore your own flesh and blood?* Therefore, I say that the insurrection at our nation's Capital by thousands of laws abiding, salt of the earth, blue grass, believing-Christians was an embarrassment to the Body of Christ in America. It showed just how for so many years the Church has not evolved in her *mind, will and emotions* towards the people color. If you ever going to advance you must change your mind-set. The mind-set of the Church is stuck. How she continues to be stuck historically with complications that prohibits its ability to produce good fruit that impacts all people *(black, white, or brown)* positively in this country is what I am explaining to you. The Church in America can no longer fast as they do today and think that their voice will be heard on high. There must be a change within us. No one could not tell me that these European Christians that established this nation and the Church really loved Black people. Let me throw this scripture in while I am on subject: *"If anyone says, 'I love God,' yet hates his brother, he is a liar. For anyone who does not love his brother, whom he has seen, cannot love God, whom he has not seen" (1 John 4:20).* Now we have hundreds and hundreds of years of the Evangelical Church in America crying out to God for revival. What they do not realize is that their lack of repentance from their historical sins has held back God's response to them. The Church loves to name throw their former spiritual giants work such as *Dr. Billy Graham, Lester Sumrall, Chuck Swindoll, Kathryn Kuhlman, Smith Wigglesworth, Aimee Semple McPherson, Charles Finney, Jerimiah Lamphier, TL Osborne, Oral Roberts, Kenneth Hagin, Sr, John Vernon McGee, Jerry Falwell,* and the list goes on. But may I ask you this question: what did either of these great revivalist and healers do to address the racism, inequality, Jim Crow law, injustice, police brutality, and terrible treatment of Black people in this country during their preaching years? Its' just a question and its' a fair one since so many of our Preacher's love to herald their work. All these preachers represented the Church in America during racially divided times. If you must think hard to answer the question, then that validates what I have been saying for 3/4s of this book. It should not be hard. One should be able to recall quickly and say it. If I asked you that same question about Dr. Martin Luther King, you would not have to hesitate but can quickly re-call what he did for us on those matters above. This is the value of *critical thinking* you go by the historical facts of what people have done and not by what someone says' to you. Did any of these ministers listed above preach vehemently from their pulpits, packed-out tent meetings, churches, or stadiums how it was wrong for America to treat black/ brown people in the way that they have for hundreds of years during their era? If we let all their cheerleaders in today's Church tell it, all these people were highly anointed and were powerful men and women of God. Where was there power from the pulpit from them when it came to racism and obvious social injustice towards people in color that were sitting in their congregations? Let me say to you, I am not against any of these preachers' efforts, work in bringing people to Christ and healing them from sickness and disease, which they did. What I am saying is that all these people lived and preached during an era of racial, social disorder and inequality towards Black people in America. They all had great followings. What did they do to help the situation other than thinking that Black people needed a healing or Jesus? The point is that I do not believe they said much about it at all, at least not openly. Like the preachers that came before them did the same thing. All these Preachers were more worried about losing their following rather than standing up against the racist issues going on in America during their time. If any of them did fight against it openly, and not behind closed doors, then I stand corrected. For the record, The Church pulpit is the safe place for the public to be corrected about its ways. It should come from their pastor, all of them. If the preachers will not correct a congregation, then who is going to do it? We must remember that many of white people was used to Blacks view as not as his equal. He was something to be used to put a yoke around his neck and make him plow his fields along with a horse. He was never meant to lead. My point is if Black people were good enough to preach to, attend their services, revival meetings and put money in the offering plate, then we were good enough for our white evangelical preachers, brothers, and sisters to take a stand against racism, violence, and social injustice against us in America. Here is a good place to put a quote from Sherlock Holmes, *"What speaks the loudest is the dog that didn't bark."* What I am saying to the Pastor, Spiritual Leaders and Evangelical Church is that we had four years of a President stoking hate, racism, militia groups, police violence, killings and you all never barked to put a stop to it. That is what we have witnessed from our evangelical Pastors and Political leaders from 2016 to 2020. You were the dog that did not bark, when you should have done so! When the racial, social injustice and inequality issues spread like wildfire in our country our Church leaders are never the ones to speak up. Very few will raise their voices against racial and social injustice. I personally used to watch America's Greatest Preacher, Dr. Billy Graham on my mother's and grandmother's television as a child in the 1960s and 1970s. As early as seven, eight, nine years old I would ardently wait for him to say anything in his sermons that would help Black peoples plight in America, stand against racism, joblessness, poverty, injustice, inequality, and police brutality. Unfortunately, from my personal experience, I can say that I never heard it come out of his mouth. Not even once that I can remember! The ironic thing that I learned from my Pastor friend from South Africa is that he certainly did deal with it over there when working with and visiting Nelson Mandela. I just shook my head when he told me that information, The Word of God say's this *"Hope deferred makes the heart sick (Proverbs 13:12).* I got sick and tired of waiting for this man to say something in one of his sermons about the issues mentioned above and by the time I was twelve, I stopped watching Billy Graham and others like him on TV. I refused to watch him as a teenager, and it is maybe the reason I did not give my life to Christ until I was in the military at 20. I did not know much about the Church back then, but what I was not going to do is be a part of something that could not speak against wrong. Thank God for grandmother's and mother's prayers that I did find the Lord and recognize his importance in my life. But here is the problem with that fact. I found the statistics on-line of a person coming to Christ after age 19 and it is not a good one. It reads: *"Adults aged 19 and over have just a six percent probability of becoming Christians"* according to the article, ***"When Americans become Christians"*** You can read it for yourself by going to the link below:

http://home.snu.edu/~hculbert/ages.htm.

If those stats are true, it looks like I just made it by my chinny, chin-chin. Please do not get nervous and stop reading now because I mentioned Dr. Billy Graham or others. God already knows that I felt this way and used to do this as a child, this does not surprise Him at all about me. I am just letting you in on it and how not standing up for justice in the pulpit can even affect the children that you overlook growing up in society. In fact, it was God's Spirit that reminded me of the experience I had with him as a child so I can write about it as an adult. Personally, I had forgotten all about it since it has been so long ago. What I am trying to say is that Dr. Graham had worldwide influence over many people when I was a child, and I cannot remember him taking an aggressive stand publicly about what I am writing. His preaching against the mistreatment of Black people in America would have made me see him in a wonderful way as a child. Knowing myself, I would have wanted to be just like him. Instead, by the time I was 12 years old, I wanted to me more like Dr. Martin Luther King, Jr. It was his messages that inspired me and gave me goosebumps when I heard his voice as a child. It was his stand against racism and the civil rights of all people that made me listen and influenced my thinking. I realized later that I was looking for deliverance of my family and community. I wanted to see simple fairness, justice, safety from the police and jobs for our people. This would have made me look at Christians, especially preachers who stood up for us in a big way. Nevertheless, I lived through the 1960s and 70s with worry every weekend for years from age 5 to 14 if my uncles *(who were young Black men in their 20s)* would get beaten or even killed by a police officer.

Gratefully, that did not happen, but no child should ever have to live with these types of concerns because of racism.

Here is a good question: who were the big-name preachers that were preaching to America in the 1960s and 1970s during such racist times? I tell you, a lot of names on my list above. That is why I looked at the church differently as a child. I hoped that these well-known preachers would say something in their sermons that would make people stop treating Black people so badly. Once again, those sermons never came. It was because the goal for the Church back then were large tent revivals and world-wide crusades. It certainly was not *justice, mercy, and faithfulness* in this nation. Although, it sounds like the fair things for Pastors to bring up from time to time back then, it went very much untouched by them. But at the same time, these believers steadily would pray for revival, set up tent meetings in Black communities and anticipated phenomenal Church growth. It just seems to me that church growth would have been much better if everyone in the congregation had a job and could participate financially. One would think there would have been some preaching towards this in America especially when it was clear that Black people loved to be in Church services. Unfortunately, the Church was distracted with other things back then. I can hear many Evangelical Preachers saying to themselves that are reading this book that their job is to only preach the Gospel. They don't realize that preaching faithfulness, justice, and mercy for everyone to be employed was a missed opportunity to call legislators into account. I think if they would have done so and been affective that we would have much stronger Churches to this day. When the atrocities of unemployment were affecting everyone back then, I am sure it was addressed from the pulpits across America. There is no place for this lack of empathy from any Church leader when any race faces injustice, violence, and unemployment. If we are kingdom minded as believers, then we would want all people healthy, working and treated right so we can build what we are commissioned to do. Once again, every-time that I saw preachers like Dr. Billy Graham preach, after a while I walked away from the television disappointed knowing he was not going to forcefully address the significant issues of the times. Again, I have nothing against his ability to bring people to Christ and maintain an evangelical message, what I am saying is that with his influence he could have done more. He could have been a great instrument to address the systemic racism that was in this nation openly. Here is a quote from an article where he too before he passed wished he would have done more to address the civil and voting rights with Dr. King. In an article written by Jay Reeves on February 25, 2018, titled: *"Billy Graham had pride and regrets on civil rights issues"* It reads: *"Still, Graham had regrets. In an interview with The Associated Press in 2005, when he held his final crusade, Graham said he wished he had fought for civil rights more forcefully. In particular, Graham lamented not joining King and other pastors at voting rights marches in Selma, Alabama, in 1965.*

"I think I made a mistake when I didn't go to Selma," Graham said. "I would like to have done more."

Unfortunately, what we saw with Dr. Billy Graham concerning these issues, it was common for many other preachers; including those in the list above who responded the same. That is what I noticed back then as a kid. I finally realized that there was no national minister that was going to forcefully stand up for what was right for Black people. They would talk around it, but they took no hard stance against it. That is what we are seeing today from them in the 21st century. Let me say, if you are a Christian, Believer or a-part of the Church please do not get upset with me for I am too apart of the Church. I am a Believer in the Lord Jesus Christ. I am just fed up with the lack of back-bone and passivity displayed by our most visible spiritual leaders. Because the leadership in the Church has been weak, I started identifying myself with the Body of Christ. I do not want people to think that I am someone who cannot speak up for right against wrong when I need to. People like justice, even unbelievers can respect a person that stands up for what is right. Unfortunately, most preachers have done what the American Church has always done when it comes to hatred towards Black people in this nation and that is Nothing! The truth is that these preachers that I listed above were doing no less then what their predecessors had done in the past in America about RACISM, which was NOTHING! I did not know this as a child, but as an adult I can now see it. The church has historically done nothing in America to condemn slavery, racism, injustice, and white supremacy. The American Church do not realize is that they can no longer ignore the infirmity of Black people, our safety, growth, development and think that their voices will be heard on high to God. Until the house of Jacob (American Church) recognizes their original sin in America is RACISM, VIOLENCE, AND INJUSTICE *(not partial birth abortion, homosexuality, the loss of prayer in schools, same sex marriage, pedophilia, satanism or the legalization of marijuana)*, there will be no revival from their fasting and prayers. When I read the Old Testament, all revivals have always started with a nation repenting of its sins first and then the revival would come.

The Prophet Joel 1:13-14 said it this way to Israel; *"Dress in sackcloth and lament, you priests; wail, you ministers of the altar. Come and spend the night in sackcloth, you ministers of my God, because grain and drink offerings are withheld from the house of your God. Announce a sacred fast; proclaim an assembly! Gather the elders and all the residents of the land at the house of the Lord your God and cry out to the Lord."* There is more from the prophet Joel in Chapter 2:12-17; *"Even now this is the Lord's declaration, turn to me with all your heart (The House of God), with fasting, weeping, and mourning. Tear your hearts, not just your clothes, and return to the Lord your God. For He is gracious and compassionate, slow to anger, abounding in faithful love, and he relents from sending disaster. Who knows? He may turn and relent and leave a blessing behind Him, so you can offer grain and wine to the Lord your God. Blow the horn in Zion! Announce a sacred fast; proclaim an assembly. Gather the people; sanctify the congregation; assemble the aged; gather the infants, even babies nursing at the breast. Let the groom leave his bedroom, and the bride her honeymoon chamber. Let the priests, the Lord's ministers, weep between the portico and the altar. Let them say; 'Have pity on your people, Lord, and do not make your inheritance a disgrace, an object of scorn among the nations (which that is exactly what has been happening since the murder of George Floyd). Why should it be said among the peoples, 'Where is their God?'"* If these self-righteous evangelicals want to see God's hand, then they are going to have to acknowledge their greatest sin from the birth of this nation which has been ignoring RACISM and REPENT! If they do so, Isaiah 29:8-12 put things in order by saying *"Then your light will appear like the dawn, and your recovery will come quickly. Your righteousness will go before you, and the Lord's glory will be your rear guard. At that time, when you call the Lord will answer when you cry out, he will say 'Here I am.' If you get rid of the yoke among you (RACISM and INJUSTICE), the finger-pointing (being judgmental towards everyone that is not living their Christian beliefs and values) and malicious speaking (seeking laws and judges to force biblical principles on everyone in this country or punish the unrighteous instead of ministering to people to come to the Lord), and if you offer yourself to the hungry and satisfy the afflicted one, then your light will shine in the darkness and your night will be like noonday. The Lord will always lead you, satisfy you in a parched land, and strengthen your bones. You will be like a well-watered garden and like a spring whose water never runs dry. Some of you will rebuild the ancient ruins; you will restore the foundations laid long ago; you will be called the repairer of broken walls, the restorer of streets where people live.*

We can see from these verses in Isaiah 29 the house of Jacob, which would be the Church in our day has been under surveillance by God? If God is not pleased as to what He sees from the House of Jacob or the Body of Christ and its leaders *(prophets and seers)* than it can stagnate His response to their prayers and fasting. When the Church does justice and do what is right, then *"their recovery will come quickly, and their righteousness will go before them and shine like the noonday sun."* They will get their good name and reputation back. When was the last time that the Church shined in this nation as such? It has been mostly *finger-pointing (being judgmental), malicious speaking and contention* in the Church for more legislation that suit believers. Nevertheless, God say's in Isaiah 59:1-4 *"Indeed, the Lord's arm is not too weak to save, and his ear is not too deaf to hear (He is always giving the Church chances to repent. It just will not in America). But your iniquities are separating you from your God, and your sins have hidden his face from you, so that he does not listen. For your hands are defiled with blood and your fingers with iniquity (watch the judgement and finger pointing Church!); your lips have spoken lies (stop telling yourself and your hearers how God built this nation and how its foundation is rooted in Judeo Christian, Godly and Biblical values. It is a lie! The only one that believe it is those who teach it) and your tongues mutter injustice (historically it was European Christians who assisted in creating laws/legislation against black people for their benefit so they can be on the top and blacks on the bottom). No one makes claims justly no one pleads honestly. They (The Evangelical Church) trust in empty and worthless words (about America's history and independence); they conceive trouble and give birth to iniquity.* If you still do not believe what I am writing about, I have more quotes for you to read. Listen to what former Governor George Wallace of Louisiana said to protest change when President Dwight D. Eisenhower sent Federal Marshalls to escort six-year-old Ruby Bridges and her mother to integrate into a white school, *"This is a people's movement, it does not make any difference if some major politicians are going to support you or not. If they do not support us in this movement, to take back our government and give it to us and let us run our own institutions, those who stand in the way are liable* to get run over." This statement was made by Governor Wallace in November 1960. That was only 60 years ago. Luke 6:45 say's *"For out of the abundance of the heart his mouth speaks."* If that was not terrible what you just read then let us look at a letter written by the Christian Slave owner from the West Indies, Mr. William Lynch. He wrote this letter and traveled here to assist the slave masters in America who were having trouble with keeping their slaves in submission in 1712. The Christian believers solicited Willie Lynch's help as they pooled their money together to get him to come to America. This speech was said to have been delivered by Willie Lynch on the bank of the James River in the colony of Virginia. Mr. Lynch was a British Christian slave owner that ran plantations in the West Indies. He was invited to the colony to teach his diabolical methods to slave owners here. The letter reads a such below:

Gentlemen,

*I greet you here on the bank of the James River in the year of our Lord one thousand seven hundred and twelve. First, I shall thank you, the gentlemen of the Colony of Virginia, for bringing me here. I am here to help you solve some of your problems with slaves. Your invitation reached me on my modest plantation in the West Indies, where I have experimented with some of the newest, and still the oldest, methods for control of slaves. Ancient Rome would envy us if my program is implemented. As our boat sailed south on the James River, named for our illustrious King, whose version of the Bible we cherish, I saw enough to know that your problem is not unique. While Rome used cords of wood as crosses for standing human bodies along its highways in great numbers, you are here using the tree and the rope on occasions. I caught the whiff of a dead slave hanging from a tree, a couple miles back. You are not only losing valuable stock by hangings, you are having uprisings, slaves are running away, your crops are sometimes left in the fields too long for maximum profit, you suffer occasional fires, your animals are killed. Gentlemen, you know what your problems are; I do not need to elaborate. I am not here to enumerate your problems, I am here to introduce you to a method of solving them. In my bag here, **I HAVE A FULL PROOF METHOD FOR CONTROLLING YOUR BLACK SLAVES**. I guarantee every one of you that, if installed correctly, **IT WILL CONTROL THE SLAVES FOR AT LEAST 300 HUNDREDS***

YEARS. My method is simple. Any member of your family or your overseer can use it. **I HAVE OUTLINED A NUMBER OF DIFFERENCES AMONG THE SLAVES; AND I TAKE THESE DIFFERENCES AND MAKE THEM BIGGER. I USE FEAR, DISTRUST AND ENVY FOR CONTROL PURPOSES.** *These methods have worked on my modest plantation in the West Indies and it will work throughout the South. Take this simple little list of differences and think about them. On top of my list is "AGE," but it's there only because it starts with an "a." The second is "COLOR" or shade. There is* **INTELLIGENCE, SIZE, SEX, SIZES OF PLANTATIONS, STATUS** *on plantations,* **ATTITUDE** *of owners, whether the slaves live in the valley, on a hill, East, West, North, South, have fine hair, course hair, or is tall or short. Now that you have a list of differences, I shall give you an outline of action, but before that, I shall assure you that* **DISTRUST IS STRONGER THAN TRUST AND ENVY STRONGER THAN ADULATION, RESPECT OR ADMIRATION.** *The Black slaves after receiving this indoctrination shall carry on and will become self-refueling and self-generating for* **HUNDREDS** *of years, maybe* **THOUSANDS.** *Don't forget, you must pitch the* **OLD** *black male vs. the* **YOUNG** *black male, and the* **YOUNG** *black male against the* **OLD** *black male. You must use the* **DARK** *skin slaves vs. the* **LIGHT** *skin slaves, and the* **LIGHT** *skin slaves vs. the* **DARK** *skin slaves. You must use the* **FEMALE** *vs. the* **MALE,** *and the* **MALE** *vs. the* **FEMALE.** *You must also have white servants and overseers [who] distrust all Blacks. But it is* **NECESSARY THAT YOUR SLAVES TRUST AND DEPEND ON US. THEY MUST LOVE, RESPECT AND TRUST ONLY US.** *Gentlemen, these kits are your keys to control. Use them. Have your wives and children use them, never miss an opportunity.* **IF USED INTENSELY FOR ONE YEAR, THE SLAVES THEMSELVES WILL REMAIN PERPETUALLY DISTRUSTFUL.** *Thank you, gentlemen."*

LET'S MAKE A SLAVE

It was the interest and business of slave holders to study human nature, and the slave nature in particular, with a view to practical results. I and many of them attained astonishing proficiency in this direction. They had to deal not with earth, wood and stone, but with men and, by every regard, they had for their own safety and prosperity they needed to know the material on which they were to work, conscious of the injustice and wrong they were every hour perpetuating and knowing what they themselves would do. Were they the victims of such wrongs? They were constantly looking for the first signs of the dreaded retribution. They *watched therefore with skilled and practiced eyes, and learned to read with great accuracy, the state of mind and heart of the slave, through his sable face. Unusual sobriety, apparent abstractions, sullenness, and indifference indeed, any mood out of the common was afforded ground for suspicion and inquiry. Frederick Douglas LET'S MAKE A SLAVE is a study of the scientific process of man-breaking and slave-making. It describes the rationale and results of the Anglo Saxons' ideas and methods of insuring the master/slave relationship. **LET'S MAKE A SLAVE** "The Original and Development of a Social Being Called 'The Negro.'" Let us make a slave. What do we need? First of all, we need a black nigger man, a pregnant nigger woman and her baby nigger boy. Second, we will use the same basic principle that we use in breaking a horse, combined with some more sustaining factors. What we do with horses is that we break them from one form of life to another; that is, we reduce them from their natural state in nature. Whereas nature provides them with the natural capacity to take care of their offspring, we break that natural string of independence from them and thereby create a dependency status, so that we may be able to get from them useful production for our business and pleasure.*

CARDINAL PRINCIPLES FOR MAKING A NEGRO

*For fear that our future generations may not understand the principles of breaking both of the beast together, the nigger and the horse. We understand that short range planning economics results in periodic economic chaos; so that to avoid turmoil in the economy, it requires us to have breadth and depth in long range comprehensive planning, articulating both skill sharp perceptions. We lay down the following principles for long range comprehensive economic planning. Both horse and niggers [are] no good to the economy in the wild or natural state. Both must be **BROKEN** and **TIED** together for orderly production. For orderly future, special and particular attention must be paid to the **FEMALE** and the **YOUNGEST** offspring. Both must be **CROSSBRED** to produce a variety and division of labor. Both must be taught to respond to a peculiar new **LANGUAGE**. Psychological and physical instruction of **CONTAINMENT** must be created for both. We hold the six cardinal principles as truth to be self-evident, based upon following the discourse concerning the economics of breaking and tying the horse and the nigger together, all inclusive of the six principles laid down above. NOTE: Neither principle alone will suffice for good economics. All principles must be employed for orderly good of the nation. Accordingly, both a wild horse and a wild or natural nigger* is dangerous even if captured, for they will have the tendency to seek their customary freedom and, in doing so, might kill you in your sleep. You cannot rest. They sleep while you are awake, and are awake while you are asleep. They are **DANGEROUS** near the family house and it requires too much labor to watch them away from the house. Above all, you cannot get them to work in this natural state. Hence, both the horse and the nigger must be broken; that is breaking them from one form of mental life to another. **KEEP THE BODY, TAKE THE MIND!** In other words, break the will to resist. Now the breaking process is the same for both the horse and the nigger, only slightly varying in degrees. But, as we said before, there is an art in long range economic planning. **YOU MUST KEEP YOUR EYE AND THOUGHTS ON THE FEMALE and the OFFSPRING** of the horse and the nigger. A brief discourse in offspring development will shed light on the key to sound economic principles. Pay little attention to the generation of original breaking, but **CONCENTRATE ON FUTURE GENERATION**. Therefore, if you break the **FEMALE** mother, she will **BREAK** the offspring in its early years of development; and when the offspring is old enough to work, she will deliver it up to you, for her normal female protective tendencies will have been lost in the original breaking process. For example, take the case of the wild stud horse, a female horse and an already infant horse and compare the breaking process with two captured nigger males in their natural state, a pregnant nigger woman with her infant offspring. Take the stud horse, break him for limited containment. Completely break the female horse until she becomes very gentle, whereas you or anybody can ride her in her comfort. Breed the mare and the stud until you have the desired offspring. Then, you can turn the stud to freedom until you need him again. Train the female horse whereby she will eat out of your hand, and she will in turn train the infant horse to eat out of your hand, also. When it comes to breaking the uncivilized nigger, use the same process, but vary the degree and step up the pressure, so as to do a complete reversal of the mind. *Take the meanest and most restless nigger, strip him of his clothes in front of the remaining male niggers, the female, and the nigger infant, tar and feather him, tie each leg to a different horse faced in opposite directions, set him afire and beat both horses to pull him apart in front of the remaining niggers. The next step is to take a bullwhip and beat the remaining nigger males to the point of death, in front of the female and the infant.* Don't kill him, but **PUT THE FEAR OF GOD IN HIM**, for he can be useful for future breeding.

THE BREAKING PROCESS OF THE AFRICAN WOMAN

*Take the female and run a series of tests on her to see if she will submit to your desires willingly. Test her in every way, because she is the most important factor for good economics. If she shows any sign of resistance in submitting completely to your will, do not hesitate to use the bullwhip on her to extract that last bit of [b----] out of her. Take care not to kill her, for in doing so, you spoil good economics. When in complete submission, she will train her offsprings in the early years to submit to labor when they become of age. Understanding is the best thing. Therefore, we shall go deeper into this area of the subject matter concerning what we have produced here in this breaking process of the female nigger. We have reversed the relationship; in her natural uncivilized state, she would have a strong dependency on the uncivilized nigger male, and she would have a limited protective tendency toward her independent male offspring and would raise male offsprings to be dependent like her. Nature had provided for this type of balance. We reversed nature by burning and pulling a civilized nigger apart and bullwhipping the other to the point of death, all in her presence. By her being left alone, unprotected, with the **MALE IMAGE DESTROYED**, the ordeal caused her to move from her psychologically dependent state to a frozen, independent state. In this frozen, psychological state of independence, she will raise her **MALE** and female offspring in reversed roles. For **FEAR** of the young male's life, she will psychologically train him to be **MENTALLY WEAK** and **DEPENDENT**, but **PHYSICALLY STRONG**. Because she has become psychologically independent, she will train her **FEMALE** offsprings to be psychologically independent. What have you got? You've got the nigger **WOMAN OUT FRONT AND THE** nigger **MAN BEHIND AND SCARED**. This is a perfect situation of sound sleep and economics. Before the breaking process, we had to be alertly on guard at all times. Now, we can sleep soundly, for out of frozen fear his woman stands guard for us. He cannot get past her early slave-molding process. He is a good tool, now ready to be tied to the horse at a tender age. By the time a nigger boy reaches the age of sixteen, he is soundly broken in and ready for a long life of sound and efficient work and the reproduction of a unit of good labor force. Continually through the breaking of uncivilized savage niggers, by throwing the nigger female savage into a frozen psychological state of independence, by killing the protective male image, and by creating a submissive dependent mind of the nigger male slave, we have created an orbiting cycle that turns on its own axis forever, unless a phenomenon occurs and re-shifts the position of the male and female slaves. We show* *what we mean by example. Take the case of the two economic slave units and examine them close.*

THE NEGRO MARRIAGE

We breed two nigger males with two nigger females. Then, we take the nigger male away from them and keep them moving and working. Say one nigger female bears a nigger female and the other bears a nigger male; both nigger females—being without influence of the nigger male image, frozen with a independent psychology—will raise their offspring into reverse positions. The one with the female offspring will teach her to be like herself, independent and negotiable (we negotiate with her, through her, by her, negotiates her at will). The one with the nigger male offspring, she being frozen subconscious fear for his life, will raise him to be mentally dependent and weak, but physically strong; in other words, body over mind. Now, in a few years when these two offsprings become fertile for early reproduction, we will mate and breed them and continue the cycle. That is good, sound and long range comprehensive planning.

WARNING: POSSIBLE INTERLOPING NEGATIVES

Earlier, we talked about the non-economic good of the horse and the nigger in their wild or natural state; we talked out the principle of breaking and tying them together for orderly production. Furthermore, we talked about paying particular attention to the female savage and her offspring for orderly future planning, then more recently we stated that, by reversing the positions of the male and female savages, we created an orbiting cycle that turns on its own axis forever unless a phenomenon occurred and reshifts positions of the male and female savages. Our experts warned us about the possibility of this phenomenon occurring, for they say that the mind has a strong drive to correct and re-correct itself over a period of time if it can touch some substantial original historical base; and they advised us that the best way to deal with the phenomenon is to shave off the brute's mental history and create a multiplicity of phenomena of illusions, so that each illusion will twirl in its own orbit, something similar to floating balls in a vacuum. This creation of multiplicity of phenomena of illusions entails the principle of crossbreeding the nigger and the horse as we stated above, the purpose of which is to create a diversified division of labor; thereby creating different levels of labor and different values of illusion at each connecting level of labor. The results of which is the severance of the points of original beginnings for each sphere illusion. Since we feel that the subject matter may get more complicated as we proceed in laying down our economic plan concerning the purpose, reason and effect of crossbreeding horses and niggers, we shall lay down the following definition terms for future generations. Orbiting cycle means a thing turning in a given path. Axis means upon which or around which a body turns. Phenomenon means something beyond ordinary conception and inspires awe and wonder. Multiplicity means a great number. Means a globe. Crossbreeding a horse means taking a horse and breeding it with an ass and you get a dumb, backward, ass long-headed mule that is not reproductive nor productive by itself. Crossbreeding niggers mean taking so many drops of good white blood and putting them into as many nigger women as possible, varying the drops by the various tone that you want, and then letting them breed with each other until another circle of color appears as you desire. What this means is this: Put the niggers and the horse in a breeding pot, mix some asses and some good white blood and what do you get? You got a multiplicity of colors of ass backward, unusual niggers, running, tied to backward ass long-headed mules, the one productive of itself, the other sterile. (The one constant, the other dying, we keep the nigger constant for we may replace the mules for another tool) both mule and nigger tied to each other, neither knowing where the other came from and neither productive for itself, nor without each other.

CONTROLLED LANGUAGE

*Crossbreeding completed, for further severance from their original beginning, **WE MUST COMPLETELY ANNIHILATE THE MOTHER TONGUE** of both the new nigger and the new mule, and institute a new language that involves the new life's work of both. You know language is a peculiar institution. It leads to the heart of a people. The more a foreigner knows about the language of another country the more he is able to move through all levels of that society. Therefore, if the foreigner is an enemy of the country, to the extent that he knows the body of the language, to that extent is the country vulnerable to attack or invasion of a foreign culture. For example, if you take a slave, if you teach him all about your language, he will know all your secrets, and he is then no more a slave, for you can't fool him any longer, and **BEING A FOOL IS ONE OF THE BASIC INGREDIENTS OF ANY INCIDENTS TO THE MAINTENANCE OF THE SLAVERY SYSTEM**. For example, if you told a slave that he must perform in getting out "our crops" and* *he knows the language well, he would know that "our crops" didn't mean "our crops" and the slavery system would break down, for he would relate on the basis of what "our crops" really meant.* **So you have to be careful in setting up the new language; for the slaves would soon be in your house, talking to you as "man to man" and that is death to our economic system.** *In addition, the definitions of words or terms are only a minute part of the process. Values are created and transported by communication through the body of the language. A total society has many interconnected value systems. All the values in the society have bridges of language to connect them for orderly working in the society. But for these language bridges, these many value systems would sharply clash and cause internal strife or civil war, the degree of the conflict being determined by the magnitude of the issues or relative opposing strength in whatever form. For example, if you put a slave in a hog pen and train him to live there and incorporate in him to value it as a way of life completely, the biggest problem you would have out of him is that he would worry you about provisions to keep the hog pen clean, or the same hog pen and make a slip and incorporate something in his language whereby he comes to value a house more than he does his hog pen, you got a problem. He will soon be in your house*

I know this letter was hard to read, it was the same for me. These were the true feelings, expressions, words, and methods of a European King James Bible believing Christian. As you can see from reading this letter by him that the Church has been way off her true mission for the *Kingdom of God* in America in the 1700s. Ask yourself, *"What in the world does this letter have to do with the real mission of the Church, which is to bring salvation to all?"* But this is how the Church perverted the gospel with Christian men in America to control black slaves indefinitely. Did you read the part when Willy Lynch taught the slave owners how to break the Black male slaves like a horse? He told them to: *"Keep the body, Take the Mind!"* I noticed how Willy Lynch kept addressing the slave owners as *"Gentlemen."* I don't see anything gentle about any man who is taught to **"Take the meanest and most restless nigger, strip him of his clothes in front of the remaining male niggers, the female, and the nigger infant, tar and feather him, tie each leg to a different horse faced in opposite directions, set him afire and beat both horses to pull him apart in front of the remaining niggers. The next step is to take a bullwhip and beat the remaining nigger males to the point of death, in front of the female and the infant.** *Don't kill him, but* **PUT THE FEAR OF GOD IN HIM**, *for he can be useful for future breeding."* This letter from Willy Lynch shows just how Christians operated towards Black people

people to keep a strong economy. If you noticed the entire letter was about the economy. It is always about the money with these folks. Even in the Trump era, it was about their money. That is why they could not see or hear the protesters in the streets. It is sad, but the Church has wasted too much time trying to sell the world a fake image of Christ. The results have been that the Church itself has become barren and fruitless in her mandate which is to be the *salt* and *light* in the earth. But the Church back then would rather listen to saints like Willy Lynch instead of God. Now her history in this nation is easily known around the world, due to cable news and social media. If America was to ever right the wrong, it is important that we all know the truth about the people who were establishing this nation. Read Willy Lynch's letter again and see their abuse towards the *thoughts, feelings, desire to control, destroy mentally, physically, psychologically, socially, and economically* Black people for hundreds of years. Think about it, the transatlantic slave ship journey took 10 to 11 months under deplorable conditions. Many Black people died from suffocation. In other words, they could breathe, sound familiar. As if that was not bad enough for Africans, we can see that the masters thought of wicked, diabolical ways to make things worse when the slaves arrived by soliciting the help of William Lynch. Therefore, I say that the Africans went *from hell to hell* coming to these American shores. These were born-again, Spirit-filled Christians that was doing these things. I certainly after reading this letter seriously question the *potency* of the Spirit inside of these people that utilized these methods taught against slaves. It could not have been extraordinarily strong. Nevertheless, many of our evangelical brothers and sisters in Christ want everyone to think that American history is great and that we need to stop talking about slavery in this nation. Therefore, I question the potency of God's Spirit that they claim to be in them this very day. When has this nation been great for Black people? It was only great for the European people that arrived here, but them slaves on those ships, not at all. To add insult to injury the Evangelical Christian Church had the audacity without hesitation or thought to embrace the slogan in 2016 *"Make America Great Again!"* Are you serious? *"Again?"* That means it was Great at one time before! Through whom lens is the Church looking through? It could not be through the lens of most Black people, yet 85% of White Evangelicals supported and voted for Trump who was clearly at minimum *"divisive, prejudice, racially insensitive, if not outright racist."* Just like they ignored Willy Lynch diabolical mindset, for the purpose of the economy, the conservatives ignored Trump's character no matter how it affected Black and Brown people. History always repeats itself, it just a matter of time for it to do so. This letter from William Lynch in *1712* to the faithful, God-fearing Christian men is an example of the garbage that the Church in America had *embraced, supported, implemented, and condoned.* And you wonder why I say the "*Church is Not Innocent!*" To this day the Evangelicals continue to have a history of turning a blind eye, deaf ear and are passive on these issues. It is all about the money to them. This passivity continues to find its way in our pulpits with preachers that should know better. It is the very reason people are becoming done with the institution of the Church in America. I have spoken to a lot of believers in the past years, and they are upset with the Church. They are starting to see the very things about which I am writing. The people that I have talked to are not done with God (they are too smart to do that), but they are too through with the Christian Church in America that looks away from racism. These people know that "*a good tree bringeth not forth corrupt fruit; neither does a corrupt tree bring forth good fruit. For every tree is known by the fruit it bears*" *(Luke 6:43).* Willie Lynch and the Church who implemented his brutal methods of controlling slaves, taking their minds, and causing division between them, their women and children can never be seen as someone who brought forth good fruit. How Willy Lynch was welcomed as a Christian man by the Church for so many years is beyond my comprehension. To let you in on how the world now looks at the *Evangelical Church*, I was sent this letter by a friend. It was written by a Christian blogger, John Pavlovitz on January 24, 2018. This is the letter that I mentioned earlier in the book that I want you to pay attention to. It is mind blowing what he says below. John Pavlovitz is a white man. The letter is entitled: ***"White Evangelicals, this is Why People are Through with You"***

Dear White Evangelicals,

"*I need to tell you something: People have had it with you. They're done. They want nothing to do with you any longer, and here's why. They see your hypocrisy, your inconsistency, your incredibly selective mercy, and your thinly veiled supremacy. For eight years they watched you relentlessly demonize a black President; a man faithfully married for 26 years; a doting father and husband without a hint of moral scandal or the slightest whiff of infidelity. They watched you deny his personal faith convictions, argue his birthplace, and assail his character—all without cause or evidence. They saw you brandish Scriptures to malign him and use the laziest of racial stereotypes in criticizing him. And through it all, White Evangelicals—you never once suggested that God placed him where he was, you never publicly offered prayers for him and his family, you never welcomed him to your Christian Universities, you never gave him the benefit of the doubt in any instance, you never spoke of offering him forgiveness or mercy, your evangelists never publicly thanked God for his leadership, your pastors never took to the pulpit to offer solidarity with him, you never made any effort to affirm his humanity or show the love of Jesus to him in any quantifiable measure. You violently opposed him at every single turn—without offering a single ounce of the grace you claim as the heart of your faith tradition. You jettisoned Jesus as you dispensed damnation on him. And yet you give carte blanche to a white Republican man so riddled with depravity, so littered with extramarital affairs, so unapologetically vile, with such a vast resume of moral filth—that the mind boggles. And the change in you is unmistakable. It has been an astonishing conversion to behold: a being born again. With him, you suddenly find religion. With him, you're now willing to offer full absolution. With him, all is forgiven without repentance or admission. With him you're suddenly able to see some invisible, deeply buried heart. With him, sin has become unimportant, compassion no longer a requirement. With him, you see only Providence. And White Evangelicals, all those people who have had it with you—they see it all clearly. They recognize the toxic source of your inconsistency. They see that pigmentation and party are your sole deities. They see that you aren't interested in perpetuating the love of God or emulating the heart of Jesus. They see that you aren't burdened to love the least, or to be agents of compassion, or to care for your Muslim, gay, African, female, or poor neighbors as yourself. They see that all you're really interested in doing, is making a God in your own ivory image and demanding that the world bow down to it. They recognize this all about white, Republican Jesus— not dark-skinned Jesus of Nazareth. And I know you don't realize it, but you're digging your own grave in these days, the grave of your very faith tradition. Your willingness to align yourself with cruelty is a costly marriage. Yes, you've gained a Supreme Court seat, a few months with the Presidency as a mouthpiece, and the cheap high of temporary power—but you've lost a whole lot more. You've lost an audience with millions of wise, decent, good-hearted, faithful people with eyes to see this ugliness. You've lost any moral high ground or spiritual authority with a generation. You've lost any semblance of Christlikeness. You've lost the plot. And most of all you've lost your soul. I know it's likely you'll dismiss these words. The fact that you've even made your bed with such*

150

malevolence, shows how far gone you are and how insulated you are from the reality in front of you. But I had to at least try to reach you. It's what Jesus would do. Maybe you need to read what he <u>said</u> again—if he still matters to you."

I could not have said half of how he explained it. Do not believe what he said in the letter, and it is still true. It is everything that I have been trying to articulate about what I have watched and seen from the Evangelicals since Barrack Obama became President in 2008. I saw exactly for eight years what he wrote about above. It was terrible! In attempt to be bring change to what has been going on in this nation I made a laundry list of things that the Christian politicians and evangelicals can do to help eradicate racism in America. Maybe it can help, I don't know, but I believe that some people just do not know where to start. Here are some ideas below, just pick two or three of them if you feel that it is too much for one to do:

The Church can start by repenting for the sins of their ancestors that solicited the diabolical slave control methods of Willy Lynch. Slaves were protesting in America with *uprisings, running away, leaving the crops in the field too long, setting property on fire and killing the slave owner animals.* The Christians back then also said that these Black people are violent, breaking the law, rebellious and disobedience. Just remember that this same type of Christians called the January 6th Insurrection at our nation's Capital *"a normal day or a regular tour of the Capitol."* The evangelical must stop being so quick to judge *"Black protestors."* They need to learn how to hear them out. Black people have been protesting from time to time since they got off the slave ships.

The Church needs to not continue to be, *insensitive, complicit, passive, deaf, mute, and blind* to the plight of Black people in America. They should start trying to understand the disease of racism and its affects. They should ask God to help them learn to show empathy when an injustice is done. If they do not understand, start asking their Black parishioners questions to get understanding. Dominique Foxworth said it best about empathy: *"Empathy and understanding are characteristics that prompt actions. Actions that give birth to progress. Without all of us acknowledging the vile germs of our history and their contribution to the dysfunction that is present-day American injustice, we cannot expect a cure. Confronting the submerged shameful actions of our past is the only way to understand their enduring societal effects and begin to address them."*

The Church needs to stop ignoring the *"Elephant in the Room."* It needs to stop doing business-as-usual on Sunday mornings when there is a big racial divide in the nation. The pastors should start preaching against it and deal with the racism that has plagued this nation for four hundred years. If they want to be recognized as the *"Moral Majority,"* Then act like it. I believe a real *Prophets, Evangelist, Preachers, Teachers, and Pastors* do not go with the crowd and will correct the nonsense. A real man or woman of God knows who they work for and will deal with a racist when necessary. These people do not keep quiet when it comes to the *attitudes, behaviors and ways* of men that are unjust. For example, here are the words of a Caucasian Pastor that I do not know. I have heard of his name down through the years but never seen or heard him preach until recently. I saw a YouTube video of him that went viral that got my attention. His name is Pastor John Kilpatrick. He is an Assembly of God's minister who said these very courageous words as a white man to his congregation that is at least 98 percent white with a few Black people in Alabama. He said to his church while Donald Trump was President on June 11, 2017 *"Let me say something right quick. I think back on the African American people in America. I think how they were taken against their wills, put in the bellies of ships, brought over here, beat, and cussed. Many of them died on those ships, thrown overboard. They were pulled from families over there. You ain't never heard of a gut-wrenching song until you hear a black person sing one of those old black Negros spirituals. 'Nobody Knows....,' see I can't sing it like they sing it because I hadn't experienced what they have. When you experience hell, it comes out of the voice. I said when you experience hell it comes out of the voice. If you're one of those people that you got problems with black people or whatever, you better shut your mouth! Because they are God's people you better hear what I am saying to you. You better shut your... you better shut your white mouth! You better shut your white mouth; I'm not kidding you. I know that some of you were raised in the deep south, and you were raised by prejudice people and bigoted people. You better get that out of your system. You better get it out of your system, it'll cause you to suffer. Right along with those masters it'll cause you to suffer right along with them. These are God's people! And I know that there is wicked in white races and wicked in black races and all that. I am not justifying none of that stuff. I'm just saying God knows what happened to the black race, He knows how they wound up over here and God is going to reimburse all the black people for all their trouble and all their labor. You watch what I tell you! Watch what I tell you!* It's when our pastors across the country sound like this that the racism in America will begin to eradicate. It must start in the pulpits, then it will flow out to the rest of the congregation and out into the streets to the rest of the world. The church has been much too silent on this problem and for far too long. To prove my point, John Sergenthalen who was the assistant to the former Attorney General Robert Kennedy and was key in helping to keep the *1961 Freedom Riders* from being beaten, imprisoned, and even killed admitted to the following: "*I grew up in the south a child of good descent parents. We had women that worked in our household, sometimes surrogate mothers. They were invisible women to me. I can't believe I couldn't see them. I don't know where my head and heart were. I don't know where my parents and teacher hearts were. I never heard it once from the pulpit. We were blind to the reality of racism and afraid I guess of change.*"

The Church needs to start preaching a moral standard in their pulpits that teaches the members to act against the racism in this nation, refused to be a part of it intentionally or passively. Former President John F. Kennedy in his speech on June 11, 1963, when calling on congress to create legislation to get rid of the Jim Crow laws that were against Black people. He wanted to give civil right protections to all people in America: President Kennedy said "*A great change is at hand and our task, our obligation is to make that revolution, that change peaceful and constructive for all. THOSE WHO DO NOTHING are inviting shame as well as violence. Those who act boldly are recognizing RIGHT as well as REALITY.*" John F. Kennedy when he was President was called a "*Nigger Lover*" because he tried to help Black people by pushing for legislation for equal justice. God has called the Church to be the light of the world, not a flicker. Unfortunately, it has been the Churches silence and doing nothing that has invited the shame and violence that we have seen in this country. Nevertheless, it would be this speech and other attempts like this to bring change that would eventually have the former President John F. Kennedy assassinated five months later in November 1963. I was barely three months old when he was assassinated by a white man. My mother told me that she was sitting on the sofa feeding me a bottle when the *Breaking News* came across our black and white television screen. She said the news shocked her so badly that she almost dropped me while falling to the floor in grief and tears.

The Church needs to implement protocols that places Black people in leadership and speaking positions in the Church. They need to raise up Black preachers who are members in their churches to preach sermons to give a balance of how the Word of God is viewed from another lens and experience. The Church need to understand that Black people are not trying to destroy a republic, but just the lies that have been told about this nation's republic for four hundred years. We are well read and are willing to share the truth and shame the devil! It is time-out for one race controlling the narrative in our churches, especially within those Churches that have mixed congregations. I believe the Church should look like heaven is going to look, but it should also sound like heaven is going to sound. That means that we all will speak and worship.

The Church should stop being gullible and allowing political leaders to derail them off their God given purpose which is kingdom. The Church needs to realize that they are being pimped for votes by people who are full of malice and hatred. Just because these political leaders say they say they are Christians does not mean that they really are believers. Stop allowing known groups and people who divide us to speak to their congregations, use their Church facilities to hold conferences and promote their racist political views. I read a very disturbing article online written by a digital journalist by the name of Fares Sabawi, published November 19,2021 with caption: *"Corner Stone Church Pastor: 'I deeply regret hosting political event after chants of 'Let's go Brandon' go viral."* One would say, what is wrong would chanting *'Let's go Brandon?'* I will include Fares Sabawi article, and you will see exactly what is wrong with this chant and why the meeting should not have been held at one of our top Evangelical Churches in San Antonio, Texas. The article reads as such: *"A prominent San Antonio pastor on Thursday distanced himself from a controversial political conference that took place at his family's church last weekend. Matt Hagee, executive pastor of Cornerstone Church, said in a statement that "it was not appropriate" to host the "Reawaken America" conference, where far-right political activists promoted baseless conspiracy theories about the 2020 election and led chants of "Let's Go Brandon" — a euphemism among Republicans that means "F--k Joe Biden." The conference was held at the church from Nov. 11 to Nov. 13. "Regrettably, the organization was not properly vetted," Hagee said. "The Church is not associated with this organization and does not endorse their views (I say, why did you let them hold the conference in your Church?)" The event featured multiple conservative figures, including Roger Stone, former national security advisor Michael Flynn, My Pillow CEO Mike Lindell and Texas Attorney General Ken Paxton. Hagee also referenced videos of the conference that showed him welcoming the crowd, praising them for their faith."*
The real problem that I have with this evangelical pastor and church that allowed this to happen. The fact that this meeting was held one year after Joe Biden was elected as President of the United States. We were

still trying to get through the mess from the Capitol Insurrection, the FBI arresting people that done that vicious act, the former President still stoking the lie that the election was stolen, Churches losing members and closing thousands of Church buildings. All these issues and more were well known by all Pastors and Churches in this nation that a lot of these people were Q-Anon conspiracy theorist, but this Pastor allows them to have the conference in his building regardless of the facts and it backfired on him. The chants of *'Let's Go Brandon'* went viral on social media for the world to see. One would think that the Church would have learned from their previous mistakes, but this just goes to show that many are stubborn, refuse to repent and will have to learn the hard way when some of their members start walking away.

The Church needs to stop being passive and pathetic. It needs to be aggressive and prophetic! Stand against injustice and inequality towards all people. Be willing to Stand Up to Power instead of looking to become their spiritual friends and megaphones. It needs to do what Frank Sesnos said, the Former CNN Washington Bureau Chief..." *we are supposed to call out inconsistencies, lies and hypocrisies"* by political and cable news leaders.

The Church needs to cease from being obnoxious *(intoxicated with oneself and its history)*. Many years ago, I remember hearing the Lord's voice while sitting in Church tell me *"That you never want to be obnoxious, be God's property and feel good about it!"* I thought that was a remarkably interesting quote. Therefore, *I* wrote it down on the front cover of my bible so I would never forget it. I realized later that is exactly where the Church has gone in America. She has become obnoxious, even though she is God's property - she feels good about it. When a person is in that state, they are full of themselves. Unfortunately, the Church has been full of herself in America for hundreds of years. It needs to humble itself like I saw in a YouTube video of several people in the south kneeling and asking a Black community for forgiveness for years and years of racism after George Floyd was killed. I will provide you the YouTube link so you can watch it yourself: https://www.youtube.com/watch?v=fdX6aVzPgHs. It is enormously powerful. It is when we humble ourselves like these people have that God can move in our lives and forgiveness can do its work.

The Church needs to stop being *double minded* by telling Black people when it comes to the history of slavery in this country to; *"Get over It!"* But when it comes to 9/11 or Pearl Harbor – *"Always Remember or Never Forget It!"* If that is not hypocritical and offensive, I do not know what is. Start showing empathy and be willing to learn from people of color how racism has impacted them. Black people are not stupid. We know the history of 911 and Pearl Harbor were devastating but each happened in one day. Slavery in America lasted 246 years and we are still dealing with the diabolical *ramifications* of it. One example is with our young Black kids doing exactly what Willy Lynch wanted us to do to each other. To this day Black on Black crime is entrenched in his methods that taught Black people to hate each other for their differences and make them *"BIGGER."* His methods of teaching Black people to *"FEAR, ENVY and DISTRUST"* one another is alive and well today. Most Black kids do not even know that they are conducting Willy Lynch doctrine, teachings, methods, and behaviors. As you read above, he trained the slave masters a method that would put us at odds with each other for the slightest of reasons. No other culture in America does that to each other but African Americans. Therefore, to all of those who love to try to challenge Black people and change the narrative to *"why so many Black people are killing each other in the inner cities* "when they are talking about the systemic disease of racism. Here is your answer: it is because of the historical methods taught by Mr. Willy Lynch, the Slave Masters, and their ancestors. The young Black people are practicing a 300-year-old *mind-set* that was passed down to Black people from the slave masters and their kin. It is a spirit that has traveled from one generation to the next within Black people. If you ask most Black kids who had been involved in Black-on-Black crimes; who is Willy Lynch? What did he teach? What were his methods? They would not know who or what you are talking about. Our educational system teaches our kids about Dr. Martin Luther King and Malcolm X; but they will not touch Mr. Lynch. Why, because they do not want Black kids to know about him. It is too much of an ugly past. Many do not want to take responsibility for what was done and taught. Therefore, it is still present today. I had a conversation with a young white lady that I went to high school years ago. I was talking to her about a movie that was coming out on the story of Emmitt Till. Even she thought that it needed to be done and shared with the world. She recognizes that it is a terrible part of our history. She feared that its existence quietly remained, and we needed reminding of it regularly. I could not agree with her more. The institutional racists know that if Black kids ever learn their history that they would not be participating in Black-on-Black crime anymore. They would know that its methods were taught to us by a white Christian man and slave masters three hundred years ago. Black kids would become awoke and no longer want to do it. Once again, I grew up in the inner city. I am quite confident that if young Black men and women were taught in our schools the methods that came out of Willy Lynch, they would think twice about Black on Black violence. Unfortunately, these kids do not know the history and are conducting his *mentality* towards each other. The facts are that Mr. Lynch predicted if the slave masters would teach his *methods* that it would last for more than three hundred years, maybe even 1000. It was 1712 when he taught his methods of *division, envy, distrust* to the Slave Master in the American South. I released this book in 2022. That means it has been 310 years since he taught those methods and our Black culture is still attacking, killing, and hurting each other out of *fear, envy, and distrust* to this very day. We are the only culture in America that does that to each other. Why? It is called learned behavior from one generation to the next. Marriages and relationships between a Black men and Black women struggle vehemently. The Black woman was to be programmed to not trust the Black man according to Willy Lynch methods. The plan was to have Black women to only trust white men. I do not have time to argue any of this, just read the letter! Nor am I getting on Black women. I am just giving you his planned methods to break down the Black culture. I love Black women. I know plenty of Black woman that love Black men and have never been brainwashed by Willy Lynch's methods. If you read my *"Acknowledgements"* in the beginning of the book it is a Black woman's life that I dreamed about, whether it was real or not, running from her slave captors that made me determined to finish this book. I gave her a name; *"The Runner."* What I am saying is that we have been conditioned as Black men and women to be at odds with each other. The man that taught us his methods was a Christian who admired the King James Bible. He passed his methods down to generations of slave masters and their families in the South that taught his principles. The point is that more of us need to become aware of what has been passed down to us as a people so we can stop the violence in our communities. The very racist people that we have a problem with for many years are the ones that have been infiltrating our neighborhoods with *guns, alcohol, unhealthy foods, and drugs*. Why, because they understand the *Willy Lynch spirit* still works and we do not. They know that Black people have been taught to be at odds with and kill each other over the simplest reason. Just look at social media post on Facebook and Twitter, there is always some young Black person posting our people fighting and even being shot in our communities. Listen to the background, you can always hear the laughing and jeering from the young people in the crowd. Once again, what other culture in American does this but Black people. Why, because we were the only ones enslaved and got taught their methods, which is why. Trust me, I am not making any excuses for our Black people not knowing better and the history of their ancestors, which is our job to now educate each other on these facts, in which I am doing in this book. My mother said to me many times and to all her children, *"once you know better than you will do better."* It is time for Black people to know better and do better. Also, before I end this section, my oldest son brought up a good point to me about this matter. Caucasian families should not sleep on this behavior because many of their children are doing what they see on social media that black kids are doing. White kids are listening, dancing, singing, and supporting the same music that Black kids are listening too. He had the conversation about Willy Lynch with his son (my grandson). He told me how after he had the conversation with him how he went down to his room. My grandson took it upon himself to dive in and read up on Mr. Lynch. He found the same letter that I included above and noticed the heinous ways Mr. Lynch would teach the slave masters. He came out of his room, and he could not believe that Black men were treated no different than a horse that needs to be broken. My grandson knows that he is not a horse, so why should a man be trained as one? The book has made him think differently about himself, his parents, ancestors, and his generation. I am so proud of my grandson for taking it upon himself to research this dark American history that he will never get in a classroom. He did not know that I had already made up my mind that I was going to have him read at-least this chapter in my book when it came out. Now he may be interested in reading the entire book. What I would say to is do not think that this *Willy Lynch/Slave Master* mentality of *fear, envy, and distrust* of each other cannot show up in your neighborhoods. It is learned behavior! It will be best that we all instruct our children, white and Black kids that this was a *demonic spirit* used to control Black people. That it has no place in our society. Finally, since Mr. Lynch was a bible believing Christian, the Church sent for him and accepted his methods, the Church needs to help clean up the mess that is in our streets with Black kids. The Church needs to be the one to teach young Black, Brown, and White kids that what Willy Lynch taught to destroy the Black culture was wrong. They need to repent and say they were wrong for taking on his methods. I think every Church should have this as an annual bible study. If the Church helped promote the mess, then they should help clean up the mess in our streets in my opinion.

Next, the Church needs to repent for embracing the racially insensitive slogan that divided us in the 2016 Presidential Campaign, *"Make America Great Again."* That campaign propaganda was so divisive amongst the races and the Evangelical Church embraced it without hesitation. But when people of all colors and backgrounds in 2020 took to the streets to stand up against racial injustice in this nation with the statement *"Black Lives Matter,"* you did not see the evangelicals. These protesters got push back from the Christian politicians and Evangelical Right. They pushed out information that the founders of BLM are not legitimate because it was started by gays and lesbians. Not going for it! It does not matter if aliens started the organization. The point of the statement that they are saying is still true. The goal of the slogan was to get a twisted minded society to see Black people as significant. I mean think about it, we have been forced in society to produce a statement to just *"matter."* I say, *"Black Lives Matter"* because they do! It is time for Americans to recognize it and repent from their hateful past. Now all sudden people want to say, *"All Lives Matter."* I say if, All Lives Mattered in America then it would not have never been necessary for any group to produce the slogan *"Black Lives Matter."* I tell everyone, it does not matter who produced the group *"Black Live Matter,"* the narrative was never about who they sleep with or not. The point is why did anyone ever have to produce such a statement in the first place? They produced the statement because they saw years of *Black Lives* not mattering. They saw how we were being treated by the police without accountability. When has America ever been great again for Black people? Ironically, 80 percent *(millions)* of evangelical Christians never used the *spirit of discernment* and filtered that statement through the lens of Black people. Because of their embrace of that statement and Donald Trump, many are abandoning the Evangelical Church and it is their own fault. Look at this article by a conservative columnist for the New York Times, David Brooks an *"Raw Story"* written on February 4, 2022, entitled *"Evangelicals Struggling After Four Years of Trump Exposed Institutional Riot:"* It reads:

In his column for the New York Times, conservative David Brooks spoke with evangelical leaders who are <u>attempting to pick up the pieces</u> after some within the church embraced Donald Trump ,which led to many <u>abandoning </u>the church. Late last year, NBC reported that polls showed that the term "born again" *has come to mean "less about faith, religion or the church and instead become a political distinction," and more about "they're against immigration, science and abortion and to signal a belief that discussions of racism in America are antithetical to their idea of America." With Christian writers lamenting <u>"The evangelical church is breaking apart,"</u> Brooks spoke with some Christian leaders who explained the past few years while Trump was president were a terrible ordeal for Christians. Writing,*

"There have been three big issues that have profoundly divided them: the white evangelical embrace of Donald Trump, sex abuse scandals in evangelical churches and parachurch organizations, and attitudes about race relations, especially after the killing of George Floyd," Brooks spoke with the president of Christianity Today, Tim Dalrymple, who came under fire after calling for the former president to be ousted after the first of his two impeachments. "As an evangelical, I've found the last five years to be shocking, disorienting and deeply disheartening," he stated. "One of the most surprising elements is that I've realized that the people who I used to stand shoulder to shoulder with on almost every issue, I now realize that we are separated by a yawning chasm of mutual incomprehension. I would never have thought that could have happened so quickly." According to Brooks, the embrace of Trump is the "proximate cause" of the turmoil among Christians. "Trump is merely the embodiment of many of the raw wounds that already existed in parts of the white evangelical world: misogyny, racism, racial obliviousness, celebrity worship, resentment and the willingness to sacrifice principle for power," he wrote. "Then there is the way partisan politics has swamped what is supposed to be a religious movement. Over the past couple of decades evangelical pastors have found that their 20-minute Sunday sermons could not outshine the hours and hours of Fox News their parishioners were mainlining every week. It wasn't only that the klieg light of Fox was so bright, but also that the flickering candle of Christian formation was so dim." "The turmoil in evangelicalism has not just ruptured relationships; it's dissolving the structures of many evangelical institutions. Many families, churches, parachurch organizations and even denominations are coming apart. I asked many evangelical leaders who are wary of Trump if they thought their movement would fracture. Most said it already has," the columnist explained. Writing that "something more fundamental is going on than a fight over just Donald Trump," Brooks suggested that the church is in dire need of reappraisal. "Institutional rot has been exposed. Many old relationships have been severed. This is a profound moment of turmoil, pain, change and, while it's too early to be sure, possible transformation," he wrote before warning, "There can probably be no evangelical renewal if the movement does not divorce itself from the lust for partisan political power. " "Over more than a century, Catholics have established a doctrine of social teaching that helps them understand how the church can be active in civic life without being corrupted by partisan politics. Protestants do not have this kind of doctrine," he suggested before adding, "Those who are leading the evangelical renewal know they need one."

I echo this article vehemently because it says everything that I have noticed about the Evangelical Church and its' politicians. If evangelicals were truly born again and filled with the Spirit of God when they came to this nation, then God would have been able to do something in their hearts towards Black people when they got here in the1600s. The problem is that they really were not who they said they were when they came to this nation, and we are seeing it again today. The truth is that the British Christian Colonizers that came to America in the 1600s according to the *Born-Again* experience where not born-again at all. History always repeats itself.   We are seeing what looks millions of evangelicals who claimed to be *Born-Again*, supported a President who perpetuated racism and division in America. People are now seeing who they really are with their greed for partisan political power and white national sentiments, many people have left their churches.

Pastors should stop standing up in their pulpits telling stories about themselves and how they over-come certain setbacks in life when we are seeing police killings of Black people on national TV. It is like they try to relate to the plight of the struggle of people of color in this nation with their own experience and it does not work. It is not the narrative and certainly not the time to be talking about themselves. People at those times are hurting and concerned if their children, nephews, nieces, and grand children can walk down the street without getting into an altercation with a police officer. They are worried if their colored or bi-racial children get pulled over by the police if they will not end up dead! When preachers do this, it only shows church members that they are out of touch with what is going on in society and avoiding the real elephant in the room. We must understand that in today's America, many white people too have Black children, nieces, nephews, and grandchildren whether it is through adoption, foster care, mixed marriages, or relationships. Many whites have the same concerns that Black people do. Preachers just need to condemn racism every time it raises its ugly head towards people of color from their pulpits. This way no one is unclear about where the Church stands on racial violence towards any race.

Pastors need to stop allowing visiting Pastors to preach in their pulpits to their congregations that are insensitive to racial issues in this nation. If they have not been proven to have taken an open and clear stance against racism towards all people in America, do not risk them preaching to your congregation and they say something stupid. It is a turn off to people of color. It is very disrespectful when they do this when Black parishioners must sit there and listen until they are done with their ignorant speech. I think one of the best things that is happening for the Church now is on-line services. Now you can just turn them off and not be disrespectful by walking out of the church while they are preaching. I have never been one to care about leaving a service while a Pastor is preaching, taking a collection, or giving an altar call. But there have been times where I did not want to listen to what was offensive and just go. People expect their Church leaders to be our partners in getting rid of this turmoil of racism in America. We know that racism is taught behavior to hate another race and the European people where the architects of it in this country. Therefore, it is up to their descendants to help all of us get rid of this problem and not deny or foster it.

The Church needs to listen to people who are crying out for justice. If you think about it many Presidents and Politicians do not live the lives of most of their constituents. One would think that at-least the Church leaders would be able to empathize with their parishioners and try to do something about the racial problems. They are closer to the people more than anyone. It was clear to me after George Floyd's murder in May 2020 and three and half years of our former President and politicians stoking racism in this country that we were grossly divided. I saw that our Evangelical Preachers had no interest in correcting American's behavior toward race. For example, I watched online a well national known Evangelical preacher for a whole week during his 2020 Summer Family Bible Conference. That July he had several evangelical panel members and not once mention the death of George Floyd by police officers, all the protest, the racial divide and rioting in the streets across America. What they did choose to discuss was the success of the former President. I watched him put his congregation under conviction that if they did not get out to vote for him again in November 2020, that if he lost, it would be their fault. When I saw this, I thought to myself now that is sick. I did not see them pray for the Floyd family, the division in the country or for the protest that was happening all over. This is the very reason America has been hemorrhaging with racial divide. The Church ignores too much that goes on right before its' eyes. Here we were in a heated summer of protest behind police shootings of Black people across this nation and this prominent evangelical pastor, several panel members and his congregation could not acknowledge what was happening in our nation. All they could do is get behind the current president at the time *(who openly did not hold his tongue back from inciting police and his followers to use force)* and ignore what was happening in the streets towards people of color. This evangelical pastor, speakers, leaders, and church members functioned as though they had not seen anything wrong with racism in our nation. Instead of addressing those issues, they were preparing themselves to get ready to win another presidential election. I watched all of them clap and applaud like everything the Trump Administration did was great. It is these kinds of Christians that I have an issue with and have been writing about in this book. They are the ones' that keep us stuck and the Church from moving forward in race relations. One would think that all Christians would have a set purpose and integrity we are to keep that has been established by Jesus. What we have seen from the Church during this time has sent the Church's influence reeling backwards. It is not about the kingdom; it is about political power. When it comes to correcting everyone in this nation who are not *Pro-Life*, involved in *Homosexuality*, *Lesbianism* and *Same Sex Marriages* these evangelicals can be heard loud and clear across the country. On the other side, when it comes to *racism, police killings of Black people, injustice, the lack of mercy* and *faithfulness* towards to people of color, you cannot get a peep out of them. In fact, which is when many off them turn and hide behind the law. They will not say one word against *"racism, injustice or police brutality."* Tell me, how can parishioners pray and praise God in Church with a big elephant in the room when police brutality and racism terrorizing our country? Lets' make it clear again; America's original sin was not with *abortion, homosexuality,* or *same-sex marriage* it was birthed out of a *slaveocracy and the greed for white power.* The fact that it keeps raising up is because we never dealt with it. Until we as Americans deal with it, we will always find ourselves catapulting backwards when we are trying to move forward. I am confused with these evangelical preachers and Christian leaders. I do not understand why they are not so dogmatic about condemning the issues that has originally plagued our nation but can be so aggressive about everything else? It is because the issues that I am bringing out in this book has nothing to do with them. It was their ancestors doing and therefore makes it uncomfortable. If they do not talk about it, then it will not require them to take responsibility for change. They do not want to have to repent of their sins and the sins of their ancestors like its say's in Leviticus 26:40-42…" *If they shall confess their iniquity, and the iniquity of their fathers, with their trespass which they trespassed against me, and that also they have walked contrary unto me. And that I also have walked contrary unto them and have brought them into the land of their enemies; if then their uncircumcised hearts be humbled, and they then accept of the punishment of their iniquity; Then will I remember my covenant with Jacob, and my covenant with Isaac, and my covenant with Abraham will I remember; and I will remember the land.*" These ministers know that there has never been a national call for them and their people to repent of racism, slavery, and white nationalism in America. They change the focus to be on different issues like abortion, homosexuality, taking prayer out of schools and same sex marriage. What it does is it give the Church something else to pray about and not what their ancestors have done. I think that they may feel it would be easier to move the nation forward if Black people just get over the issue of slavery and racism. The *M oral Majority* would rather for us to forget about our past and support their agenda in fighting all these other issues. They really do not want to deal with their historical issues of *slavery, racism, and greed.* What these evangelicals do not understand is that many believers who are Black do not see the nation through the same lens that they do. We are no longer in slavery and forbidden to the read the scriptures in the bible. We know the word of God just as much as they do. We know right from wrong. We know what *"an unjust weight, unequal scale (Proverbs 20:23 and Proverbs 11:1)* looks like. We do not see equality, justice, mercy, faithfulness, the condemnation of systemic racism, and white nationalism from many of our evangelical brothers and sisters in Christ. It is very noticeable. It is time for the silence to stop. It is time to speak the truth about it all and how it has plagued Black people for hundreds of years. It does not matter if others do not want to hear us talk, sing, preach or write about it. If we do not hold our brothers and sisters in the Church to account no one will. It is unfortunate that many politicians, preachers, and people who live across America in blue grass communities that claim to be law-abiding citizens, the true believers and real Americans are so blind to these issues. Just as this well-known Evangelical preacher chose not to address the killing of George Floyd and all the protest at his Summer Bible Conference in July 2020, I will tell you that he was not the only preacher that behaved in that way. Once again, quoting a portion of an article written by Gabriel Sherman on January 24, 2022, who is with Vanity Fair about Jerry Falwell, Sr son, Jerry Falwell, Jr. It speaks of his personal problems, support of a race-baiting former President. It shows his mindset two (2) days after the death of George Floyd, his ignoring all the protest in the summer of 2020, his insensitivity towards how Black people feel about black face jokes and the Ku Klux Klan.

It reads: *"On August 24, 2020, Falwell resigned from Liberty in the wake of a sensational tabloid scandal that could have been dreamed up in the writers' room of* The Righteous Gemstones. *A former Miami pool boy named Giancarlo Granda claimed he had a nearly seven-year affair with Falwell's wife, Becki—and that Falwell often liked to watch them*

164

have sex. Granda went on a national media tour—he gave interviews to ABC News, CNN, Reuters, Politico, and The Washington Post—*and said the Falwells began "grooming" him when he was 20 and bought his silence with luxury vacations, rides on Liberty's private jet, and an ownership stake managing a Miami Beach hostel. To bolster his claims, Granda released screenshots of Facetime calls and text conversations with Becki ("I'm not wearing any panties," she allegedly wrote Granda in one message). Falwell released a statement that acknowledged Becki and Granda's relationship, but he vehemently denied watching the trysts. Instead, Falwell said* he *was the real victim of a* "Fatal Attraction–*type" extortion plot after Granda demanded $2 million to keep the affair secret. Viewed in hindsight, the scandal was the combustion of a self-immolating fire that Falwell had been stoking for months, if not years. Liberty had spent the better part of 2020 lurching from one PR crisis to the next brought on by Falwell's boorish and reckless behavior, his race baiting, COVID-19 denials, and slavish devotion to Donald Trump. Two days after George Floyd's murder in May 2020, Falwell tweeted a picture of a COVID mask that showed a man in blackface posing with a man in a KKK hood. In early August 2020, Falwell posted a photo on Instagram of himself aboard a yacht with his pants unzipped, a drink in one hand, and his other arm wrapped around a pregnant Liberty employee with her belly exposed. The controversies turned Falwell into an avatar of the rank hypocrisy, know-nothingism, and toxic masculinity that explained why 81 percent of white evangelical Christians voted in 2016 for Trump, a thrice-married reality TV star who literally boasted of grabbing women by the private."*

What the Evangelical Church does not realize is that there are millions of believers who are just as dead set against these things that I mention more than the ones that they promote for us to stand against. Black and Brown people are sick of the injustice, the lack of mercy, insensitivity, and unfaithfulness to us from our brother and sisters in Christ. Just because someone rises to power and shouts *'Let us Make American Great Again'* it does not mean that they were including Black and Brown people. Once again, this message and man exposed the true hearts of many believers just like Jesus did the teachers of the law and pharisees. Although they claimed to be the true followers of God, obeyed the law of Moses, and gave the tithe from their land, they neglected the more important matters of the law that had to do with the treatment of people. Let us read the exact words of Christ concerning this in Matthew 23:23-28; *"Woe to you, teachers of the law and Pharisees, you hypocrites! You give a tenth of your spices, mint, dill and cumin. But you have neglected the more important matters of the law – justice, mercy and faithfulness. You should have practiced the latter without neglecting the former. You blind guides! You strain out a gnat but swallow a camel." "Woe to you, teachers of the law and Pharisees, you hypocrites! You clean the outside of the cup and dish, but on the inside are full of Greed and Self-Indulgence. Blind Pharisees! First clean the inside of the cup and dish and then the outside will also be clean" "Woe to you, teachers of the law and Pharisees, you hypocrites! You are like whitewashed tombs, which look good on the outside but on the inside are full of bones of the dead and everything unclean. In the same way, you appear to people as righteous but, on the inside, you are full of hypocrisy and wickedness."* It does not matter if you are a president, politician, pastor, or blue grass resident. To refer to yourselves as the true Americans who are righteous law-abiding citizens is ridiculous. The slave masters said the exact same things to the natives and blacks. To act like when Trump became President as though God had raised up a Moses to lead his people into the promise land was foolishness for all the world to see. The man's character and integrity were clearly deplorable, but the Church seemed to not mind. This only clarifies all what Jesus taught about the Pharisees and Teachers of the Law in Matthew Chapter 23. His point was that it is not what is on the outside of a man that makes him clean, but it is what is on the inside of him that makes him unclean. For God to make this subject clear to me, I dreamed while writing this section one night that: *I was standing in a building getting ready to walk out the front door down some steps when an older Caucasian man was calling me to come back inside. I recognized the man who was a Pastor. He is known for his work in three different states across America. I knew the Pastor had passed away several years ago but recognized him in the dream and came back in the building so he could talk to me. He wanted me to promise him that I would look out after his wife who was still living, and I promised him that I would do so. Then he moved over by what seemed to be a kitchen sink and he started talking to me about an experience that he had with the Lord. I did not know if this was an experience he had with the Lord while he was living or after he had passed away, but it did not seem to be relevant as to what he was starting to tell me. He told me that he had experienced the Lord taking him all around this country flying over all the rives of this nation. They were incredibly beautiful from the sky and then allowing him to dip down from the sky to taste and drink out of each one of them. He was still standing by the sink with me and telling me how when he had tested the waters...all of them tasted very nasty and foul. Then he began to speak of a certain river where he had been taken by the Lord in this nation and that water tasted the worse of them all. It was so foul and filthy that he began in the dream to spit out some of what he had tasted in the sink while he turned on the tap water so it could wash it down the drain. Then I could hear another voice in the dream ask if any one of us had ever been to what I thought he said, Omaha? The older Pastor who had spit in the sink had pointed his finger towards me for it was like he knew I had been there in the past; therefore, I slightly raised my hand and it seemed like there were other people around who a few of them had raised their hands as well. It was some of those waters that the older Pastor had spit out in the sink for me to see how foul and nasty they were beyond any other waters across this nation. When I woke up from the dream and started meditating on what I was dreaming. I realized that I had been to Omaha a few times, more than what I had considered in the dream. I had been their two or three times on a government work project and another two or three times while coaching on the road a few semi-pro football games from Colorado. The next morning, I got on the internet and Googled rivers running through Omaha and saw that the Missouri River runs from there and it is the longest river in North America. It rises in the Rocky Mountains over western Montana. The Missouri River flows east and south for 2,341 miles before entering the Mississippi River north of St. Louis, Missouri. That is when I realized that I had taken my sons to two summer football camps from Colorado to St. Louis, Missouri back in the early 2000s when they were young. I had not only been a few times where the Missouri river runs to Omaha, but I had been a few times in where it ends in St. Louis, Missouri. The older Pastor in the dream was my wife's father who put in years of work in the Church and was known to march during the civil rights movement.* If we look at this dream it goes right in line what Jesus was saying about the Pharisees and Teachers of the Law. On the outside everything looks *clean, perfect, and beautiful.* In the dream, the rivers, and waters as he was flying around this nation above with the Lord looked beautiful, clean, and fresh until he went down to taste each one of them, everything was foul and nasty. What my wife's father was trying to show me in the dream is what has been going on across this nation in the hearts of people in the Church for an exceptionally long time. If no one has ever told you, know that water always represents the Word in the bible. In this dream it was plenty of it from the sink to the riverbeds being shown to me. What I got from this dream is that we look nice, beautiful, and clean on Sunday morning in the Church, but on the inside of us we are like what Jesus said to the scribes and pharisees: *"Woe unto you, scribes and pharisees, hypocrites! For ye are like whited sepulchers, which indeed appear to be beautiful outward, but are within full of dead men's bones, and of all uncleanness*

(Matthew 23:27)." Christians look great until the world gets a good taste of them. Then they will find that many are full of everything that is foul and unclean. Not to keep picking on Mr. Willy Lynch, but I know from his letter that the inside of that man was most definitely *foul* and *unclean* as a Christian, but the Church followed his methods regardless for over a hundred years.

Our Church Pastors need to stop being petty about the young protesters that are putting their lives on the line to bring change in America. It is ridiculous. These kids are not rabble-rousers, disobedient and lawless as preachers tag them. These kids just want to see change in this nation. As I look around the country, the protesters have done more than the Church and caused several police chief's and their top administration to resign. They have caused police officers to be suspended, fired, or charged with crimes. What has the Church done to bring change? I am incredibly old school; actions speak louder than words to me. The pastors spend their time judging and being critical about everything these young people did. They criticize them for protesting, cursing, and standing up against the police. The pastors are too busy consuming themselves with miniscule matters but ignoring the important things that are destroying this nation. That is why I say that they are petty. Matthew 23:24 say's it this way: *"You blind guides! You strain out a gnat but swallow a camel."*

Here is a big one: The Church need to stop trying to legislate the work of God by getting the government to do what we should be doing as people of righteousness. Instead of fighting so hard to get politicians, judges, and legislators to pass certain laws, especially overturning the Supreme Court decision in 1973 Roe v Wade; why don't we do what we are called to do and let God's spirit deal with people on what is right and what is wrong? How about giving the holy spirit room to convict and judge when they come to Christ from our witness? That way what people change to do is genuine and not forced by law. How about these lazy evangelicals get off their behinds and win the world around them to Christ, disciple them with the Word of God and teach them to live a new life of godliness. Stop putting it on the American government to produce legislation that make Christians feel good. You cannot legislate righteousness. I know that every civilized nation needs laws to govern society, but some of this work we need to be doing ourselves as believers. We as believers cannot force people to live a godly and righteous life, that only comes through the work of the holy spirit through Christ. The Church gets too over the top about wanting what scripture teaches us to be to be in our national laws. Bringing people to Christ so one can experience a changed mind and heart is the Church's job, not the government. Christians want to legislate everything and then claim that they are law abiding citizens that follow the rule of law and doing the work of Jesus. Well, it was Christians that came to this country, stole the land from the natives, and created laws that made Black people slaves indefinitely and devised method to destroy a entire Black culture up to a thousand years. It was Christian legislators that made these laws to keep people of color with no rights and made it impossible for them to thrive. Until Evangelical Christians get people of color best interest at heart, the last thing that I want to hear from the conservatives as President Biden said in a press conference on May 4, 2022: *"Is about the deficits and their ultra–M.A.G.A. agenda. I want to hear about fairness, I want to hear about decency, I want to hear about helping ordinary people."* I want to hear them talk about ending racism and putting down white nationalism. That will be a good start.

The Church should stop bragging on the history of their founding fathers and the establishment of this country's republic as if it were so great. It needs to stop embellishing how we are a nation who was built on a core belief in God and Judeo-Christian values. There was nothing Christ like that supports the establishment of this nation. If you do not believe me, ask the descendants of the Native Americans that was were here first and murdering of their family members by the Godly British Colonials. It is sickening to hear evangelicals amplify this rhetoric so proudly and try to make it believable as if we do not know the true history of the establishment of this nation. Just stop it, it sounds ridiculous for many that hear you say it with much pride. In other words, people know better. The history of the establishment of this nation is bloody and we might as well accept it. The Evangelicals cannot even sell it to their children and grandchildren anymore because this young generation have cell phones and they can Google whatever they want to know. The days of hiding things in a book is over. Young people know better now, that is why they are protesting. As I mentioned earlier, even my young grandson got on his I-Pad and learned everything he needed to know about Willy Lynch. There is not an adult, white or black that can tell him anything different. He now knows for himself from his own research, not even mines.

The Church needs to stop whining about God's name no longer in our courts and no prayer in school as if these things make us a Christian nation. The bible says, *God is a Spirit and they that worship Him must worship Him in spirit and in truth (John 4:24).* If Christians start worshipping God properly, they will not need to see His name on a dollar bill, in a court room or a classroom. He is a Spirit. He lives inside of you, that means you can take Him anywhere you go. One can take Him on a Space Shuttle to the Moon if that is where you are going. The truth is that God was never in control of our nation's money, courts, or classrooms. Man has always controlled those things. That is why this country was built on a slaveocracy and not a democracy. That was sold to us as a bunch of crocks to control what people think about America. The Christian politicians wanted put God's stamp of approval on what they did to be justified in whatever they wanted to do. Once again, just because God's name or logo is on it, it does not mean that He is in it. You can paint the largest cross on the hood of your car, but it doesn't mean that Christ is in there. Remember, wherever you go there YOU are!

The Church needs to start being the light of the world and live as the salt of the earth. We need to live in a way that people see our good works and glorify our Father in heaven as to who we are showing ourselves to be. How about that idea saints? Jesus walked amongst the lowly, the demonically oppressed and the most ungodly folks on the face of the earth for 33 years. He never had God's name on his T-Shirt, Ballcap, or wore a cross around his neck. Jesus walked and lived among them in a way that the lowly, demonically oppressed and most ungodly came to him asking to be delivered, healed or what must they do to be saved. Evangelicals just need to stop it with needing God's name posted every-were in society. We are the salt of the earth, live something and the world will ask you how they too can have the peace that they see in you. I have always known even as early as a teenager that if I could find some way to bottle up "Peace" and sell it, I would be a trillionaire within one year. That is what people want, Peace! Then give it to them through you. Why don't you stop being a religious *hell raiser* and thinking we need more crosses and Jesus' logos everywhere?

The Evangelical Church need to really stop acting like they care so much about the unborn babies when history shows that they did not care about the born Black babies on the plantations or in the south. Did the Church care when they participated in what black babies went through being used as bait to catch alligators in our southern swamps in Florida? Oh, you do not want to talk about those facts. I will show that they can care less about Black babies that are unborn since they had no concern for the ones that were born. Yes, Christians in this country used to use Black babies to catch alligators in the south all the way up to the 1960s, but they want us to believe they now care about all unborn babies. No, they just want your vote and support. How many Black babies were traumatized and eaten behind these heinous crimes that no one wants to talk about that Christians participated in America? Instead of me talking about it, I will let you read part of an astonishing article I found on-line entitled *"The gut-wrenching history of Black babies and alligators"* written by Domonique Foxworth, on June 22, 2016, *"The Undefeated"* But, here is where I draw the line. I started to include this entire write-up in this book, but it is too horrible to read what Christian people in the south were doing with Black babies and alligators as late as the 1960s. It was all greed, no two-ways about it. Therefore, I will just include a small portion of the article and the online link where you can go read what they were doing in what was called *"The Maafa."* Feel free to put this link in your internet browser to pull up the article, I am not convinced that everyone should need to read terrible history in our nation in my book .Here is just a snippet of the article as to what it says: *"Was using Black children as gator bate unacceptable? No. Unbelievable? No. The idea that Black Children are acceptable gator bait was not born in the head of one zookeeper, it was a practice in the American Everglades that inspired lore and occasioned memorabilia. In 1923, Time Magazine reported that colored babies were being used for alligator bait in Chipley, Florida. The infants were allowed to play in the shallow waters while expert riflemen watched from concealment nearby. When a saurian approach the prey, he is shot by the riflemen. This tactic was more humane than the one described in a Miami News Times article. Alligator hunters would sit crying Black babies who were too young to walk on the water's edge. With a rope around their necks and waists, the babies would splash and cry until a crocodile snapped on one of them. The hunters would kill the alligator only after the baby was in its jaws, trading one child's life for an alligator skin. They made postcards, pictures and trinkets to commemorate the practice."* Click on this link to read the full article: The gut-wrenching history of black babies and alligators — Andscape.

For those of you who took the time to read it, did you catch the last part of the article where Dominique Foxworth said, *"The Christian people responsible for centuries of Maafa justified their sins by convincing themselves that blacks were an inferior race?"* I wonder where they got that from? And we wonder why the Church has not seen revival in our nation. Go ahead, keep praying, but until it repents its' not happening. I am saddened to inform you that this kind of mess went on in America with Christians until around 1960. Legislation had to be written against it to put a stop to it. This is what happens when you let the self-righteous Evangelicals dictate what is right and wrong without challenging it. I have no problem at all protecting the rights of unborn babies, but my question is where were these Christian's concerns about the Black children that were born being fed to alligators for their skin? The Church need to stop acting like they care so much about the unborn babies when history shows that they showed no mercy or concern at all for the born Black babies for economic reasons, especially in the south. I hope everyone got through that part. If this was too gross, I do apologize.

Nevertheless, the Church needs to learn how to have a heart for other peoples' pain that comes from injustice and inequality. If Jesus can be touch with the feelings of our infirmities, then the Church should be able to do so as well. The bible says, *"For we have not a high priest which cannot be touched with the feeling of our infirmities; but was in all points tempted like as we are, yet without sin (Hebrews 4:15),"* It needs to stop being so calloused! Unfortunately, the Church has not been empathetic on issues of race and social injustice. It prefers to be *Right* rather than *Righteous.* It has always taken a self-righteous stand towards these things and claims to be about the *rule of law* but cannot see the suffering of Black/Brown families. There are only a few White Preachers in America that will have the boldness to stand up in their pulpits and rebuke the *spirit of RACISM, White Nationalism and Police Violence* in America. Many of them will not do it no matter how many opportunities they have had to address it in this nation. If they do speak about it, it is always reduced to sin, problems, or issues in America. Even the President of the Southern Baptist Convention said in a statement about *"critical race theory"* is *"antithetical to the bible and only the Gospel can save… it is dangerous to view humans and conflict primarily through the lens of race, gender, or sexuality instead of via scriptural concepts such as sin."* Again, reducing everything down to sin and avoiding having the conversation because they know it is one that cannot win. In which you can read the full article online in the Washington Post written by Sarah Pulliam Bailey and Michelle Boorstein on December 23, 2020, entitled: *"Several Black pastors break with the Southern Baptist Convention over a statement of race."* The problem with this is that it gives these preachers an excuse to not call out racism like they have no problem doing other matters of the flesh that is not in agreement with their politics. I think you should really find time to read the article above. It will help you understand how big this problem has been even at the legendary Southern Baptist Convention with Black pastors who have decided to leave the national organization. Its' one thing to talk about something, its' another thing to make a commitment to get something done and destroy its works. What I see most evangelical preachers end up doing is changing the narrative and the conversation becomes about their individual experiences with racism. They show no interest of what it may be like to be a Black person in this country. What they fail to realize that the issue of racism in America is not about them, its' about the people of color who have been held down by its virtues since the establishment of this nation. Historically, the Church has never stood up during times like these when it should have been the loudest voice. The Church was mute back in the 1600s and it is mute now on the issue in the 21 Century. It would much rather stay quiet, marginalize, or defend the government on many issues instead of being touched with feelings of the infirmities of Black people in America and bring change. Because the Church have been quiet on these issues, now it looks like God has taken the platform from the preachers and have given it to every-day people who have no reputation. Ordinary people can now use social media, Facebook, Twitter, You-Tube, Facetime, etc. to get their message out to the masses. Every-day people have found their voice and now use these platforms to defy the bigotry in America and the Church does not like it because the focus is no longer on them to speak to *moral issues* in society for which they have neglected.

In summary, the Evangelical Church in America need to stop being a Harlot with political leaders that wink their eye, smile at them, tell them what they want to hear about fighting for religious rights, banning abortion, installing conservative judges, re-awakening America, meeting all their needs, filling up their heads to makes them run off with the self-righteous and sell their souls. Just stop being such a harlot and follow rabble-rousers. The Church in America needs to know the difference between a *"Pimp and a Prophet."* It needs to stop being so quick to crown someone as *"sent by God"* and others who are not of their political persuasion *"the Devil."* Its' ridiculous! If we are going to offer prayers, respect, and petitions for one Presidential leader, we should offer up prayers for every President. The Church needs to learn how to deal with its inconsistencies and hypocrisies that others do see. Stop thinking that the world is blind and stand up for justice, godliness, and righteousness with all leaders…Black, Brown, or White.

Chapter Seven

Back To the Spirit of Greed

"What Made Americans Greedy Again"

W.M.A.G.A

"A King, A Cult and The Idolatrous"

"In fact, all who want to live a godly life in Christ Jesus will be persecuted. Evil people and seducers will become worse, deceiving, and being deceived"

2 Timothy 3:12-13

Three days after the 2016 Presidential Elections in America a very respected friend of mines asked me *"Ken, who does the new president remind you of in the bible?"* Without hesitation I told her *"Nebuchadnezzar."* She asked me why I chose him? I told her that I watched the entire 2016 campaign that year and saw an arrogancy in him that he was going to have to be humbled like God did King Nebuchadnezzar, King of Babylon in the book of Daniel. Also, I saw early was that he talked too much and loved attention. I told her something that my grandmother used to tell all her grandchildren when we were young. Grandma would say to us *"don't let your mouth write a check that your behind can't cash!"* I discerned that this man, although rich, had a severe case of *"mouth-i-tis."* I told her that his mouth would eventually find him in a world of trouble. The bible is noticeably clear about controlling the tongue, in which I saw early that he had none. *James 3:1-6 say's "Not many of you should become teachers, my fellow believers, because you know that we who teach will be judged more strictly. We all stumble in many ways. Anyone who is never at fault in what they say is perfect, able to keep their whole body in check. When we put bits into the mouths of horses to make them obey us, we can turn the whole animal. Or take ships as an example. Although they are so large and are driven by strong winds, they are steered by a very small rudder wherever the pilot wants to go. Likewise, the tongue is a small part of the body, but it makes great boasts. Consider what a great forest is set on fire by a small spark. The tongue also is a fire, a world of evil among the parts of the body. It corrupts the whole body, sets the whole course of one's life on fire, and is itself set on fire by hell".* Of course, my friend looked at me and laughed when I said all this, but I was serious. Now she texts me regularly and says, you were right. You said that his mouth was going to get him in a lot of trouble, and it happened. He not only lost the 2020 election, but he is being investigated for possible criminal charges in several states. I explained to my friend that this man did not behave like a President but much more like a king. That is why I said Nebuchadnezzar who was a Babylonian King. As a former Supervisor for the White House Air Force Presidential Honor Guard, I got to see President Ronald Regan up close on many occasions and how his wife Nancy behaved. Also, I got to see some of President George Bush, Sr and his wife Barbara for about six months before I left service. This new president was clearly no Ronald Reagan or George Bush. The new President in 2016 had a bravado overconfident attitude and tone that none of these former presidents had that stoked white nationalism, the Christian Right and divided us in America. I knew from my own military experience and training that when it comes to leadership *"Leadership Starts at The Top, Tone is Everything and Words Do Matter!"* His words and tone during the 2016 campaigning were despicable, disgraceful, disrespectful, divisive and race baiting. The evangelical church and the GOP Republicans knew it but ignored it and said nothing! I understood in November 2016 that his leadership inequalities would reveal itself over time. I had no idea it would take four years, I figured more like 18 months. Like David French said in his article written in the *Atlantic* on March 28, 2022, entitled: *The Third Rail, "I deeply underestimated the continued prevalence and malignant legacy of American racism."* Regardless of these facts, even though losing the popular vote to Hillary Rodham Clinton, he still won the most electoral votes due to his promises he made to White Nationalist, the Evangelical Church and *"dog whistling"* to those who are racist at heart in our nation. The fact of the matter is that 85 percent of the White Evangelical Christians and Pastors in our nation still voted for him. They chose to ignore the violent words and hateful rhetoric from this man. They refused to acknowledge

175

that divisive rhetoric and lies can lead to violent actions from followers eventually. I watched for four years how the Evangelical Church showed no regard as to how this was affecting their Black and Brown Christian brothers and sisters in Christ. Many of them sitting right there in the same congregation along with them and the Pastor's still did not denounce this man's racist rhetoric during his term. Dr. Malcom X once said, *"The Clergy Politician Leadership that has been handpicked for the so-called Negros by the White man himself. This Clergy Politician Leadership does not speak for the Negros majority or the black masse., They speak for the black bourgeoisie, the brain washed, white minded, middle-class minority."* Is that what has been happening in America with our Evangelical Right preachers for the past years. I will let you reflect and judge that for yourself. What I will say is that they have had nothing to say to defend the cause of the Black woman or men in America as a whole, including their own black brothers and sisters in Christ that sit in their churches or listen to their television broadcast. Nevertheless, I watched the new president's attitude and behavior during the campaign and election, bragging that he could do anything and get away with it, including shooting someone in Central Park. I could clearly see that here was a President that he and his followers *(including the Church)* were in for a huge humbling. This kind of humbling could only come from God, not man. To learn more about this President I had watched a documentary on him prior to his election where his father Fred Christ Trump had raised him as a young man and taught him that *"He (his son) was a King and everyone else were subordinate to him."* This would explain his cockiness, brashness, and rude behavior. It would explain his talking down to others and how he treated all who campaigned or spoke against him. I personally watched him walk right behind and almost on top of Hillary Clinton on national debate seething with hate as to try to intimidate her while she was speaking against him. How he got away with that one, I have no idea. Unfortunately, many of our spiritual and political leaders thought that this style of bullying was permissible, excusable, necessary and a show of strength. It was what America needed in the White House. Remember what Will Rogers said in 1935, *"A fool and his money is soon elected."* The Conservate Politicians and the Evangelical Church needed to be humbled and they would be proven wrong in their choice over the next four years. The truth is that this experiment with a man who was not qualified to be Commander In Chief was foolishness for the Church to get involved in. When I had compared him to Nebuchadnezzar, King of Babylon I had already read the book of Daniel many times before. I saw the same foolishness that was in Nebuchadnezzar's heart. I knew King Nebuchadnezzar's start and I knew his end. This man to me was heading in the same direction of destruction that he and his followers could not see coming.

The story of King Nebuchadnezzar starts in 2 Kings Chapter 24 and Chapter 25, but the details are in the book of Daniel Chapter 1 thru Daniel Chapter 4. I will give you a synopsis of these writings about King Nebuchadnezzar just in case you have never read these books. Nebuchadnezzar was simply an enemy king to the Jews that God used to punish the evil Kings of Judah for a time. His first conquest was during the reign of King Jehoiakim of Judah who became his vassal for three years and Nebuchadnezzar sent foreign armies into Judah to destroy it. All this was done to remove Judah from the Lord's presence at the Lord's command because of the prior sins of King Manasseh which had to do with all the innocent blood he had shed. King Manasseh had filled Jerusalem with innocent blood shed and the Lord was not willing to forgive (2Kings 24:1-4). Then, during another King of Judah reign by a different name Jehoiakim, Nebuchadnezzar marched up to Jerusalem and the city came under siege. King Jehoiachin of Judah, along with his mother, his servants, his commanders, and his officials surrendered to Nebuchadnezzar. He also carried off from Judah all the treasures of the Lord's temple and the treasures of the king's palace. He cut into pieces all the gold articles that King Solomon of Israel had made for the Lord's sanctuary. He took the king's mother, the king's wives, his officials, the leading men of the land, seven-thousands of the best soldiers, craftsmen, and metalsmiths into exile from Jerusalem to Babylon. Also, he made Jehoiachin's uncle Mattaniah, who he renamed Zedekiah, king of Judah in his place. Later, Zedekiah rebelled against Nebuchadnezzar and once again he laid siege against the city with his army and this time built a siege WALL all around it. Nebuchadnezzar blinded King Zedekiah, bound him in bronze chains and took him back to Babylon. Later, Nebuchadnezzar and the captain of the guards, his servant, entered Jerusalem and burned the Lord's temple, the king's palace and all the houses of Jerusalem. Nebuchadnezzar would then appoint Gedaliah son of Ahikam son of Shapan over the rest of the people in Judah. Gedaliah would be killed by Ishmael son of Nethaniah, son of Elishama of the royal family with ten other men. Eventually, Nebuchadnezzar would pardon King Jehoiachin of Judah and released him from prison and set his throne over the thrones of the kings that were with him in Babylon and paid him an allowance of a portion for each day for the rest of his life (2 Kings 24:8-20 and 2 Kings 25:1-30).

To learn more about Nebuchadnezzar you would have to read the book of Daniel Chapters 1 through Chapter 4. During King Jehoiakim reign of Judah and when Nebuchadnezzar sieged against Judah, he ordered his chief eunuch to bring some the Israelites from the royal family and from the nobility, young men without any physical defect, good-looking, suitable for instruction in all wisdom, knowledgeable, perceptive, and capable of serving in the king's palace. Those instructions would find a number Israelite young men in the king's realm and among them from Judah was four young men: Daniel, Shadrach, Meshach, and Abednego. God gave the four men knowledge and understanding in every kind of literature and wisdom, and they stood out above all the others in the king's palace. Daniel was the only one that understood visions and dreams of every kind and at the end they were presented to King Nebuchadnezzar. The king was pleased with these four young men, and they began to serve and attend the king in every matter of wisdom and understanding. They were ten times better than all the magicians and mediums in the king's entire kingdom. In his second year of his reign, Nebuchadnezzar had dreams that troubled and disturbed him, and he could not sleep. So, he gave orders to summons all the wise men in his kingdom to tell him what he had been dreaming and to interpret the dreams for him and or they could be executed. Unfortunately, this was too hard for the magicians and mediums, and they tried to get the king to tell them what he dreamed so they could give him an interpretation. The king refused to tell them of the dreams for he feared they would lie and give him some interpretation to keep from being executed. Daniel had heard about what was going on and did not want himself and friends (Shadrach, Meshach, and Abednego) to perish with the other wise men. He went to the king and asked for some time to reveal his dreams and interpret them. God had favor on Daniel, and he was able to do exactly just that for the king sparing his life, his friends and all the wise men in the kingdom. Later Nebuchadnezzar made a golden statue ninety feet high and 9 feet wide. He set it on the plain of Dura in Babylon and sent word to all the leaders to assemble for a dedication. The people of every nation and language when they heard the music were supposed to immediately fall and worship the golden image. Word got back to the king that Shadrach, Meshach, and Abednego did not fall and worship when the music played, and he summoned the three men and asked them about it. The three men replied to the king and said *"Nebuchadnezzar, we do not need to give you an answer to this question"* (Daniel 3:16). The king was filled with rage on his face and had them thrown into the fiery furnace. Because the king did it with such haste the very men that threw them in were consumed by the flames. Suddenly, the king realized that the three men were walking around in the fire unburned and there was a fourth person in the flames with them. He summoned the three men to come out of the flames and they were not burned or even smelled like smoke. King Nebuchadnezzar honored the God of Shadrach, Meshach and Abednego and recognized that the three men risked their lives rather than serve or worship any god except their own God. The king would then issue a decree that *"anyone of any people, nation or language who says anything offensive against the God of Shadrach, Meshach and Abednego will be torn limb from limb and his house made a garbage dump"* (Daniel 3:29). The King would later have one last dream and it frightened him while he was in his bed for the images and visions in his mind had alarmed him. He issued a decree once again for all the wise men to come to him to explain the matter of the dream. Finally, Daniel came before the king to interpret the dream and the king trusted Daniel for he knew the spirit of God lived in him. The king began to tell Daniel the dream and when he was finished Daniel was frighted for the king for, he knew the dream had everything to do with the king and his reign over the kingdom. Daniel told the king that he would be driven away from the people to live with the wild animals and feed on grass like cattle and be drenched with dew from the sky for seven periods *"Let his mind be changed from that of a human and let him be given the mind of an animal for seven periods of time"* (Daniel 4:16). In other words, the king would lose his mind for seven years. He told him that this will happen until the king acknowledges *"that Heaven rules"* (Daniel 4:26). He would then give the king his advice *"Separate yourself from your sins by doing what is right and from your injustices by showing mercy to the needy. Perhaps there will be an extension of your prosperity"* (Daniel 4:27).

Knowing this above is the reason I told my friend that the new President reminded me of King Nebuchadnezzar. As the new president came into office many voters and notable psychologist could see that he was a man of unstable mind and character. In fact, one Harvard Psychologist observed from a distance and said that he was a *"malignant narcissist."* His four-year term would prove that this Harvard elite was correct. Nebuchadnezzar too was a man who had lost his mind and believed that he was the Almighty. God had to humble him for seven years before his mind was restored to him and he realized that *"Heaven Rules."* Like Nebuchadnezzar, he was a president that wanted to dominate, control and rule all his subjects. If any official were found to be disloyal to Nebuchadnezzar, there would be a price to pay with imprisonment or death. The Former President had too made it clear that he would take actions to imprison, fire or even threaten the life of any government officials that did not do what he wanted. He had called for the investigation and imprisonment of Hillary Clinton who ran against him in 2016. Also, he had called for the investigation and imprisonment of Barrack Obama who was the president before him along with countless firings of other government officials. This man clearly demanded loyalty to himself and his administration. What he did not realize, is what the late former First Lady Barbara Bush who died on April 17, 2018, said about the President's antics for loyalty that *"loyalty goes both ways!"* You cannot expect others to be loyal to you if you are not loyal to them. Besides all this thirst for loyalty, he needed to understand that *"Heaven Rules"* and not him. I have never witnessed such bizarre behavior from so many God-fearing, levelheaded people when Donald Trump took the oval office. It was almost cultic like in which I will talk about next. Let start with:

What is a cult? According to the dictionary, a cult is *"a misplaced or excessive admiration for a particular person or thing."* We have watched during his four years him do and say many offensive things during his administration. People in Washington, all around the country support his unruly thoughts, emotions, and behaviors as I mentioned in previous chapters. Not only our Republican Senators were entangled in his debauchery for four years, but 126 House Republicans and 17 Republican Attorney Generals were willing to put their names on a list to support the overturn of the 2020 election on his way out the door. When we look at his rallies and who were in the crowds. It was millions of Caucasians who were willing to support his ways and do anything he said *(including violence, sedition, and insurrection)* to keep him in office. He could easily encourage his followers at his campaign rallies to harm protesters. He told them that he will pay their legal fees and they would believe him. I watched pastors defame their character and ministries with unwarranted preaching, prayers that defended this man for his whole term. Some preachers even went as far as blaming the devil for stealing the election from him, the church is being persecuted, and praying *"foolish"* prayers publicly for God to overthrow the voting results. I mean it was crazy cultic like behavior on his behalf everywhere, including within the Church. Evangelicals all over the country banded together promoting a false prophecy that God said Donald Trump was going to be re-elected as President. I watched a YouTube video of one pastor, Kenneth Copeland who has been respected and well known since the 1970s say six days later after Joe Biden was declared 46th President of the United States *"The media said that Joe Biden is President… (He then laughs) Ha, Ha, Ha. Look at your neighbor and say…Ha, Ha, Ha."* All his congregation turned to each other and starts laughing. He started laughing and mocking at the presidential results of Joe Biden getting 306 electoral votes five days after the election. Even the President's *so called* personal spiritual advisor Pastor Paula White, went viral on social media praying insane prayers calling for angelic forces, angelic reinforcements, on the assistance of angles from Africa and South Africa. She was prophesying that *"she heard the sound of abundance of rain and the sound of victory, victory, victory…and the Lord say's it is done"* … all this meaning that Donald Trump will not have to leave the White House. They were believing that congress would overturn the results of the election and Trump will remain President. It was like false prophets and soothsayers were popping up all over the Church across the nation. She clearly knew the votes were counted and Trump lost the presidency, but she kept up a lie and false prophecy. All of this was nonsense and many Christians followed her and supported the *"Big Lie"* only to be embarrassed later. It was like she refused to believe that the country voted against and wanted him out of office. This was the kind of ardent cultic behavior by the Evangelicals that was going on in America. This kind of behavior kept Christians and followers thinking that the election was a fraudulent and stolen from Donald Trump. They were led to believe that he would win in court. This too is another reason the Church is not innocent and just as guilty in what happened in our country on January 6, 2021. They echoed the lies that many of the politicians and journalist were guilty of doing. The evangelical republican right believers who claim to be more in line with the teachings of Jesus could not live with the results of the 2020 election. Therefore, they began preaching, teaching, and praying all kinds of foolishness and heresies against the results. Many leaders seduced their congregations to believe that God was going to turn things around for them. I could not believe what I was hearing and seeing. They were all deceived and being deceived. I then saw a video trending on social media of our Christian evangelical brothers and sister praying in front of the buildings where they were still counting the votes. They were kneeling, praying, speaking in tongues, laying hands on the doors and windows for workers to stop counting the votes. Talk about some outright foolishness! It was plain craziness in America in what I was seeing our White brothers and sisters in Christ doing publicly to embarrass themselves, the Church, the Body of Christ and not listen to the will of the people. I have no idea how the wise and discerning Christian Right could not see something like this coming since November 2016 when Trump won the election is beyond me. I am reminded that the word of God talks about an evil people and seducers that will become worse and worse. Deceiving the people and being deceived themselves. It says, *"In fact, all who want to live a godly life in Christ Jesus will be persecuted. Evil people and impostors will become worse, deceiving, and being deceived (2 Timothy 3:12-13).* In other words, it is not going to get better, but worse. That is what we saw in America is a bunch of people and clergy that put that lie out that Trump was going to win the 2020 election, or have it overturned by congress. Many of them went as far as to say that God was going to intervene. Every one of them must come clean and repent. They promoted the false prophecy openly therefore they should have to repent openly. Their blasphemy led so many people astray and almost derailed our nation's democracy. Likewise, all the church goers that went to these churches and supported the *"Big Lie"* from their leaders need to repent as well because they took pleasure in the false prophecies that took place. It is not only he that does the wrong is guilty but he that has taken pleasure in him that do it…is guilty. It was sad to see these people for years be seduced and deceived by their Christian leaders. This is something that nobody wants to talk about when you bring it up. If God really told these so-called *prophets, teachers, pastors, and evangelist* that Donald Trump was going to win the 2020 election He does not need a mob to storm the Capitol Building to make it happen. Then they had the nerve to have a prayer meeting on the Senate floor after they broke in (SMH). Nevertheless, after all this foolishness from our clergy and church goers went on for seven hours that day. Joe Biden was still inaugurated as the 46th President of the United States on January 20, 2021. Many preachers got caught up in this in America to the point that now they are not qualified to write or preach honestly against what happened because they participated in it. They were heard over their pulpits for four years promoting their support of this man who is responsible for five people dying because of his desire to forcefully take over the White House for another four years. His followers were too blind to realize that black, brown, and white Americans went to the polls and legally voted him out. They voted against racism, bigotry, white nationalism, social injustice, and anyone who flirted with its agenda. That spirit is not wanted in this country anymore and the Christian Right knows it. That is the reason the former President loss. What these people were doing to resist what happened at the voting polls was very cultic in nature. When Hillary Clinton lost the 2016 election you did not see Democratic Christians out in public embarrassing themselves praying to overturn the election. They were upset at the loss but took it in stride and dealt with the results. If Obama would have lost his second term, I do not think you would have seen Black Pastor's, Senators and Congressman doing everything they could to discredit the election as fraudulent and taking legal actions to overturn the results. All I am saying is the behavior of the *Christian Right and our Born-Again* legislators has been very bizarre and cultic like during those four years. The sad thing about it is that they cannot see what it has done to the reputation of the Church. Their true colors came out once a Black man came to office in the White House in 2008. Unfortunately, there are still many whites in America that believe that white men by nature were created to lead. Barrack Obama becoming the 44th President was not the end of the world but obviously struck a nerve and challenged that belief in those who are covertly prejudice in America. Donald Trump becoming that 45th President made the prejudice incredibly happy that a white man was back in power, and you could see it on their faces. What they did not see was Kamala Harris coming, who would be the first woman and Black woman to become Vice-President in 2020. I know that my evangelical brothers and sisters in Christ do not like getting a bible study but let me remind them. The bible is noticeably clear about God and His love towards all His people. We can be here all day reading and writing about it. But He is also clear about what He hates that many of the Evangelicals seem to forget.

Let us take a few minutes to remember. In Proverbs 6:16-19, its say's *"There are six things that the Lord hates, seven are detestable to Him: haughty eyes, a lying tongue, hands the shed innocent blood, a heart that devises wicked schemes, feet that are quick to rush into evil, a false witness who pours out lies and a person who creates discord between the brethren.* When I look at this list, the former president could be said to have engaged in all seven of them now that five people are dead. I will let you be the judge of that one yourself. It is looking like that he may be held responsible for the attack on our nation's Capital Building. Nevertheless, the evangelicals and self-righteous lawmakers will not talk about any of this in their news stations, conference meetings, social media platforms, newspapers, periodicals, or pulpits. To me this scripture fits so well for I have never seen one President in my day that has so much pride and arrogancy *(which are haughty eyes).* I never seen a President tell countless lies including one is about a porn star, his former attorney, his former campaign manager, a longtime friend, the Corona

Virus, the election results were rigged, that he won the 2020 Presidential Election just to name a few *(which was no less than a lying tongue)*. He was being investigated for bank, insurance, tax, and campaign fraud. He was impeached on charges of *abuse of power, obstruction of Congress and inciting an insurrection on the Capitol Building.* He was caught on tape with a pressuring phone call to Georgia's top election official to overturn his defeat. He was caught saying *"There is nothing wrong with saying that you have recalculated...All I want to do is this, I just want to find 11,780 votes. Flipping the state is a great testament to our country"* *(this was no less than devising wicked schemes)*. He used the military, state police, national guard, and militia groups to intimidate and abuse protesters in major cities across the nation. He desired to invoke martial law and appointing special counsel as part of efforts to overturn the 2020 Presidential Election results *(feet quick to rush to evil)*. He casted doubt on the knowledge and ability of our Generals, military, national intelligence agencies such as (CIA, NSA, FBI...etc.) and judges to be able to do their jobs. He did not speak the truth about the work of Center for Disease Control (CDC), Scientist, Medical Professionals, the severity of COVID-19 and the need for the public to wear mask *(which was being a false witness who pours out lies)*. Then we have the whole Charlottesville, SC incident where the president said *"there were very fine people on both sides"* when a young lady was run down by a white supremacist in vehicle during a protest. This caused even further discord between Black people and whites in America. The former President never condemned the White Supremacist groups *"The Proud Boys, The Three Percenters, Oath Keepers, Buggy Boy's.* What he did do is asked them to *'stand back and standby'* like he was giving them orders that was significance to his administration. This was a clear sign even back then in August 2017 that he was collaborating closely with those white nationalist groups. Later, these would be the same people that would tear up the Capitol Building in Washington, DC on his behalf. He was constantly *dog-whistling* to groups that believe this nation is being taken away from them. In December 2020 he invited the leader of the Proud Boys to the White House for a meeting. January 6, 2021; was one of the most embarrassing chapters in US History when Pro-Trump supporters breached the U.S. Capitol forcing a lockdown. They did this when lawmakers were convening to count the electoral college votes and several people were killed, including a Capitol Police Officer, *(not only was he a person who creates discord between the brethren, but may be responsible for having innocent bloodshed)*. Remember that creating discord between the brethren is the seventh thing that is detestable to the Lord, and we all have lived through that chaos during his term. My question is: where do our pastors and Evangelical Church leaders get off endorsing and supporting a President like this for four years? Have they not paid attention to his actions and words? Or did they just ignore them? May I remind them of what Jesus taught the disciples during his ministry on earth – He said *"Leave them, they are blind guides. If the blind lead the blind, the two will fall in the ditch (Matthew 15:14)."* This is a fair warning for any of us who choose to ignore these seven things mentioned above emanating out of leadership. That leader will not only himself fall into a ditch but everyone who follows their ways will fall with him. American's must open their eyes and admit that their bigotry, prejudice, social injustice, and systematic racism is a dead end for any civilized nation. If we are going to be the beacon of light to others across the globe, then we are going to have to stop dismissing the sins of our past. I am not writing about making people today pay for the sins of their ancestors. What I am saying is that denying, ignoring, marginalizing and not working to make real change can no longer exist. Lastly, I will talk about the *idolatrous.* They too were very apparent during his term. What does it mean to be idolatrous? The dictionary explains it as *"worshipping idols or treating someone as an idol."* I could not refrain from the fact as to how I have personally witnessed many people in America worshipped this president without them recognizing their idolatrous behavior. He has come as close to an idol to people than what I have read about in the bible. Once again, he bragged that he realized that he can *"shoot somebody in the middle of 5th avenue and he would not lose any voters"* and he was right. Even though he never shot anyone he certainly tested the waters in every aspect to see what he could get away with while keeping his followers. In fact, during his second race he gained another ten million voters than what he had in 2016 election. GOP government officials on every level across the nation were willing to stand with him at all costs no matter how awful the president behaved, lied, or dismissed his oval office duties. To add insult to injury, I watched a well-known television evangelist, Pat Robertson from the 700 club miss it with this man. Pat Robinson has been highly respected preacher in America for more than 50 years. Even he made excuses for him and said how the president believes in alternative reality. Instead of saying that the President believes in telling lies, he called it an alternative reality. Are you serious? This powerful Christian Right evangelist had the boldness to say this on his national television program. Millions of people watch his broadcast daily around the world. Although this President is largely immoral, I thought to myself here is this well-known international preacher who is making excuses for the president believing in an alternative reality *(which is a softer way to not say that he makes*

185

up lies) but this same preacher is very direct about the sin of men and women who engage in the lesbian or gay lifestyle. Doesn't he realize that these people say that their alternative sexual lifestyles are their alternative reality? This makes the Church look bad when we have preacher's tolerating presidential leadership foolishness while in the same breath judging everyone else's sin. The point is that even Christian leaders and preachers of reputation across America had gotten caught up into this idolatrous behavior towards this president like so many American constituents. If America cannot trust its priest, pastors, preachers, and prophets to call a spade a spade than who can we trust? Pat Robertson has been around long enough to know when to call a liar a liar. The unwillingness of this national televangelist to call a spade a spade has caused him to lie on his television broadcast viewers on January 4, 2021 *(two days before the House was to confirm the outcome of that vote and the insurrection that happened on Capitol Hill on January 6, 2021).* I watched him lie about what would happen to the results of the 2020 electoral votes. This prophecy that he gave on national TV was ridiculous and only proves my point about the bizarre idolatrous behavior I have seen. To make sure what I heard on his television broadcast is correct I dictate his words for you to read. He said: *"As we start this program today, I have a word from the Lord. You can judge it and when it is over you can say you were either right or wrong. But I want to lay it out right now. The election of Joe Biden and Kamala Harris is not official until the electors are certified by the congress. Now that takes place on Wednesday that is the 6th. That is the most important day. Now the word that I believe I have is that so many people have been praying and there is so much that has been irregular about this election and outright fraud and just the irregularities that are not in accordance with the constitution. I have been praying and I am sure that you have been praying. I have felt in my heart that Donald Trump won the election, and it has been stolen away. But what is going to happen, I believe…and you can judge it now and you can see what happens in a few days from now. I believe something dramatic is going to happen before the congress votes on those electors. Something dramatic is going to happen that is going to change the outcome of that vote. Mark it down, when it is all over you can say; well, oh buddy, you were right on, or you missed the Lord. But anyhow, watch it! Something dramatic, The Holy Spirit of God is going to intervene to this situation, and it is going to be something very dramatic. So, keep an eye on that ok!* He would later in the same broadcast double down by saying *"As I said at the beginning of this program; keep your eyes open in the next couple of days. The Holy Spirit of God is going to move in great power to bring something about to keep this whole election fraud from being carried out. And God was going to step in and not let it happen"* The problem with this prophecy is that Pat Robertson thought out of his own volition. It was he who thought that God was going to have congress not accept several states electoral votes and do a recount. He obviously had inside knowledge that there would be a recount, but I do not think that knowledge was from God. Do not be fooled, a lot of these Evangelical Right preachers are well connected to legislators on Capitol Hill. Many of these congressmen and senators have their cell phone numbers. Pat Robinson clearly knew something on January 4th, 2021, but it was not from where he tried to say it was coming from, which was the Lord. This is the kind of mess that I have noticed that these conservative evangelicals have been doing in their pulpits and broadcast for years. They have been telling their listeners outright lies. They have been pro-phet-lying to the church and people who believe their words. They have been culpable with Donald Trump's divisive ways and are just as guilty in spewing out falsehoods that radicalized many people in our nation to violence. Pat Robinson was correct that something dramatic was going to happen before congress counted the electors. There was a plan to delay it or push it out 10 days for investigation while Trump Supporters had organized to meet up in Washington DC to protest and disrupt congress. Therefore, that was not hard to predict when everyone knew what the Trump followers had been planning for weeks. What he did not see coming was the breaking in the Capitol Building by pro Trump supporters. Secondly, the lie was that this *"something dramatic was going to change the outcome of that vote and keep this whole election fraud from being carried out."* We all know that is not what happened a few days later January 6, 2021. The fact is that the outcome of the vote was not changed or stopped. They tried to do it, but it did not happen. The dramatic event was an *insurrection* of Trump protestors that broke into the Capitol Building, overwhelmed the police, took over the senate floor, broke in their offices. They threatened to find the speaker of the House – Nancy Pelosi and the Vice President – Mike Pence to hang them on the gallows that they had built outside the Capitol Building. There were white nationalist videotaping themselves, having prayers on the Senate floors as if they were doing God's will. The piousness of the Christian Right was on display for the entire world to see. None of this behavior changed the outcome of the vote, it only accelerated it to be confirmed by Congress by 3:40am the next morning Joe Biden as President after they reconvened. One would think that these preachers know that God in His word speaks against false prophecy and false prophets? Here are a few verses: in Deuteronomy 18:21-*22* its say's

"And if thou say in thine heart, how shall we know the word which the Lord not spoken? When a prophet/prophet speaketh in the name of the Lord, if the thing follows not, nor come to pass, that is the thing which the Lord hath not spoken, but the prophet hath spoken it presumptuously: thou shalt not be afraid of him." Also, in Jeremiah 23:31 *"I am against the prophets who wag their own tongues and yet declare, 'The Lord declares.' Indeed, I am against those who prophesy false dreams, declares the Lord. 'They tell them and lead my people astray with their reckless lies, yet I did not send or appoint them."*

All this false prophecy from preachers, lies from the Republican GOP is what lead people astray. They are just as much at fault as to what happened on January 6, 2021, as the people who stormed the building. These people love to use preaching to control the narrative and the minds of the people. The conservatives believed them and the *Big Lie* they were promoting. The bottom line is that all of this was about White power. The church refuses to acknowledge and condemn it. How Pastor's all around this country could ignore the fact that many of the Black and Brown people in their congregations were being offended by the former Presidents mouth on a weekly basis is beyond me. Very few of them stood up in their pulpits to protect the sheep. It was like they idolized him, and Pastors allowed their Black and Brown sheep to suffer his racist and insensitive rhetoric for four whole years. Tell me, what parents sits there and let a bully put their mouth on their child for four years without saying anything? Not the parents that I grew up around. Eventually someone is going to check you about it. To this there must be accountability moving forward. All of us in our communities must act against the racism and be willing to call others out that should know better into account. I will say that I did see Pat Roberson from the 700 club try to clean up his words the day after the insurrection and say, *"Evil is good to the god's it would destroy. The Romans had it a little differently, whoever the gods would destroy they first drive mad. There was a madness yesterday and it came on Donald Trump and people had been hoping and hoping. He had his own people in the senate ready to fight for him. Congress, Ted Cruz was ready and what does Trump do, he goes crazy. He urges this huge crowd that came to Washington to support him to march on the Capitol. There may have been some ringers that gone into that group, we do not know. They took over the Capital.*

They invaded the offices and just done horrible things. Now instead of supporting him, now the people who were all lined up to have a hearing on every one of those voter frauds claims. They could not do anything, and they could not wait to vote against him." So instead of him taking responsibility of the false prophecy that he gave on television three days before, he chose to blame Donald Trump of messing things up because he went mad. Thankfully, not all clergy would keep quiet about what was happening in our nation. Just so you know that it was not only me that noticed the duplicity of our church leaders. The theologian Russell Moore wrote these words in his article in *Time* on-line magazine on January 21, 2021. It reads; "Theologian Russell Moore has a Message for Christians who Still Worship Donald Trump:"

"'The past few years have not been an easy time to be God's lobbyist. A lot of folks claiming to represent the Almighty have been jostling for space in the corridors of Washington, with a lot of conflicting agendas. Their methods often seem mutually exclusive with the Christian tenet that one should love one's neighbor. So perhaps it's not surprising that shortly after the events of Jan. 6, the guy whose actual paid job it is to try to get those in power to think about a higher power got about as ticked off as a polite Southern gentleman of faith is allowed to get. "If you can defend this, you can defend anything," wrote Russell Moore, a theologian who is also the president of the Ethics and Religious Liberty Commission (ERLC) of the Southern Baptist Convention (SBC), in an excoriating editorial to his fellow evangelicals about the breach of the Capitol. The intruders displayed Jesus Saves signs next to those calling for the hanging of Vice President Mike Pence and, once in the building, thanked God for the opportunity "to get rid of the communists, the globalists and the traitors" within the U.S. government. "If you can wave this away with 'Well, what about ...'" added Moore, "then where, at long last, is your limit?" Many Christian leaders and thinkers decried the attack on the Capitol, but few went as far as Moore; he laid the blame squarely at the feet of a man many evangelicals believe to be their hero: President Trump. "This week we watched an insurrection of domestic terrorists," Moore wrote, "incited and fomented by the President of the United States." When asked about that statement

during an interview from his book-lined Brentwood, Tenn., home office a week later, he doubles down. "He called them to the rally. He told them that the future of our country was at stake, that the election had been stolen from him and that weakness could not be an answer," Moore says. "And after the attack took place with our Vice President under siege, with people calling for him to be executed, the President continued to attack the Vice President on Twitter. It's indefensible." In criticizing President Trump, Moore has diverged from such influential evangelicals as Franklin Graham, who compared Republicans who voted for Trump's second impeachment to Judas Iscariot; Jerry Falwell Jr., who said he'd give Trump a third honorary degree if he were still head of Liberty University; and author Eric Metaxas, who devoted almost his entire Twitter feed after the election to increasingly bizarre and implausible conspiracy theories on the method by which it was stolen. Moore's position differs even from that of the guy tipped to be the next head of the SBC, the Rev. Albert Mohler, who voted for Trump in 2020 and said–even after the events at the Capitol–that he'd do it again. "It's–it's been lonely," says Moore of his stance. "But I think many people have experienced that sort of loneliness over the past four or five years. I don't know a single family that's not been divided over President Trump, and politics generally. I don't know a single church that hasn't been." Moore's opinions are not new. He has been a Never Trumper since at least 2015 and scoffs at the notion put forward by many evangelical leaders that Trump converted to Christianity just before being elected. "It is not a position that I find rational," he says. "Especially when Mr. Trump has been very clear about his own spiritual journey, or lack thereof." The usually mild-mannered author's stance has come at a cost. He says both he and his family have been the subject of threats and that people have tried to dig up information that would prove he is a liberal. (Heaven forfends!) In February 2020, the executive committee of the SBC formed a task force to look into whether the ERLC was fulfilling its "ministry assignment" after reports that churches were withholding their giving, citing Moore's political positions. Moore's loneliness is of a particular sort, however, since unlike most of Trump's most vocal critics, he is a dyed-in-the-wool social conservative, staunchly opposed to same-sex marriage, abortion, and premarital sex, and he has worked to limit the spread of the first two. (He acknowledges he's walking into a cold breeze on the third.) In a way, he is a weathervane for the cold front much of the evangelical church is now facing. What is the future for a group that preaches truth, peace, and moral living, after it gambles all its chips on a man who embodies none of those but will play along–and loses? The pushback against Moore is surprising. Born in Biloxi, Miss., and ordained at 23, he checks dozens of typical conservative boxes, from his gentle demeanor to his five sons, two of whom are adopted from Russia to the family photos he posts of the entire clan clad in khaki pants and navy sport coats. He publicly supported the right of a Colorado baker to decline to make a wedding cake for a gay couple. He would love to see Roe v. Wade overturned. He believes gay Christians should remain celibate. He has also championed protection for Deferred Action for Childhood Arrivals recipients, undocumented immigrants, and refugees. He helps guide church thinking on living wills and end-of-life decisions, weighing in on the role of doctrine if people are in terrible pain. In many ways, Moore's job is to pull his fellow Baptists into the future. In others, it is to try to prevent the culture from abandoning convictions that are several millennia old, some of which–like celibacy outside marriage–no longer seem to make sense to most people. "I think the problem with evangelical Christianity in America is not that we are too strange but that we are not strange enough," says Moore. "We should be countercultural in loving God and loving our neighbors in ways that ought not to make sense except for the grace of God." Often Moore has to tap-dance around the gap between his church's beliefs and its behavior. He dismisses as a "manufactured controversy" the criticism of six SBC seminary presidents who in November released a public condemnation of critical race theory. "I don't find any postmodern theory motivating those who are concerned for racial reconciliation and justice," says Moore. "I find that what motivates such things is the Bible." And while Moore has set himself apart from those who support the President, he declines to condemn those who opted to vote for Trump because they believed

*in the platform, not the man. Moore thinks reports of the death of
American Christianity are overblown. But as increasing numbers
of Americans tell pollsters that they are not affiliated with any
kind of religion, and in the wake of Trump, he wants the church
to take a harder look at its priorities. "The biggest threat facing
the American church right now is not secularism but cynicism.
That is why we have to recover the credibility of our witness," he
says. It is one thing to dismiss the teachings of his faith as strange
and unlikely, he notes, but "if people walk away from the church
because they don't believe that we really believe what we say, then
that's a crisis." This is what he fears will be the legacy of an era in
which people of faith put so much faith in a President. "There is an
entire generation of people who are growing cynical that religion
is just a means to some other end."*

As you can see from his article that he too believes that the Church
worshipped the former President and needed to be reminded of a few
things. Regardless of all our national problems, the Church worshipping
a man, behaving cultic, becoming idolatrous, excusing carnal behavior,
embracing lies, false prophecies, and prophets – is a problem with God.
Over the years I have learned that there is one book in the bible besides
Revelations that most people do not spend -time reading and that is
Leviticus. I highly recommend that we spend some time in that book. In
chapter 26 there is an interesting conversation that God is speaking to
his people about making idols, obedience, disobedience and repenting
for their own sins and their ancestors' sins. Here is some of what it says:'
*"'Do not make idols or set up an image or a sacred stone for yourselves,
and do not place a carved stone in your land to bow down before it. I am
the LORD your God. "'Observe my Sabbaths and have reverence for my
sanctuary. I am the LORD. "'If you follow my decrees and are careful to
obey my commands, I will send you rain in its season, and the ground
will yield its crops and the trees their fruit. Your threshing will continue
until grape harvest and the grape harvest will continue until planting,
and you will eat all the food you want and live-in safety in your land. "'I
will grant peace in the land, and you will lie down, and no one will make
you afraid. I will remove wild beasts from the land, and the sword will
not pass through your country. You will pursue your enemies, and they
will fall by the sword before you. Five of you will chase a hundred, and a*

hundred of you will chase ten thousand, and your enemies will fall by the sword before you. "'I will look on you with favor and make you fruitful and increase your numbers, and I will keep my covenant with you. You will still be eating last year's harvest when you will have to move it out to make room for the new. I will put my dwelling place[a] among you, and I will not abhor you. I will walk among you and be your God, and you will be my people. I am the LORD your God, who brought you out of Egypt so that you would no longer be slaves to the Egyptians; I broke the bars of your yoke and enabled you to walk with heads held high. "'But if you will not listen to me and carry out all these commands, and if you reject my decrees and abhor my laws and fail to carry out all my commands and so violate my covenant, then I will do this to you: I will bring on your sudden terror, wasting diseases and fever that will destroy your sight and sap your strength. You will plant seed in vain because your enemies will eat it. I will set my face against you so that you will be defeated by your enemies; those who hate you will rule over you, and you will flee even when no one is pursuing you. "'If after all this you will not listen to me, I will punish you for your sins seven times over. I will break down your stubborn pride and make the sky above you like iron and the ground beneath you like bronze. Your strength will be spent in vain because your soil will not yield its crops, nor will the trees of your land yield their fruit. "'If you remain hostile toward me and refuse to listen to me, I will multiply your afflictions seven times over, as your sins deserve. I will send wild animals against you, and they will rob you of your children, destroy your cattle and make you so few that your roads will be deserted. "'If in spite of these things you do not accept my correction but continue to be hostile toward me, I myself will be hostile toward you and will afflict you for your sins seven times over. And I will bring the sword on you to avenge the breaking of the covenant. When you withdraw into your cities, I will send a plague among you, and you will be given into enemy hands. When I cut off your supply of bread, ten women will be able to bake your bread in one oven, and they will dole out the bread by weight. You will eat, but you will not be satisfied. "'If in spite of this you still do not listen to me but continue to be hostile toward me, then in my anger I will be hostile toward you, and I myself will punish you for your sins seven times over. You will eat the flesh of your sons and the flesh of your daughters. I will destroy your high places, cut down your incense altars and pile your dead bodies[b] on the lifeless forms of your idols, and I will abhor you. I will turn your cities into ruins and lay waste your sanctuaries, and I will take no delight in the pleasing aroma of your offerings. I myself will lay waste the land, so that your enemies who live there will be appalled. I will scatter you among the nations and will draw out my sword and pursue you. Your land will be laid waste, and your cities will lie in ruins. ³Then the land will enjoy its sabbath years all the time that it lies desolate, and you are in the country of your enemies; then the land will rest and enjoy its sabbaths. All the time that it lies desolate, the land will have the rest it did not have during the sabbaths you lived in it.

"'As for those of you who are left, I will make their hearts so fearful in the lands of their enemies that the sound of a windblown leaf will put them to flight. They will run as though fleeing from the sword, and they will fall, even though no one is pursuing them. They will stumble over one another as though fleeing from the sword, even though no one is pursuing them. So, you will not be able to stand before your enemies. You will perish among the nations; the land of your enemies will devour you. Those of you who are left will waste away in the lands of their enemies because of their sins; also because of their ancestors' sins they will waste away. "'But if they will confess their sins and the sins of their ancestors—their unfaithfulness and their hostility toward me, which made me hostile toward them so that I sent them into the land of their enemies—then when their uncircumcised hearts are humbled and they pay for their sin, I will remember my covenant with Jacob and my covenant with Isaac and my covenant with Abraham, and I will remember the land."

If the evangelicals want to change their witness and have influence over people in America, then they would want to pay attention to the scriptures above, repent of their sins and the sins of their ancestors that caused division in this nation hundreds of years ago. It sounds and seems simple, but unfortunately as I said earlier most of them prefer to be *right* rather than *righteous.* Nevertheless, the one thing that did happen and saved our democracy that evangelicals did not foresee coming was on January 12, 2021. All the Chairmen of the Joint Chiefs of Staff and Joint Forces *(Army, Navy, Marines, Air Force, Coast Guard, Space Force and National Guard)* wrote and signed the following memorandum to shut down the chaos in our nation 6 days after the insurrection: *"On January 20, 2021, in accordance with the constitution, confirmed by the states and the courts and certified by congress, President-Elect Biden will be inaugurated and will become our 46th Commander-in-Chief. The US military will obey lawful orders from civilian leadership…and remain fully committed to protecting and defending the constitution of the United States against all enemies, foreign and domestic. We support and defend the constitution. Any act to disrupt the constitutional process is not only against our traditions, values, and oath; it is against the law. The violent riot in Washington D.C. on January 6, 2021… we witnessed actions inside the Capitol Building that were inconsistent with the rule of law. The rights of freedom of speech and assembly do not give anyone the right to resort to violence, sedition, and insurrection."* It would be this letter that would put the kibosh on the argument of whether Joe Biden and Kamala Harris would take over the White House. Far as I am concerned, if the white nationalist, militias, racist and preachers could not hear the voice of the people on November 3, 2020, when they voted. What they would hear is all these military Generals above that signed this letter that allowed the new administration to come to power on January 20, 2021, without incident. In other words, none of those militia groups wanted none of that smoke! God always has the last Word! Ecclesiastes 7:8 says, *"The end of a matter is always better than the beginning and patience is better than pride."* This letter is what put an end to the matter. Now it is time for people to be held accountable for their actions. History will not view the Trump presidency and those who supported it kindly. The Evangelical Church in America was certainly involved! One of their own GOP representatives spoke the truth when she said, *"The President of the United States summoned this mob, assembled the mob, and lit the flame of this attack. Everything that followed was his doing. None of this would have happened without the President."* Rep Liz Cheney ® Wyoming January 12, 2021

For far too long *White Supremacy Terrorism* and *Extremism* has gone unnamed, unmasked, and unchecked in America. Racism and hate have been with us as an infectious disease throughout the fabric of our society. Racism and hate were used as a strategy during Trump's administration. It fueled their policy and agenda. He clearly appealed to a base that his administration knew his message would resonate. Groups like the Proud Boys, Oath Keepers, Buggy Boy's, and Three Percenter Militias, responded to his dog whistling. We must understand that unchecked evil without accountability spreads likes a virus! When terrible things happen without accountability it only produces more dreadful things. There are several Senators, Congressman, Christian Leaders, Radio Talk Show, News Reporters, and military people who were operatives of Donald

Trump promoting the *Big Lie*. It also appears to have been a network of churches, national radio talk show host and television ministry leaders who too were complicit about voter fraud that fomented this chaos in our country. What we saw on January 6, 2021, I say was the tipping or boiling point. We must understand that Donald Trump came to the White House on an agenda that white nationalist heard loud and clear. What he has said and promoted with his vile language against people of color was wrong. How he has fueled and worked up these white nationalists into a frenzy to do violence was unnecessary. Also, the majority of the Republican GOP who supported him no matter what he said and done were no less than co-conspirators of this attempted Quo in our nation. All who were involved must be held accountable so that it never happens again. Likewise, the preachers, should be ashamed of themselves for the damage they have done by misleading God's people. Either you are shepherd of the sheep or a hireling. The shepherd protects the sheep and knows when it's been wounded or hurt. The hireling does not protect the sheep but uses them for his/her own purpose. No shepherd should ever support or marginalize a President who stokes, condones, and supports racism that comes from any group. We expect pastors and spiritual leaders to protect the sheep and refute any politician or president that stirs-up racial offenses. We should not hold these yahoos in high esteem, regardless of their policies. Our pastors and spiritual leaders had plenty of time to do this, but many never did so during his four-year term. Only after what happened on January 6, 2021, did some of them start to change their tone and sound more pastoral about what was going on in this nation. We now have all the disturbing video and bodycams of Capitol Police officers being attacked with all sorts of weapons. The Capitol Police were trying to push the people back and five (5) people end up dead, four officers who responded to the insurrection committed suicide. That day you could see TRUMP 2020 flags, American flags, Confederate flags, and huge JESUS banners in the crowds. The Republican GOP has been trying to sweep all of this under the rug and say let's move on. Unfortunately for them it is not going to work this time. The Christian politicians always want to move on when people notice their wicked deeds. They said the same thing with slavery and now with what happened at the Capitol. It is their way to minimize the trauma of the results of what they have promoted to marginalize its affects. People are tired of embracing their teachings of moving on whenever they tell us to do so. It is time start holding them accountable to what they do. We must realize is that there is no reconciliation without accountability! That horrible day will too forever be a part of our negative history if we do not deal with it. When a country does not deal

with its past sins, it will find a way to repeat itself in another generation. Now is not the time to turn the page and move on. It is the time to confront and hold people's abject way of thinking accountable. I can only imagine what our FBI agencies are going through trying to unravel this mess. This is the time that we should be confronting our history to make sure that this never happens again. All these pastors and politicians should be ashamed of themselves for putting their faith behind a man who promoted white extremism that caused much more division in American society. I think they all can take the advice of Anna Marie Cox - Podcast called *"With Friend Like These"* who is white, and she said, *"I started wondering, 'why is it that we allowed Trump to get elected?' I have been working in progressive causes as a teenager. Yet nothing that I have done have been able to prevent this incredible catastrophe. So, maybe as a well-meaning white person, maybe I wasn't doing all the well-meaning things I thought I was doing. Maybe the stuff that I thought was well meaning turned out not to be that much help at all. So why not listen to the people who may be the objects of this well-meaning progressiveness. Why not listen to people of color? Why not listen to people who are not set. Why not listen to people who we need to raise up in this moment for leadership? Because you know what, us well-meaning white people, we are part of what led to Trump! I think listening is a big part of it. I think white people in the political space, often assume, because they mean well – think that they are going to do the right thing. And we often don't listen to the people who we are trying to help and that is one good reason why representation is so important."*
I could not agree with Anna Marie Cox more. Listening to the people who is the object of all this racism, social injustice and police brutality would be a suitable place for the politicians and evangelicals to start. I would like to say, if you are white and have been reading this book, I want to thank you. That means that you have been listening to a Black man for about 85 percent of his book. That too is a good place to start. You can also listen to the words from U.S. State Rep of District 5 in Massachusetts., Katherine Clark. She was born the same year I was in 1963. Katherine said on MSNBC Politic Nation on January 31, 2021; *"We have to call out this White Supremacy wherever we see it. Whether it is in the halls of congress or in our community. We know that if we are going to heal this country it starts with addressing our history racism and how institutional racism and bias infects every single institution in our country. We have to stand up and say that this is enough! That at this moment of racial reckoning that equity has to be the center of everything we do. Recently the Speaker spoke about the enemy within and one of the enemies within is White Supremacy."* I also could not agree with

Katherine more. The Republican GOP, Right Wing Journalism and the Evangelical Church are all guilty of coddling, embracing, and ignoring white nationalism in this country. It is pitiful to hear white nationalists now wanting to play victim by saying that they are the forgotten man in America. The truth of the matter is they are not victims, they have been terrorists. And no, we have not forgotten them as Black people in America. We can never forget a racist. Donald Trump was just the right person that came along to fan the flames of prejudice and racism. He got many whites fired up and it revealed to us who they really were. Racist and prejudice people have chosen their path, belief system and are the ancestors of generations of not patriots, but what I call hatriots! Once again, many preachers supported this President up until the very last month of his Presidency. They were still giving him their prayers and prophecies. Donald Trump would be Impeached again for the second time the next on January 13, 2021, and 64% of Evangelical Republicans still said in a poll that they supported Trump's recent behavior after the insurrection of the Capitol Building. The Righteous Republican GOP may have still supported him but Major Corporations all over country the next day said differently. Major Corporations began suspending all its political contributions to his campaign. Corporations like Verizon, Walmart, MasterCard, American Express, AT&T, Marriott, BlueCross BlueShield, Commerce Bank, Amazon, and others said: *"to those elected officials who voted against certification of the electoral college votes, which will give us the opportunity to review our political giving policies and practices."* Here is a list of some companies that have opted to suspend donation to all politicians, regardless of whether they voted against upholding the Electoral College results: 3M, Bank of America, Charles Schwab, Citigroup, Coca-Cola, Deloitte, Facebook, Ford, Goldman Sachs, Google, Hallmark, Hilton, JP Morgan, Microsoft, Salesforce, Target, Tyson, UPS, Visa. I thought to myself, that not even the black slaves of the south that were being tormented and persecuted here in this nation ever attack the Capitol Building with an insurrection attempt. They never did such thing. If we look at all the legislation that came out of this nation since 1641 against Black people, the slaves could have been angry enough to do this due to all the policies written against them, but they never did. First, we all know that if black people would have attempted what we had seen at the Capitol Building that the police would have shot them off the walls, out of the door and windows like animals. The *clergy politicians* (as Malcolm X called them) would have had every one of them hung from a tree on the Washington Mall. There would have been Black dead bodies everywhere, inside, and out of that building. That said, the people who stormed the building, went inside, and scaled the walls should be held accountable and brought up on federal charges. Who would have ever thought that the leader of the Oath Keeper's and nine others would be brought up on federal charges of "*seditious conspiracy and other charges for crimes?* " People like him that would do this in our country call themselves: *capitalist, patriots, and Christians.* I do not think so!

Chapter Eight

Back To the Spirit of Greed

"What Made Americans Greedy Again"

W.M.A.G.A

Dreams, Visions and Warnings to America

"I the Lord, reveal Myself in visions and speak through dreams"

Number 12:6

It is not like this country has not been warned about its ways by Godly members of the Church in the past, they just have not listened. I have read something that explains what going on in America that was noted by a well-known Evangelist by the name of AA Allen. He was an respected Evangelist in the 1950s who received a vision from God on the 86th floor of the Empire State Building while looking through a telescope. His vision was widely published and discussed amongst believers all over this country as to what it meant. I have heard a lot about AA Allen ministry, especially in my younger years. I have even had a first-hand witness from one of my exceptionally good friends who was present when Evangelist AA Allen came to his aunt's home in Brooklyn, New York. He told me how his aunt was delivered from demonic oppression while he and his cousin stood outside the door of the bedroom where it happened. I want you to read AA Allen's account of the vision he had about America on top of the Empire State Building in 1954 and really think about what he saw. I have been on the 86 floor of the Empire State building and thought about AA Allen and which telescope that he may have been using when he got the vision below. Let me remind you that he had this vision during a heightened time of racism, inequality, injustice, the adoption of Jim Crow law, segregation, and police brutality towards Black people in America. Personally, from what I have seen of AA Allen's recorded services and firsthand testimonies from other people, I believe that AA Allen did hear from God. God was using him to try to get the attention of this nation to turn from their wicked ways or a national humbling was inevitable. Here is the written account of his vision that was published so widely to for you to consider about our nation and its fulfillment.

Vision Given to AA ALLEN in 1954

"As the elevator shot upward to the first of the Empire State Building observatories, 86 floors above the ground, my ears began to close as the altitude increased. This was my first time to go up the great ascent to the top of the Empire State Building, and I was thrilled with the expectation of seeing all of New York City, New Jersey, Manhattan, the Bronx, and on across the Hudson River to Westchester, in a great panoramic view. But little did I realize that God had an even greater view awaiting me, as through a supernatural vision. He would let me see that which is soon to take place on the whole North American continent." -----*I saw a giant telescope*------ *"As I stepped off the elevator and went onto the outside terrace, just to the south of me, on Bedloe's Island, I could see the Statue of Liberty, illuminating the gateway to the "New World" as She held aloft her torch. To the north extended Manhattan Island, and although there was some fog, I was able to see glimpses of the city stretched in every direction."* *"As I looked about me, I saw a giant telescope, of the kind into which one may drop a dime and for a certain period of time, be able to see everything distinctly for a distance of about 15 miles (24 km). With my dime in hand, I stood waiting for the man in front of me to be through viewing the scene. Suddenly, he swung the telescope in such a way that its giant eyes seemed to look directly at me. To my amazement, I felt a great surge of the Spirit and power of God."* *"Then suddenly, I heard the voice of the Lord, clear and distinct. It seemed to come from the very midst of the giant telescope. But I knew it was a voice directly from heaven. It said, "For the eyes of the LORD range throughout the earth to strengthen those whose hearts are fully committed to him. You have done a foolish thing, and from now on you will be at war." (ref. 2 Chronicles 16:9)"* *"The ticking of the telescope had stopped. The man before me had used up his dime's worth. I was next. As I swung the telescope to the North, suddenly the Spirit of God came upon me in a way that I had never thought of before. Seemingly in the spirit I was entirely caught away."* *"I knew that the telescope itself had nothing to do with the distance which I was suddenly enabled to see, for I seemed to see things far beyond the range of the telescope, even on a bright clear day. It was simply that God had chosen this time to reveal these things to me, for as I looked through the telescope, it was not Manhattan Island that I saw, but a far larger view. That morning, much of the view was impaired by fog. But suddenly as the Spirit of the Lord came upon me the fog seemed to clear, until it seemed that I could see for*

thousands of miles." "But that which I was looking upon was not Manhattan Island, it was all of the North American Continent spread out before me as a map is spread upon a table, it was not the East River and the Hudson River that I saw on either side, but the Atlantic and the Pacific Oceans. And instead of the Statue of Liberty standing there in the bay on her small island I saw her standing far out in the Gulf of Mexico. She was between me and the United States." "I suddenly realized that the telescope had nothing to do with what I was seeing, but that it was a vision coming directly from God. And to prove this to myself I took my eyes away from the telescope, so that I was no longer looking through the lens, but the same scene remained before me." "There, clear and distinct, lay all the North American continent, with all its great cities: Chicago, New York, Seattle, Portland, San Francisco, Los Angeles, New Orleans, and the Gulf Coast cities. There were the towering ranges of the Rocky Mountains, and I could trace with my eye the Continental Divide. All this, and more, I could see spread out before me as a great map upon a table. And as I looked, suddenly from the sky a giant hand reached down toward the Statue of Liberty. In a moment her gleaming torch was torn from her hand, and instead was placed a cup." "And protruding from the cup, a giant sword, shining as if a great light had been turned upon its glistening edge. Never had I seen such a sharp, listening, dangerous sword! It seemed to threaten all the world!" "As the great cup was placed in the hand of the Statue, I heard these words: "Thus says the LORD of hosts; Drink, and be drunken, and vomit, and fall, and rise no more, because of the sword which I will send among you." I was amazed to hear the Statue of Liberty speak out in reply, "I WILL NOT DRINK!" Then as the voice of the thunder, I heard again the voice of the Lord, saying, "And it shall be, if they refuse to take the cup from your hand to drink, then shall you say unto them, thus says the LORD of hosts; YOU SHALL CERTAINLY DRINK." (Jer.25:28) Then suddenly the giant hand forced the cup to the lips of the Statue of Liberty, and she became powerless to defend herself." "The mighty hand of God forced her to drink every drop from the cup. As she drank the bitter dregs, these were the words that I heard, "should you be utterly unpunished? You shall not be unpunished: for I will call for a sword upon all the inhabitants of the earth, says the LORD of hosts." (Jer.25:29)" "When the cup was withdrawn from her lips, the sword was missing from the cup, which could mean but one thing. The contents of the cup had been completely consumed! And I knew that the sword merely typified war, death, and

201

destruction, which is no doubt on the way. Then as one drunken on too much wine, I saw the Statue of Liberty become unsteady on her feet and begin to stagger, and to lose her balance. I saw her splashing in the Gulf, trying to regain her balance. I saw her stagger again and again and fall to her knees. As I saw her desperate attempts to regain her balance, and rise to her feet again, my heart was moved as never before with compassion for her struggles." "But as she staggered there in the gulf, once again I heard these words, "You shall drink and be drunken, and spue, and fall, and rise no more because of the sword that I shall send among you." As I watched, I wondered if the Statue of Liberty would ever be able to regain her feet - if she would ever stand again. And as I watched, it seemed that with all her power she struggled to rise, and finally staggered to her feet again, and stood there swaying drunkenly. I felt sure that at any moment she would fall again - possibly never to rise. I seemed overwhelmed with a desire to reach out my hand to keep her head above water, for I knew that if she ever fell again, she would drown there in the Gulf. "Then as I watched, another amazing thing was taking place. Far to the Northwest, just out over Alaska, a huge, black cloud was arising. As it rose, it was as black as night. It seemed to be in the shape of a man's head. As it continued to arise, I observed two light spots in the black cloud. It rose further, and a gaping hole appeared. I could see that the black cloud was taking the shape of a skull, for now the huge, white, gaping mouth was plainly visible. "Finally, the head was complete. Then the shoulders began to appear and, on either side, long, black arms. It seemed that what I saw was the entire North American Continent, spread out like a map upon a table with this terrible skeleton-formed cloud arising from behind the table. It rose steadily until the form was visible down to the waist." "As the awful form stretched forward, I could see that the entire attention seemed to be focused upon the U.S., overlooking Canada at least for the time being. As I saw the horrible black cloud in the form of a skeleton bending towards America, bending from the waist over, reaching down toward Chicago and out towards both coasts, I knew it's one interest was to destroy the multitudes. "As I watched in horror, the great black cloud stopped just above the great lakes region and turned its face towards New York City. Then out of the horrible, great gaping mouth began to appear wisps of white vapor which looked like smoke, as a cigarette smoker would blow puffs of smoke from his mouth. These whitish vapors were being blown toward New York City. The smoke began to spread, until it had covered all the eastern part of the United States. Then the skeleton turned to the West, and out of the horrible mouth and nostrils came another great puff of white smoke. This time it was blown in the direction of the West Coast. In a few moments time, the entire West Coast and L.A. area was covered with its vapors." "Then towards the center came a third great puff. As I watched, St. Louis and Kansas City were enveloped in its white vapors. Then on it came towards New Orleans. Then on they swept until they reached the Statue of Liberty where she stood staggering drunkenly in the blue waters of The Gulf. As the white vapors began to spread around the head of the statue, she took in but one gasping breath, and then began to cough as though to rid her lungs of the horrible vapors she had inhaled. One could readily discern by the coughing that those white vapors had seared her lungs." "Then I heard the voice of God, as He spoke again: " Behold, the LORD makes the earth empty, and makes it waste, and turns it upside down, and scatters abroad its inhabitants. And it shall be, as with the people, so with the priest; as with the servant, so with his master; as with the maid, so with her mistress; as with the buyer, so with the seller; as with the lender, so with the borrower; as with the creditor, so with the debtor. The land shall be utterly emptied, and utterly spoiled: for the LORD has spoken this word. The earth mourns and fades away, the world languishes and fades away, the haughty people of the earth do languish. The earth also is defiled under the inhabitants thereof; because they have transgressed the laws, changed the ordinance, broken the everlasting covenant. Therefore, has the curse devoured the earth, and they that dwell therein are desolate: therefore, the inhabitants of the earth are burned, and few men left." (Isaiah 24:1-6) "As I watched, the coughing grew worse. It sounded like a person was about to cough out his lungs. The Statue was moaning and groaning. She was in mortal agony. The pain must have been terrific, as again and again, she tried to clear her lungs of those horrible white vapors." "I watched her there in the Gulf, as she staggered, clutching her lungs and her breast with her hands. Then she fell to her knees. In a moment, she gave one final cough, and made a last desperate effort to rise from her knees, and then fell face forward into the waters of The Gulf and lay still as death. Tears ran down my face as I realized that she was dead! Only The lapping of the waves, splashing over her body, which was partly under the water, and partly out of water, broke the silence." "Suddenly the silence was shattered by the screaming of sirens. The sirens seemed to scream, "RUN FOR YOUR LIVES!" Never before had I heard such shrill, screaming sirens. They seemed to be everywhere - to the North,

South, the East and the West. There seemed to be multitudes of sirens. And as I looked, I saw people everywhere running. But it seemed none of them ran more than a few paces, and then they fell. And even as I had seen the Statue struggling to regain her poise and balance, and finally falling to die on her face, I now saw millions of people falling in the streets, on the sidewalks, struggling. I heard their screams for mercy and help." "I heard their horrible coughing as though their lungs had been seared with fire. I heard the moaning and groanings of the doomed and the dying. As I watched, a few finally reached shelters ... and above the moaning and groaning, I heard these words: "A noise shall come even to the ends of the earth for the Lord has a controversy with the nations. He will plead with all flesh; He will give them that are wicked to the sword, says the Lord. Behold evil shall go forth from nation to nation, and a great whirlwind shall be raised up from the coasts of the earth... and the slain of the Lord shall be at that day from one end of the earth even onto the other end of the earth: they shall not be lamented neither gathered nor buried; they shall be dung upon the ground." (Jer. 25:31-33)" "Then suddenly I saw from the Atlantic and from the Pacific, and out of the Gulf, rocket-like objects that seemed to come up like fish leaping out of the water. High into the air they leaped, each headed in a different direction, but everyone towards the U.S." "On the ground, the sirens screamed louder. And up from the ground I saw similar rockets begin to ascend. To me, these appeared to be interceptor rockets although they arose from different points all over the U.S. However, none of them seemed to be successful in intercepting the rockets that had risen from the ocean on every side." These rockets finally reached their maximum height, slowly turned over, and fell back toward the earth in defeat. Then suddenly, the rockets which had leaped out of the ocean like fish all exploded at once. The explosion was ear-splitting. The next thing which I saw was a huge ball of fire. The only thing I have ever seen which resembled the thing I saw in my vision was the picture of the explosion of the H-bomb in the South Pacific. In my vision, it was so real I seemed to fell a searing heat from it." "As the vision spread before my eyes, and I viewed the widespread desolation brought about by the terrific explosions, I could not help thinking, " While the defenders of our nation have quibbled over what means of defense to use, and neglected the only true means of defense, faith, and dependence upon the true and living God, the thing which she greatly feared has come unto her! How true it has proven that "Except the Lord keep the city, the watchman watches but in vain." "Then as the noise of the battle subsided, to my ears came this quotation from Joel, the second chapter, " Blow a trumpet in Zion, and sound an alarm on my holy mountain! Let all the inhabitants of the land tremble, For the day of the LORD is coming; surely it is near, a day of darkness and gloom, a day of clouds and thick darkness. As the dawn is spread over the mountains, so there are a great and mighty people; there has never been anything like it, nor will there be again after it to the years of many generations. A fire consumes before them and behind them a flame burn. The land is like the garden of Eden before them but a desolate wilderness behind them, and nothing at all escapes them. Their appearance is like the appearance of horses; And like war horses, so they run." (Joel 2:1-4)." "Then the voice was still. The earth too was silent. Then to my ears came another sound a sound of distant singing. It was the sweetest music I had ever heard. There was joyful shouting and sounds of happy laughter." "Immediately I knew it was the rejoicing of the saints of God. I looked, and there, high in the heavens, above the smoke and poisonous gases, above the noise of the battle, I saw a huge mountain. It seemed to be of solid rock, and I knew at once that this was the Mountain of the Lord. The sounds of music and rejoicing were coming from a cleft high up in the side of the rocky mountain. It was the saints of God who were doing the rejoicing. It was God's own people who were singing and dancing and shouting with joy, safe from all the harm which had come upon the earth, for they were hidden away in the cleft of the rock. There in the cleft they were shut in, protected by a great, giant hand which reached out of the heavens, and which was none other than the hand of God, shutting them in until the storm be over passed."

Remember this, the statue of liberty represents *"Freedom."* It has the inscription that say's *"Give me your tired, your poor, your huddled masses yearning to breathe free, The wretched refuse your teeming shore. Send these, the homeless, tempest-tossed to me, I lift my lamp besides the golden-door!"* Could God have given Evangelist AA Allen this very descriptive vision because He saw for 350 years that European Americans and His Church was not being a people who properly cared for the *tired, poor, those yearning to breathe-free, the wretched, homeless, and tempest-tossed?* Did God see the injustice being done to people of color, especially Black people? Did all the opposition, social injustice, and resistance to the Civil Rights Act for Black people cause

God to give this Evangelist a vision? I know that a lot of people do not want to think about or address this issue, but what I have seen the bible is that God always gave his prophets a dream or vision during national crisis. All I am trying to say is that could God have been trying to use AA Allen to reach his people through this vision that has very much national implications in it, and they would not listen? The man was a notable national evangelist at the time. If anyone could warn the Church and political leaders of their attitudes towards people of color in this country, it would have been AA Allen. The real question is: How in the world could these born-again, spirit-filled, fire baptized in water, tongue-talkers run around the church and praise God in the 1950s with all this discrimination going on in the country? How could they be so *devout in faith* when it came to healings, deliverances, miracles, casting out devils, and faith towards God while at the same time be so *anorexic in love* when it came to the plight of Black people? Black people were sitting right next to them in tent meeting and pews. How could the Church in this climate not be moved to correct this nation for its refusal to treat blacks in the way that the constitution reads: *"We hold these truths to be self-evident, that all men are created equal, that they are endowed by their Creator with certain unalienable Rights, that among these are Life, Liberty, and the pursuit of Happiness?"* We must remember that many of these Church members would not be caught alive outside the church sitting having a meal at a restaurant with one of their Black brothers or sisters in Christ. They would not be found at one of their homes at a dinner table sharing a meal. Yet they would sit in church with them and praise the Lord. Racism was widespread in America despite what the Church said back then. We must understand that these churches were very much invested into these large tent and stadium revivals across the nation. There were some instigators that tried to prevent Black people from coming to them. There was no room to preach truth about racism and risk people not showing up. Therefore, the acceptance of Black people attending *(not preaching)*, seeking healings, deliverances, giving and praising God was very much the focus of the church meetings everywhere in America. Once these Christians were outside the Church meetings, these same mostly white worshippers had no real regard for the welfare of the Black people that they just praised God. Right outside these Church walls was the racial injustice and hatred towards Black people. How was the Church able to do this for so long and not do something about it? I can tell you how, it was because there was *no real respect* for Black people, not even the Black ministers. When you have no respect for a people, how they are being treated will no effect on you. Only people who have respect for them will stand up and say anything about an injustice. It is called being humane. General respect for people, any person should be like a reflex. The fact that they are a human being should be enough to grant our reflex of respect towards them. Unfortunately, Black people back then had not been granted that reflex in America. I think everyone should be given respect until they show you that they are not respectable. I mean when did the Church think that it should help end Black people not having the rights to vote, the power to purchase property, and cease the police brutality towards them? When did the church and political legislators think it was time for Black people lives to matter? Could this be the wrong that the Church and national leaders have been guilty of and why God was showing AA Allen the vision? Do forget, it was a very racist time in this country in 1954 when he had this vision. Could this be the reason we read in the article that *Lady Liberty* was thrown into the Gulf of Mexico gasping for air because *"She Couldn't Breathe,"* ready to drown, sounds familiar? I asked myself, why is she drowning in the Gulf of Mexico and not in the New York Harbor where it sits? Let us remember that the *statue of liberty* was forced to drink a sharp sword in which she refused to drink. A sharp sword is the word of God. It is like a two-edged sword. Man has a tough time swallowing the truth of the word when they hear it and will therefore refuse to swallow it. Is that what happened in America? I think God was trying to get this nation to swallow the truth of His Word and they would not do it. The nation was clearly racially divided in the 1950s and many whites were not trying to swallow the truth of the Word about loving your neighbor as yourself. The vision that AA Allen had was showing that America could not even be forced to swallow the Truth of God's Word and because of its refusal it would topple over for what she stood for, which was Liberty.

My Dream on November 28, 2016

"God visits us in the night and gives our hearts counsel and instruction while we sleep"

Psalms 16:7

For four years I sat on this dream that I know was given to me by God. On the onset of Donald Trump winning the election on November 8, 2016, republican evangelicals stormed their pulpits, news media, television broadcast, radio stations, Twitter, and other social media mechanism to declare that the newly elected president was *"God's Choice, God's Doing, God's Man, God's Anointed...etc. for such a time as this. Therefore, everyone might as well accept it and do what the bible say's and pray for those that has rule over you...etc."* Being a very watchful person, I found it amazing that all these prelates can rush to this kind of judgement about a man they did not even know. A man who had no relationship with the Church but suddenly find religion right before he ran for President. This was after watching for eight years the evangelical preachers seeing them not even mention President Barrack Obama's name at all. Looking at the apparent racial divide that the newly elected president was coddling, I never brought into what these preachers were saying about him on all their media outlets and from their pulpits. I found this to be inconsistent and very hypocritical as I observed their lack of appreciation, acknowledgement, and respect for the former President Barrack Obama, who is a Black man. Instead, I went on my own quest asking God right after his election, *"How does He see what is going on in America with the new President and the obvious racial divide?"* Twenty days later I had a dream on the early morning of November 28, 2016, in which I will not go into large details. I was shown that there were Congressman, Senators, Military Officials, Militia Groups and Church Leaders that was part of the division that was going on in America. These politicians and spiritual leaders had been speaking out of their own emotions about this new President and was lying on God. Therefore, it would show at the end of Trump's term that they had been leading the people astray and speaking lies. I had known for four years at the time of this writing that the division that came to this nation *was not God's doing* no matter what the preachers, prophets and priests in the pulpits were saying. I knew that it wasn't God's doing because He told me in that dream that *"it was not my doing."*

"Therefore, I took what I heard, kept it close to my heart and maintained a watchful eye on the Church and the Politicians that was saying differently. I kept my mouth closed, watched, and prayed as we have been taught to by Jesus to do (Matthew 26:41). He also taught us that *"A tree is known by the fruit it bears" Luke 6:45.* I watched the fruit that was coming off this man's tree long before he became the president elect and knew that he was going to be trouble in the oval office. Unfortunately, a sizable portion of my evangelical brothers and sisters in Christ saw differently. What we do not understand as believer's is that we cannot use our faith to talk the world into believing that a person's is qualified to be President of the United States and work in the White House. We have no idea if that person will be a just or unjust President once they take the office. All the kings in the Old Testament scriptures had opportunity to lead with righteousness or not. Likewise, each President has the same opportunity to lead humanity in a just or unjust manner. The Church cannot step in and try to cover up as Presidential leaders lack of integrity and think that folk will look past the obvious. There is no pastor/preacher that can speak for any president. If I read the bible correctly, the ungodly kings were all judged harshly by God for their wickedness. The just kings were not judged by God but blessed by the Him for their faithful leadership. I do not believe that the Lord has changed from dealing with national leaders in this way. Only that person can determine the success of their Presidency based on how they lead the nation that is favorable in God's eyes, not some preacher that want to sell you, their pick. Our former president was no different when it comes to how God deals with a leader over a nation of people. If the spiritual advisors that had access to him would have had some real backbone, they would have encouraged our former president to humble himself and act justly. Instead, they were too excited to be in the White House around him themselves and was spiritually useless. To me, I think the Evangelicals failed Donald Trump for they did not provide him with sound wisdom and good spiritual advise in how to treat all Americans. They helped him look like a fool for they were too scared to have him put and check on his words and behaviors for four years. The Evangelicals should have told him to ask God for what King Solomon asked Him for in a dream that he needed so badly…and that was an understanding heart to lead the people! In, 1 King 3:5-15 *"In Gibeon the LORD appeared* to Solomon in a dream by night: and God said, Ask what I shall give thee. And Solomon said, thou hast shewed unto thy servant David my father great mercy, according as he walked before thee in truth, and in righteousness, and in uprightness of heart with thee; and thou hast kept for him this great kindness, that thou hast given him a son to sit on his throne, as it is this day. And now, O LORD my God, thou hast made thy servant king instead of David my father: and I am but a little child: I know not how to go out or come in. And thy servant is in the midst of thy people which thou hast chosen, a great people, that cannot be numbered nor counted for multitude. Give therefore thy servant an understanding heart to judge thy people, that I may discern between good and bad: for who is able to judge this thy so great a people? And the speech pleased the LORD, that Solomon had asked this thing. And God said unto him, Because thou hast asked this thing, and hast not asked for thyself long life; neither hast asked riches for thyself, nor hast asked the life of thine enemies; but hast asked for thyself understanding to discern judgment; Behold, I have done according to thy words: lo, I have given thee a wise and an understanding heart; so that there was none like thee before thee, neither after thee shall any arise like unto thee. And I have also given thee that which thou hast not asked, both riches, and honor: so that there shall not be any among the kings like unto thee all thy days. And if thou wilt walk in my ways, to keep my statutes and my commandments, as thy father David did walk, then I will lengthen thy days. And Solomon awoke; and behold, it was a dream. And he came to Jerusalem and stood before the ark of the covenant of the LORD, and offered up burnt offerings, and offered peace offerings, and made a feast to all his servants." Solomon asked God in the dream to give him an understanding heart to judge the people and God found favor with him for asking this very thing. He wanted to do the right thing. It is clear during the former president's reign and after he lost the election that "an understanding heart" is not what he obtained to do the right things. In fact, he has done more to display his bad understanding attempting to get the election overturned in his favor, find ways to pardon himself, friends, and his children from any criminal charges. Unfortunately, this behavior has not only been with him, but we have several republican legislators (126 House Representatives and 17 Republican Attorney Generals) from various states filed and backed a Texas frivolous lawsuit that went all the way up to the Supreme Court to overturn mail in ballots from Wisconsin, Pennsylvania, Michigan, and North Carolina (Key battle states clearly won by Joe Biden). Which we all know that the Supreme Court denied to even hear their case. These Christians Politicians were willing to put their reputations on the line supporting a lie from a man who was described by a Professor at John Hopkins Medical School an American Psychologist as a *malignant narcissist*. These republican legislators from various states who filed provable false claims will all say that they are *born again* yet support a lie. There have been 55 cases filed, none has uncovered election fraud, have been denied and thrown out of court. Isn't ironic that all these *born-again* politicians, the votes that they wanted overturned were all in Black people districts in the states they were filing against? No, these politicians are not born again, what they are is prejudice. What do you think that say's to Black people? It says that they believe that voter fraud only happens in Black communities. Give me a break! If that effort by these born-again legislators was not racists, I do not know what is racist for that matter. Even the Christian right Vice President Mike Pence got in on this insane and atrocious attempt to overturn the will of the people that voted for Joe Biden and Kamala Harris presidential ticket. He would just only go so far with it. Can you see how all this makes Christians look stupid and racist? This kind of behavior from our legislators only proves that racism/prejudice is a cancer that exist in our country that permeates throughout government all the way up to the top. This is a classic case of when those who claim to be righteous and are not winning, they change the rules and use the courts to get their way. We wonder why people do not trust the Church in America. We are heading right back to how this nation got started. This time Black people have information and have found their voice to refute this nonsense. Not even preachers can sell us what is false anymore, they must speak the truth. Black people now have worldwide social media outlets to fight against the inconsistencies, lies and hypocrisy from the Evangelical Christians who love to have legislative power. It starting to look like that it has never been about the Evangelicals building the kingdom of God when it comes to who is going to maintain legislative power in this country. It looks more like many of them just want to influence the government for their needs. To end this chapter and show that I am on the right path. Exactly one year after starting this book, I just so happen to be visiting one of my good friends at his home the day after Christmas in 2020. Something came on his television that caught my attention. It was the *Reverend Al Sharpton* anchoring his MSNBC Politics Nation show. He was speaking with two prominent African American Pastors who head large churches in the United States. The conversation just happened to be on everything I have been writing about for the past year. The three ministers were having a conversation on *"The Separation of the Church and Race."* To paraphrase some of what was discussed they talked about the way we talk about race relations has now changed and not everyone in the Church is happy about how the conversation is sounding. They discussed how in 2020 that an *anti-racist* sentiment was mainstream in America and how there has been a push back from the right to dismiss its argument. They spoke about how there is emerging in our country *a critical theory of racism on black people* and a lot of folks don't like it and want to change the narrative. They were discussing how the nation's largest Protestant denomination *(The Southern Baptist Conference)* was wrestling with the literal exodus of Black ministers and their flocks leaving due to an incentive letter that was written by the SBC Seminary President and its leaders on racism that offended many SBC African American Pastors and Parishioners. They discussed how easy it is for white church leaders to dismiss that there is no systemic racism when you are not Black, Brown, poor, or marginalized. How easy it is for white church leaders to disown racism and the impact that it has had on Black people. These three preachers talked about how *"Trumpism"* exposed the white church and how this mentality has invaded American culture. It is being conducted now, communicated in the church and in their actions. The behavior that is being conducted in the church where we made progress on inclusion and now white church leaders want to turn the clock back behave like race has nothing to do with the condition of people's lives in this country. I will stop here to say that *racism and prejudice* are first cousins, therefore it has everything to do with the condition of people's life. The two go hand in hand. These three men discussed how this conduct is not anything new and that our white church leaders have always given us rhetoric that is not backed up with real change and action. It has always been some forces in the white church that have been resistant against dealing with race and change.

We are seeing some of the same resistance in the 21st Century after the death of George Floyd from leading white ministers. These men address the fact that it is hard for them as Black Pastor's to stand up in their pulpits every week, especially after a summer of racial unrest in 2020 and deny the racism that people in their congregations deal with every day. We must remember that Dr. Martin Luther King's historic letter while incarcerated in a Birmingham jail was to *white ministers in America.* I wonder why? It is because he knew that many of them are prejudice. Therefore, they discussed: *Is it that the white church leaders do not understand the reality of racism or is it that they are intentionally taking a blind eye to what goes on in American life every day?* Are they in deliberate denial of what Black and Brown people experience in America or is it a matter of insensitivity? They talked about how the white church will cry out *"abortion, abortion and that they are Pro-Life,"* but what about that life and how you treat it after it is born? How you educate it, how you clothe it, how you hospitalize it, where does it live and how does it eat? That is Pro-Life! The three men discussed how the white church is anti-abortion, but they are not *Pro-Life* when you can dismiss the treatment of people of color in this nation. Nevertheless, these same people who say they are *Pro-Life* are for Capital Punishment, you cannot have it both ways. Either you are standing against racism, or you are complicit with it!

Chapter Nine

Back To the Spirit of Greed

"What Made Americans Greedy Again"

W.M.A.G.A

The Finale

"The end of a matter is better than its beginning, and patience is better than pride. Do not be quickly provoked in your spirit, for anger resides in the lap of fools."

Ecclesiastes 7:8

Now that we have the facts about slavery, racism, white nationalism, police brutality, the Republic GOP, the complicities of the Evangelical Church, the laws that were implemented to control Black people in America and much more. We can finally look to see what happened that explains how we got to all this racism and division that we have seen in our country for the past several years. How we got here is simply about something that most of us fail to understand. I periodically get into conversations with men on the other side of the spectrum of what I am writing about in this book. The consistent thing that I hear that comes from them is that they have no clue of the history of their own ancestors in this nation. If they do know the history of their people, they will much rather ignore it as if it has nothing to do with today. Listen, our constitution was written to give those who were white *(especially males)* opportunity and special privileges that no other race could have in this nation. The Constitution was designed for all European men to have a chance at becoming successful in this country no matter where they came from around the world. It was not only a constitution, but it was a covenant, an agreement, or contract that the rich ruling elite would have with European men. Once we start looking at the constitution as to what it really was, which was a *covenant, contract, and agreement with European men,* then we will be able to have the proper dialog. The constitution was not written for Black and Brown people. Every debate needs to have a good starting point to discuss the facts that get answers and change. It stated right in the beginning of the constitution that it was written for their *"general Welfare and secure the Blessings of Liberty to* **themselves** *and* **their** *Prosperity."* One would simply have to ask themselves when you read it: *"who is* **themselves** *or* **their** *referring to in the Constitution?"* It is certainly not referring to Black people, because Black people didn't write the constitution. Nor did they have citizen rights at the time of its establishment. It does not take a brain surgeon to figure out that the framers were not talking about Black people. The certain *"unalienable rights of life, liberty and the pursuit of happiness"* that the framers were referring to was to European people, particularly white men. The reason we know this is because white women also had to fight for the right to vote in the early 1900s. Stick with me on this do not abort ship. We are near the close of this book. The Colonial British Elite were developing a constitution that would not only keep them in power but also appeal to their own European men abroad to come to this nation. They were focused on building a new nation that had nothing to do with British or European rule. Therefore, they needed people that would come here to work, start businesses, and build the economy. It was written in a way that these European men would accept their policies and legislations. Therefore, they made an agreement with them inside the constitution in which most people cannot see, but I see it when I read it. Each European male was promised to have a chance at being successful in America if they played by the rules. One of the rules would be for them to keep their mouths shut about the slaveocracy that they were building, and the injustice being done to people of color in this country. The European men coming to America knew that the constitution was written for them and not others. They knew it was a covenant or agreement between them and the rich ruling elite. That is why they came running. As you read earlier, you can see my family's slave Master came here by ship and landed in Charlestown, SC in1684 with his pregnant wife. He could not even wait until she delivered the baby because the opportunities were so great. He immediately started slave plantations in South Carolina and birthed their first child that same year. The agreement put the framers in power without much opposition from its own people. It allowed them to frame legislation in this country for hundreds of years with little opposition from their own people until the Civil War. The problem with this agreement is that the British Rich Ruling Elite were completely in control and if you wanted to have success as a European male, you better not as I hear some of my oppositionist say, *"get out of line!"* Trust me, they knew how to deal with their own that did not follow the status quo. These established laws and policies came with an ultimatum. If broken by anyone, including the European males that came to America with prosperity on their minds there could be consequences. To me it was more like a *bully/conditional* type relationship more than the liberty that they like to project. Therefore, European men in America became conditioned to playing by the rules and not ruffling any feathers with the British Ruling Elite. These men coming to these shores ignored all the injustice done to Blacks and Brown people and we were invisible to them. European men learned to keep their heads straight ahead and worked hard towards their own success. In other words, they did not realize at the same time they were selling their souls, character, integrity, God consciousness on the account of greed and prosperity. We are all human beings and when we ignore our God conscience, we are not as free but are in bondage. No one needs a bible class to know if people are being treated properly. Our God conscience will kick in that reality for us on its own. In fact, greed even caused European men to not acknowledge the human rights of their own white women. Once again, they ignored their God conscience and played the game with the rich ruling elite for their own success. The certain unalienable rights promised to them was for *food, shelter, clothing, land, work, business, and an opportunity* to generate wealth. These men knew that they had a right to these things and no one else in this country. They knew with these rights that they could come here, start from nothing, and end up well off or rich. What the British Ruling elite really did to men that came here is have them *"drank the Kool-aide."* Fortunately, it would backfire on them. Let me explain it to you. When you look at all the laws that the British Ruling elite wrote 1600s, 1700s and 1800s you will see that what I am saying. The laws were written in the beginning for them to keep their class in power and men that came here seeking prosperity understood it. The very laws that the British Ruling elite wrote in their early days favored only European men. Even if you look at the first anti-miscegenation laws that I spoke about earlier and how it was written: *"In 1664, Maryland criminalized such marriages—the 1681 marriage of Irish-born Nell Butler to an enslaved African man was an early example of the application of this law. The Virginian House of Burgesses passed a law in 1691 forbidding free Black people and Whites to intermarry, followed by Maryland in 1692"*. Ask yourself, *"who did these laws favor and what was its intent?"* The anti-miscegenation laws only favored white men. White men did as they pleased with Black women back then. Its intent was to make white woman solely available to them by law which would guarantee them a dominate white posterity to increase in number as the majority in this nation. Nevertheless, a lot of these early laws backfired on the rich ruling elite years later. Firstly, with the abolishment of slavery in 1863, then the 19th Amendment passed by Congress that guaranteed Women's Right to Vote in 1920, the 1954 Supreme Court decision in Brown vs Board of Education, the 1971-1973 Supreme Court decision in Roe vs Wade and the Civil Rights Act of 1964. All these laws attacked the very thing that the British elite was trying to keep from Black men which was the white woman. The abolishment of slavery immediately gave Black people more access to whites. The 1920 Women's Right to Vote gave white women a voice for her own freedoms at the voting polls. The 1954 Brown vs Board of Education put Black and White kids in the same classrooms. The 1971 Roe vs Wade gave women the right over their own bodies and could choose to have an abortion. This would lead to fewer white children being born since abortions have historically been done by more white women than any other race. Just looking at the May 9, 2016, statistics on abortions in America you will find by race that White Women at 39%, Black Women at 28%, Hispanic Women at 25% and Asian/Pacific Islander Women at 6% and Other had 3% of the abortions in America. The Civil Rights Act of 1964 prohibited discrimination in public accommodations and federally funded programs. This too brought Black people and whites together in social settings like jobs, classrooms, bars, and restaurants. These laws would legally bring Black people and whites together to form relationships. Therefore, the original intent of the British Ruling Elite to keep Black people and whites separate backfired over time with modern legislation. Now all women can vote and voice their needs. They can marry and form relationships with whoever they want without being punished. Today, woman have been promoted to the highest office as executives, judges, district attorneys, chief of police, head coaches, professional referees, athletes, sports analysts, the Supreme Court Justice, and the Oval Office. There are more bi-racial children today than in the history of this nation. America has been getting less white and browner in the past 50 years. The truth is that white men have been genuinely concerned about it. Black and Brown people have become educated and legislatively adept. We now use that same constitution that was written for their rights, liberty, and prosperity to create our own. This too has caused the prejudice conservatives to fear the new America that is on the horizon with so many Black and Brown people that they tag as liberals. Just because one is Black or Brown it does not mean that we are liberal in our views. It can mean that many of us are not crazy and know when a certain race is wanting to gain back control of us. That is why we have all these storms of race wars popping up at various times in this country.

But out of every storm there is something to learn and appreciate even more from it. I have become much more appreciative of several things after dealing with this last racial upheaval in this nation that started with our former President. The fact is that 2016 to 2020 was a crazy four years in America. I understand how it may have affected all of us in one way or another. I have always believed that you may not be able to control what you go through, but you can take advantage of the moment and get out of it what you can. I got a lot out of the divisive Trump Administration as you can see by reading this book. But there were some other *hidden treasures* that I will acknowledge in the close of this book that helped and made me more appreciative of certain people and things. The first thing that I want to acknowledge that I noticed that I have become much more appreciative of the importance of *journalism* and *free speech*. Never in my lifetime have I found myself so attached to the news than these years. I regularly watched the news before 2016, but not at the intensity that I did in these years. There was so much going on it was important to not turn on the basketball or football game in the evening and watch the news first. There were times I missed the news for a few days and when I finally did turn it on there was a lot to ponder and digest. Things were happening so rapidly in America during this time that you could not afford to go more than a day without the news. I have learned to appreciate many journalists that I felt did their best every night to bring America the facts. Some of my most respected journalist were young people who were not old enough to have lived through the sixties and seventies. These journalists were in their thirties and had a grasp on this nation's history, legislation and political issues that was impeccable. Many times, I saw them put their older colleagues to shame with the facts and not emotions in the news studio. Young Black journalist like *Bakari Sellers, Angela Rye, Yamich Alcindor and Abby Phillips*…all made me proud. This new young Black journalism that is on the horizon in our nation was no joke nightly during the Trump era. I was impressed on how knowledgeable they all were on the policies and race issues that came up during those years. All of them had clearly done their historical and legislative homework. Then there was the veteran journalist *like Don Lemon, Andrew Cuomo, Rachel Maddow, Joy Reid, and Anderson Cooper* who I know did not get much sleep during Trump's term. It seemed like they were working day and night to bring the news as factual as possible. I really appreciated the senior veteran journalist like *Wolfe Blitzer, Brian Williams, Rev. Al Sharpton, Lawrence O'Donnell,* and a host of others that weighed in nightly to balance out the facts as to what was happening in our nation. Because of people like these above, I see the much importance of *journalism/free speech* in America more than I ever did before. If I were to do life all over again, I would probably come back as a journalist or news reporter. It is so paramount to be heard and give people the facts when there is so much chaos. Also, I want to include a powerful article/confession that was in my email from a journalist that I did not know anything about. His name is *David French* who writes for the Atlantic. I mentioned a quote from him in the beginning of this book but let us see what he says in the full article. It is immensely powerful for this man write about his own mistakes and blind spots as a conservative Christian. As you will see that he is striving to be better. Let us read what he sent to my email:

"Dear reader,

I'd like to introduce you to an obscure but commonsense statement about human nature. It's called Miles's law, *and it's contained in a single, simple sentence: "Where you stand depends on where you sit." It originated as an observation about behavior in bureaucracies— that bureaucrats often defend their agencies' narrow interests over the common good—but it works as a description of how we all tend to form our positions and join our tribes. It speaks to the immense power of experience and kinship. I'll explain by referring to two of the worst mistakes of my professional and personal life. Despite living in the heart of red America and spending much of my career deep in the heart of the conservative movement, I dramatically underestimated Donald Trump's political appeal. The next one is worse. Despite growing up in the South, I deeply underestimated the continued prevalence and malignant legacy of American racism. How was that possible? In part because my experiences helped me miss reality. Even though I spent most of my childhood in small-town Kentucky, I lived in a college town. My dad has a math Ph.D. and is a retired professor. My mom has a master's degree in education and is a retired elementary-school teacher. They're both faithful Christians. They both taught me to abhor racism. And so, from the very beginning I was raised in the small world of highly educated evangelicalism. I went to a Christian college, and my social circle in law school was almost exclusively evangelical. The conservatism I grew up with was alive with the power of ideas. I was and am a pro-life classical liberal who believes strongly in the defense of liberty, not just as a matter of human dignity but also as a means of unleashing human potential. I can't even begin to tell you the number of conferences I attended where at least one person argued, "Conservative's appeal to reason. Progressives appeal to emotion." And we'd all nod along. Then someone would say, "Conservative's appeal to opportunity and possibility. Progressives appeal to identity." And we'd applaud. It all seemed right until it was proved wrong. Without even realizing it, I had let my experience shape too much of my worldview. Bit by bit, year by year, it had colored my perceptions until I couldn't see what others could plainly perceive. I had grown so comfortable where I sat that it* *had made me too secure in where I stood. I knew racism existed, but like many conservatives I underestimated both its individual prevalence and its systemic effect. I knew angry populists had a persistent presence on the American right, but I underestimated the extent to which their furious spirit had captured Republican hearts, and when push came to shove, the party would choose anger over ideas. It's a humbling thing to be wrong. But it's also eye-opening. It taught me that understanding this nation requires understanding where people sit before, we can even begin to debate where they stand. It requires, as much as possible, trying to sit in different spaces, with different people. It meant creating and applying a few simple rules. First, try to learn about an idea from its proponents before seeking out its opponents. Take critical race theory, for example. Don't know what it is? Read a critical race theorist. Then read his or her critics. Think of yourself as a judge, deciding a case between advocates, not as an advocate who's always looking for ammunition for argument. Second, intentionally seek out the best expression of the opposing side's point of view. I say this knowing that there are times when there is no truly good opposing idea. The "Stop the Steal" movement was based on lies from start to finish. But one way we can discern merit is by earnestly looking for it. Third, prioritize real relationships. One of the most <u>important and insightful reported pieces</u> in the entire 2020 election cycle came from The New York Times' Nate Cohn and Kevin Quealy. They analyzed data from the <u>Hidden Tribes Project</u> and concluded that "the outspoken group of Democratic-leaning voters on social media is outnumbered, roughly 2 to 1, by the more moderate, more diverse and less educated group of Democrats who typically don't post political content online." Spend too much time online, and you'll emerge with a <u>distorted view</u> of your opponents and your allies. This is how I've tried to learn from my mistakes. This is how I approach the world of ideas. This newsletter will likely touch on most of the third rails of American politics. The Supreme Court is going to issue its most important abortion decision in a generation. Arguments about race and gender are turning neighbor against neighbor. For the first time in my lifetime, tens of millions of Americans are even <u>open to the idea of secession</u>.*

We have to be able to talk about all of these things, no matter how fraught. But how we approach each issue matters a great deal. Do we walk into the marketplace of ideas humbly? Do we even try to understand our most bitter opponents? Do we reject complexity in favor of false simplicity? Can we create a community based on a spirit not of "moderation" (which is another way of demanding that everyone agrees, just at a different point on the political spectrum) but of shared inquiry? That's my goal, to speak with you and not at you, to explain what I know and to learn what I can. If we can't truly escape Miles's law, perhaps we can learn to apply it constructively. Let's sit together, and then see where we stand."

—David French

In all actuality, David has done exactly what the word of God teaches us to do as believers in the book of James 5:16 *"Confess your faults one to another, and pray for one another, that ye may be healed."* He has confessed his own faults as a conservative Christian openly in a news article. I am not sure if he knew this, but the reality is that what he wrote for any Black person that reads it can bring healing. I know that I was blessed by his article, which is why I included it for. The next statement in that same verse says that *"The effectual fervent prayer of a righteous man availeth much."* David's prayers will be productive and avail much. What the Apostle James is trying to tell us is that any person who can confess their sins/faults to another they are considered a righteous man or woman and their prayers can do much. Their prayers can do much for the healing of one another. If we are going to see healing in this nation, there is going need to be more than one David French. Just knowing that a man like this is out there in times like these at least attempting to listen to people of color, put himself in another man's seat and bring healing to this nation with people who may see racism differently was exciting. I also, learned to appreciate during this time of racial division was the power of the arts and theatre. Where would we be without these two that have the platforms to speak to us? Theatre and the Arts gives us a story whether you are watching it on Broadway, Television, a Concert Stage, or a large painting on a Building with an image of a fallen victim to police misconduct like an *Eric Garner, Michael Brown, Briana Taylor, Elijah McClain, Philando Castille, Daniel Prude or George Floyd...etc.* It has been said, *"A picture says a thousand words."* Thank God for all our artist who know how to say those thousand words through their paintings. I think of the William Shakespeare play that I got to see in Central Park in 2017 that got a lot of people upset at the time because of the Trump-like *Julius Caesar* play that was displayed. Now looking back at that play, it was right on target and almost prophetic. None of us knew it when we were watching it in June of 2017, but a lot that it depicted would later happen or come close to happening in this country during Trump's Administration. The play depicted protest, government upheaval, insurrection and innocent protesters being killed by the police. Look what happened on January 6, 2021, at our nation's Capital. Think about all the protest across this nation behind Black individuals being killed by police officers. Think about how the protestors were putting their lives at risk and some of them were harmed and even killed. My friend John who I spoke about earlier in the introduction also played that summer the role of Casius in the park. If you have not seen that play it is worth trying to find someone who has recorded it. This play was done live in Central Park *directed by Oskar Eustis* that ran during the summer of 2017. Many conservatives, right-wing news stations and several corporations were highly offended by it. I found it interesting for it displayed what can happen in a democracy when you have an autocratic leader in charge. The play disposed a crooked senate that conspired to kill Julius Cesar who looked and behaved like Donald Trump. It was comical, serious, and thrilling. It had a lot of possibilities in it for the viewers to think about. In hindsight, the country would eventually experience some of the things depicted in the play during the former President Trump's four-year term. There is no way that the producer of this play could have known what would happen in America. It was too early in the administration to know what would happen in America, but Oskar obviously had some divine foresight on all these possibilities and was criticized about it in the media. In his 1599 Shakespeare Play in the Park he strongly warns those who commit political violence, even in service of their country, about the futility of their actions. We can all now know just how close that depiction of protestors being killed in this play almost came to a reality since we now have the inside information from the former Secretary of Defense, Mark Esper. In his new book – *"A Sacred Oath; Memoirs of a Secretary of Defense During Extraordinary Times";* he unveils that *"As Black Lives Matter protestors swarmed outside the White House in 2020, then President Donald Trump reportedly proposed solution:* **"Just shoot them."** Therefore, the power of theatre and art is paramount for any nation to have to get our attention and cause us to think. Which brings me to the next thing that I have learned to appreciate during this time and that is great historian work. When I was younger in school, I thought history was boring, but it is not if you dig like I have done for this book. By now you would have read all the articles of history that I have included in this book. I know that some of it was hard to swallow. I am especially appreciative of the work of Historians Jacqueline Battalora PhD that I was able to find. I am also appreciative of the ambitious historical work done by journalist Nikole Hannah-Jones and the entire team of The New York Times on the 1619 Project. But there is one historian that I have come to know that I appreciate and respect mostly of his work and that is the Jon Meacham. I never knew of John before all these racial events developed in our news over the past few years, but I have had the opportunity to watch, listen and evaluate everything he has said about America for the past few years. He is deeply knowledgeable on the Confederacy and its icons that many people have celebrated and worshipped in this nation. He talks about the problem is that we still have not confronted the intimacy of our hatred towards Black people in America. That hatred is rooted in families that we have never dealt with since the Civil War. A lot of those families still do exist in our country, and they have taught several generations to hate Black and Brown people. Listening to John talk about this I saw that he is a fair, honest and conscious man about our nation's history. He has a very keen sense on what we need to do to move forward. His work is impeccable, and I cannot wait to read his new book *"The Soul of America"* after I finish writing this one. History and historians are especially important to every man's culture regardless of the generation. My appreciation for good historians has accelerated even higher because of these people named above. The next thing that I appreciate more is that all Professional Sports have taken a stand on Racism in America. For example: In the NFL on the back of many professional helmets, you see the words *"End Racism"* including in the endzones at stadiums. The NFL is now wanting to be a part of the solution of the racism that is in America and no longer look away from it. They have pledged to donate over $250 million in the next 10 years towards this effort. The funds owners have approved is specifically intended to *'combat systemic racism and support the battle against the ongoing and historic injustices faced by African Americans'* written by Jason Reid @JReidESPN, June 11, 2020. The NBA, NHL, WNBA, and MLB have taken a stand for change. Also, I am appreciative of corporate CEOs all over America who have stepped up and denounced racism in our nation. I appreciate the ones' that took the time to address their employees on the measures that they are planning to take to bring equality in the workplace. It was a such a blessing to hear these reports. It is one thing to speculate how a corporations may feel about these things that bring racial division in society, it's another thing when they go public about racial issues to make things better for their brand and employees. What we must realize is that the racial and violent behavior that we have seen on this nations soil for the past years did not come to us because of the *Russians, the Chinese, the Canadians, the Europeans, or the Latinos*. It happened because we did it to ourselves. As one my former supervisors in the United States Air Force said to me while I was still drafting this book: *"This is what happens when we wink at sin that we should have been working hard a long time ago to get rid of!"* As Abraham Lincoln said, *"America will never be destroyed from the outside. If we lose our freedoms, it will be because we have destroyed ourselves from within."* Whether we admit it or not, the *2008, 2012 and 2016* Presidential Elections exposed the hearts of many people in this country. This would make any reasonable minded person know that we have some serious work to do towards race in our nation. We have seen that amongst blacks and whites that our values, purpose, hope, and dreams are different. When it comes to the gospel that the Apostle Paul preached, we are to be one of the same heart and mind. Paul says in 1 Corinthians 1:10 *"I appeal to you brothers and sisters in the name of our Lord Jesus Christ that all of you agree with one another <u>in what you say</u> and that there be no divisions among you, but that you be perfectly united in mind and thought."* Regardless to what anyone of us says, we are not united perfectly in mind and thought not even in the Church in America. When it comes to racism, white nationalism, social injustice, police brutality, policy, and leadership we are clearly different in mind and thought. Therefore, where do we go from here? I leave you with a letter written to the Church of Corinthians by the Apostle Paul. If I have hurt anyone while reading this book, especially in the Church. I will say: *"Make room for us in your hearts. We have wronged no one, we have corrupted no one, we have exploited no one. I do not say this to condemn you; I have said before that you have such a place in our hearts that we would live or die with you. I have spoken to you with great frankness; I take great pride in you. I am greatly encouraged; in all our troubles my joy knows no bounds…I see that my letter hurt you, but only for a little while— yet now I am happy, not because you were made sorry, but because your sorrow led you to repentance. For you became sorrowful as God intended and so were not harmed in any way by us. Godly sorrow brings repentance that leads to salvation and leaves no regret, but worldly sorrow brings death. See what this godly sorrow has produced in you: what earnestness, what eagerness to clear yourselves, what indignation, what alarm, what longing, what concern, what readiness to see justice done (2 Corinthians 7:2-16).* Finally, I would say: *"Therefore, since we have these promises, dear friends, let us purify ourselves from everything that contaminates body and spirit, perfecting holiness out of reverence for God" (2 Corinthians 7:1).* This includes *"Racism"* children of God! We need to reimagine a different America with more equality. The average income disparity in a white family is $30,000 per year higher than a Black family. Bishop TD Jakes said, *"you can drive a freight train through it."* We need to move on the evidence of millions of whites marching in the streets around this nation with Black people. Acknowledging that *Black Lives Do Matter*. I like to thank each of you for your precious time, patience, and attention. I pray that you are all able to stand for justice, fairness, peace, and general RESPECT for all people.

Stay Kingdom!

KB

Ingram Content Group UK Ltd.
Milton Keynes UK
UKHW020024100323
418330UK00009B/491

9 781958 176856